John Henry Grose

A Voyage to the East Indies

Vol. 1

John Henry Grose

A Voyage to the East Indies
Vol. 1

ISBN/EAN: 9783337319229

Printed in Europe, USA, Canada, Australia, Japan

Cover: Foto ©Andreas Hilbeck / pixelio.de

More available books at **www.hansebooks.com**

A
VOYAGE
TO THE
EAST-INDIES;

BEGAN in 1750;
With OBSERVATIONS continued till 1764;
INCLUDING
Authentic Accounts of the MOGUL Government in general, the Viceroyalties of the DECCAN and BENGAL, with their several subordinate Governments under their respective Nabobs, and independent States;
Particularly those of
ANGRIA, the MORATTOES, and TANJOREANS.

OF THE
RELIGIONS in INDIA; the MAHOMEDAN, GENTOO, and PARSEES.

Miscellaneous Customs; and general Reflections on the
TRADE OF INDIA.
OF THE
EUROPEAN Settlements, particularly the ENGLISH Presidencies of BOMBAY; MADRASS, or Fort St. GEORGE; and CALCUTTA, or Fort WILLIAM; with their respective Factories: Their Government, Trade, Fortifications, and public Buildings.
The Rise of the WAR in INDIA between the ENGLISH and FRENCH in 1754; and the Continuance thereof to the Conclusion of the General PEACE of EUROPE in 1763.

Illustrated with VIEWS drawn on the Spot.

By JOHN HENRY GROSE.

In TWO VOLUMES.

The SECOND EDITION, greatly Improved.

VOL. I.

LONDON:
Printed for the AUTHOR; and sold by S. HOOPER, at the East Corner of the New Church in the Strand.
M DCC LXVI.

THE

CONTENTS.

BOOK I.

The Author's Voyage from ENGLAND *to* BOMBAY,
Page 1

CHAP. I.

Voyage from the Downs *to* Johanna. *Account of some sea-fish: the flying-fish; bonitos; albacore; dorado; shark; sucking-fish; pilot-fish; yellow-tails. Account of some sea-birds; the tropic-birds; albatrosses; noddies; and boobies. Account of a water-spout,* ——— ——— ——— 1

CHAP. II.

The five Comro *islands. Account of* Johanna. *View of it from the road. Boats come off, and their nature of dealing. Of the other four islands; Comro, Mayotta, Mohilla, and Angazeja. Landing of the sick men for refreshment.——— The town of* Johanna. *Of the founder of that government in the present family. Soil and trade. A trip into the country. The king goes on board the* English *vessels. His subjects way of begging: their houses; diet; dress; treatment of infants; language, and religion. Their land and sea animals; their fruit. Departure from* Johanna; *and arrival at* Bombay, ——— ——— 12

A 2 BOOK

CONTENTS.

BOOK II.

Of BOMBAY, — — Page 28

CHAP. I.

Author waits on the governor. Situation and latitude of the iſland. Advice for preſerving health. Former unhealthineſs of the iſland, and its preſent melioration in that point accounted for. Diſtempers. Seaſons, — — 28

CHAP. II.

Of the government of Bombay: *its charter. Of the military and marine forces: militia. The piratory on that coaſt: meaſures to oppoſe it. Mildneſs and tolerancy of the* Engliſh *government,* 35

CHAP. III.

Of the ſtate of landed property on the iſland. Engliſh, *how ill uſed by the* Portugueſe *in the ceſſion of this iſland. Land-proprietors.* Parell *the governor's country-houſe. Coconut-oarts: rice-fields. Brab-trees; toddy-birds. Cultivation improved; to what owing,* — — 45

CHAP. IV.

Of the fortifications, public works, and buildings of Bombay. *The caſtle might have been better ſituated: the town walled round: out-forts: the breach:* Engliſh *church. Private buildings and* Gentoo *pagodas.* Malabar *hill. Story of a* Gentoo Gioghy. *Rock of purification,* 49

CHAP.

CONTENTS.

CHAP. V.

Of the iflands adjacent to Bombay. *Old* Woman's *ifland.* Hanara *and* Canara. *Butcher's ifland.* Caranja. *Elephanta, and its famous cave.* Salfett.—*The ceffion of* Bombay *farther explained.* Queen Catherine's *dower liquidated.* Japan-trade *loft by it.* Salfett *conquered by the* Morattoes. *Inconveniencies of that change of mafters to* Bombay. *Ruins of* Canara. *Diftrefs of the* Portuguefe; *forced to feek refuge on* Bombay, — — — Page 57

BOOK III.

Of the MORATTOES, *and* ANGRIA, — 74

CHAP. I.

Of the Morattoes. *Derivation of their name.* Aborigines Gentoos : *conduct of the* Moguls *towards them.* — *Rife of the* Saha *or* Sow-Rajahs. —*Difpofition of the* Morattoes. *Proficients in engineering; nature of their troops. Curious in their arms.*——*Situation of* Bombay *with refpect to them. Opinion of the wealth of* Bombay. *Rapacioufnefs of the* Morattoes : *frank acquiefcence in their character of perfidioufnefs: not fanguinary: their ufage of captives in war. The fort of* Raree, *the refidence of the* Saha, *or* Mar-Rajah: *his fubjects credulous in aftrology. Story of the* Mar-Rajah *and a reputed forcerefs. Defcription of the* Morattoes *perfons and drefs. Their women; and the charge againft them of poifoning their hufbands groundlefs,* — 74

CHAP. II.

Of Angria *and his* Succeffors, — — 93

CHAP.

BOOK IV.

Of the MOGUL *Government,* —— Page 97

CHAP. I.

Of Surat: *its situation: disturbances there. History of* Mahmud Ally. *Character of the* Banyans. *Style of the* Mogul *governors. Ship-building: navigation: buildings and streets of* Surat: *provisions: odd names given to spirituous liquors. Account of the practice of champing: bathing: jugglers: toleration of religions: manufactures: commodious method of sale. Singular method of securing the caravans. Intercourse between* Surat *and* Bombay *by land. Opium: story of its paradoxical operation:* Patna *sends the best to market: story of an* English *gentleman dying of having sucked a poppy. Of the use of bang.*—— *Of the* Parsees.——*Of the* Mogul *government, and its declension. Religion of* Tartary *is deism. Of seraglios, and the* Moors *taste of beauty. Buildings and gardens of the* Moguls. *Dancing-girls. Dress of the* Moors: *manners: slaves: diet: equipage and carriages. Luxury of the Orientalists,* —— —— 97

CHAP. II.

Of the state of the Roman Catholic religion in India, *Missions more political than religious. Qualifications of a Buon-Christian: quality of their concerts. Papists have borrowed several points of worship from the Orientalists, Mahometans and Heathens: points of resemblance: inquisition imitated from the*

CONTENTS.

the Mahometans: *inhumanity of the inquisition: precaution of the* English *against* Portuguese *priests: story of cardinal* Tournon: *lying miracles of the papists: ignorance of the* Portuguese *clergy: character of the jesuits: nunneries in* India: *false pretensions to merit in the Romish missions: reason of the* English *not attempting conversions in* India, — — — Page 158

CHAP. III.

Of the Mahometan *religion. How introduced into* Indostan: *relaxation of zeal for* Mahomet: *character of the* Koran. Popes, *their resemblance to the* Khaliphs. Mahometans, *their zeal for the unity and reverence of God. Gross conceptions fittest for the palate of the* Arabs *in the time of* Mahomet, — — p. 174

CHAP. IV.

Of the Gentoo *religion. Paradox of their zeal and tolerancy, and how to be accounted for. Their veneration for* Cows: *story on that occasion of* Ecbar-Shah, *great* Mogul, *and a* Bramin. Metempsychosis. *Tenacious of their points of religion: story of* Loldafs Vituldafs, *a* Banyan, *on that occasion. Nicety of civil distinctions: story thereon of a* Nayr *and* Thyvee. *Impracticability of recovering the cast when lost. Story of a* Gentoo *and his wife: fidelity of the* Gentoo *wives, to what owing. Suicide not so common now among the* Gentoos *as formerly: story of one who drowned himself. Account of the* Gymnosophists *or* Gioghys: *story of one. Trials by ordeal on the* Malabar *coast: story of an* English *lady on that occasion. Dis-*

A 4 *tinction*

tinction *of the* Gentoos *into tribes or casts. Account of the* Bramins: *antiquity of their religion: conjectures on the* Paphian Venus: *a prayer of the* Bramins: *devotions to* Jaggernaut. *Conjecture on the pyramidal form of certain idols. An objection to* Herodotus *attempted to be solved*; *as also another to* Plutarch *and* Justin. *Indians probably initiated by the* Egyptians. *Quotations in favor of the wisdom of the* Indians: *their polytheism resolveable into the unity of God,* Page 181

CHAP. V.

Of the religion of the Parsees. *Division of the religion of the* Parsees *into two states, ancient and modern. Introductory mention of* Zoroaster, *or* Zaratoosht: *he reforms the religion of the* Persians. *Their horror of ditheism: their accounting for the appearances of evil: their notions of fire; and of the human soul: their belief of the immortality of the soul: doctrine of rewards and punishments.* Zoroaster's *books being lost, his religion undergoes an innovation. The* Parsees *scandalized as fire-worshippers in a literal sense: their innocence of manners. Account of the* Souffees,
212

CHAP. VI.

Of the Gentoo *funerals. Ceremony of interment: of cremation: and similarity of customs therein with the antient western world* — 226

BOOK

CONTENTS.

BOOK V.

MISCELLANEOUS OBSERVATIONS, Page 230

CHAP. I.

Variety of the Gentoo *cuſtoms, and of the weather in the peninſula of* Indoſtan. *Account of a ſpecies of* Pigmies *in the* Carnatic *country. Remarks on the* Gentoos *to the north of proper* Malabar. *Story of a female warrior challenging a* Morattoe *general.* Gentoos *expenſive in their marriages; affect corpulence; fond of high-ſeaſoning, pepper, myrabolans, creeatt, and ſagoe : practice of chewing betel; cachoondah, cachoo, confectionary. Some caſts drink ſtrong liquors, and eat fiſh and other animal food. Effects of a fiſh diet. Reſervedneſs of the* Gentoo-women. Bramins *and* Banyans *revengeful. Poiſoining in* India *has been exaggerated. Account of a particular poiſon.* Bramins *in ſecular employs; confeſs the unity of God. Great difference of the proper* Malabars *from the more northern* Indians. *Plurality of huſbands : nudity of breaſts. Story thereon of a queen of* Attinga : *the ſovereigns of* Attinga *always females. Manners of the* Malabars: *articles of their dreſs. Miſſionaries ſcheme of paſſing for* European Bramins : *ſtory of the hypocriſy of one.* Malabar *feaſts. Rajah of* Sarimpatam's *forces trained up to noſe-cutting.—Of* European *ſettlements on the* Malabar *coaſt.—Plagues and earthquakes not common in* India. Bramins *treatment of bloody fluxes : Mordechin, barbees : ſun-riſe, its unwholſome effect. Chronical diſtempers rare in* India,

230

CHAP.

CONTENTS.

CHAP. II.
Summary reflections on the trade of India. *That trade of advantage to the nation. Certain objections to it discussed,* — Page 252

CHAP. III.
Of the protestant mission in Malabar, — 259

CHAP. IV.
Of some particular animals of India. *The* Elephant *and* Rhinoceros. *The* Camel, Dromedary, *and* Camelopard. *The* Lion *and* Lioness. Leopard *and* Panther. *The* Tyger. *The* Ape, 268

CHAP. V.
A description of the country of Tranquebar. *Of the coins, money of account, weights and measures of* India. *With a list of our* East-India *company's present forts and factories,* — — 279

CHAP. VI.
Of the principal companies in Europe *trading to* India, — — — — 287

CHAP. VII.
Of the other European *companies trading to the* East-Indies. *The* Dutch East-India *company.* *The* French East-India *company.* Danish East-India *company.* Ostend East-India *company.* East-India *company of* Sweden. Embden East-India, *or* Prussian-Asiatic *company*, — — 301

CHAP. VIII.
Of ancient India: *its inhabitants; their religion; government; and of the* Brachmans, — 326

CHAP. IX.
Of the ancient revolutions in India, *from the conquests of* Bacchus *to those of* Alexander *the Great. Of the settlement of the* Mahomedans *in* India: *and of the* Mogul *government. Of the climate of* India, *and its present inhabitants. With some remarks relative to trade,* —— 335

A GLOS-

A

GLOSSARY, or EXPLANATION,

OF

PERSIAN, MOORISH, and INDIAN Names mentioned in this WORK.

A.

Amdanny, IMPORTS.
Arzdafht, or Argee, A petition.
Affammees, Dealers in different branches of trade.

B.

Bang, An intoxicating juice of a vegetable.
Banka Bazar, Formerly the Oftend factory.
Batta, An extraordinary allowance to the army in the field, or where garrifon provifions are fcarce.
Begum, Princefs; meaning without care.
Betel, A leaf, fomewhat like that of a kidney-bean, growing on a vine in the fame manner, and commonly ufed by all degrees of people; who chew it mixed with Chinam and the Betel-nut, which is the produce of a different plant.
Bootans, The inhabitants of Affam.
Bramin, A prieft.
Buckferrias, Foot-foldiers, whofe common arms are only fword and target.
Buckfhee, or Buxey, Treafurer to the Mogul, or paymafter of troops.
Bundar, A Cuftom-houfe.

C.

Cawn, or Khan, A title of dignity.
Chinam, or Chunam, Lime, fine and unflacked.
Chop, A fmall feal, on which is engraved the name of the Mogul, and the year of the Hegyra.

Choultry,

A GLOSSARY.

Choultry,	An open house for all travellers.
Chout,	A fourth part; but commonly used for the tribute exacted by the Morattoes.
Chowkeys,	Or Chokeys, Barriers or turnpikes; or the guards at the stairs, or landing-places.
Chubdaar,	An usher.
Circar,	See Sircar.
Coffres, or Caffres,	Negroes brought to India from Africa, and trained up as soldiers by the Europeans.
Colleries,	Inhabitants of the woods, under the government of the Polygars.
Cooley,	A porter, or laborer of any kind.
Corore, or Crore,	Of rupees, an hundred lack, or near 1,250,000 l. sterling. See lack.
Cofs, or Corse.	A measure of distance from two miles to two and half.
Cossid,	A foot-messenger, or post.
Cowle,	A protection.

D.

Dawgahs,	Or Darugahs, Custom-house officer, or collectors.
Decoyt,	A robber.
Dewan,	King's treasurer.
Dewanny,	Superintendency over the royal revenues.
Dooley,	A woman's chair, like a sedan.
Dummadah,	A river.
Durbar,	The court, or council, of a Mogul prince.
Duffutary,	An impost of ten per cent.
Duftuck,	An order.

F.

Firman,	Or Phirmaund, A patent signed by the Mogul; a royal mandate, or grant.
Fouzdar, Fowj'dar,	Or Phousdar, A governor, military officer, or renter.

Gentoo,

//
A GLOSSARY.

G.

Gentoo, or Zentoo,	Native Indians, who remain in a state of idolatry.
Gomaftah,	A broker, factor, or agent.
Gunge,	Grain-market.
Gwallers,	Carriers of Palanquins.

H.

Hackeries,	Carts or coaches drawn by oxen.
Harkarahs,	Spies.

J.

Jageer, Jaghire,	Or Jaqueer, A territory or diftrict, granted as a mark of honor, or allotted as a penfion.
Jaggernaut,	The Gentoo pagoda.
Jemidar, Jemmautdaar, or Zemidar.	Officers of horfe or foot, of the fame rank with the Roman centurion: fometimes it implies people of rank employed about the principal perfons in the government.

K.

Khan,	See Cawn.
Killedar,	The governor of a fort.
Kiftbundee,	Times of payment of the country revenues.

L.

Lack of rupees,	About 12,500 l. fterling. See Corore.

M.

Mackulka,	An obligation with a penalty annexed.
Maund,	A grofs weight between 70 and 80 pounds: but variable in different places; for at Surat it is only 37 pounds one half.
Moonfhee,	Or Moonfkee, A Perfian fecretary.
Moories,	Writers.

Moors,

Moors,	The Mahometans of India; but they are improperly so denominated.
Muchulcas,	Bonds of obligations.
Musnud,	The throne of an Indian Prince.
Muxadabad, Muckfadabad,	Or Moorshadabad, The capital of Bengal.

N.

Nabob, or Navob,	A governor of a province, appointed by the Soubah. See Soubah.
Naib, or Neabut,	A deputy to the governor of a place.
Nobut,	A drum, or mark of royalty assumed by the Soubahs of Bengal.

O.

Omrahs,	Privy-counsellors to the Mogul, and men of the first rank in the empire.

P.

Paddy,	Rice in the husk.
Paddy-grounds,	Rice-fields.
Pagoda,	An Indian temple.
Pagoda,	An Indian coin, worth seven shillings and eight pence sterling.
Palankeen,	A kind of canopy-bed for travelling.
Paragana,	A district of country.
Parsees,	Worshippers of fire.
Patamar,	A messenger, or post.
Peons,	Foot soldiers armed with a broadsword, or a match-lock.
Pergannahs,	Villages.
Perwannah,	A letter, order, or command; and sometimes a grant from the prince.
Pettah,	The town surrounding an Indian fort.
Phirmaund, Phousdar.	See Firman and Fouzdar.
Podor, or Shroffs,	A money-changer.
Polygar,	The Lord of a district.
Pondary, Foorea,	Farmers distinct allowances on grain at the Gunge.

Ponsways,

A GLOSSARY.

Ponſways,	Guard-boats.
Pettahs,	Grants.
Pykes,	Officers relative to the ſervice of the lands.

R.

Raja,	The higheſt title claimed by the Gentoo princes.
Royran,	The king's officer for receiving the revenue.
Rafftanny,	Exports.
Rumnah,	Diſtrict for the royal game.
Rupee, or Roupee,	A ſilver coin, about two ſhillings and five pence ſterling.

S.

Saneds, or Sunnuds,	Grants, or commiſſions from the Mogul, Soubahs or Nabobs.
Sardar,	An officer of horſe.
Seapoys, or Sepoys,	Indian foot ſoldiers, hired and diſciplined by Europeans.
Seer,	A meaſure, forty of which is a Maund. See Maund.
Shroff,	A banker. See Podor.
Siccas,	Coin of the country.
Sircar,	A general name for the government, or perſons concerned in the adminiſtration.
Sirpah,	A rich dreſs of the country, beſtowed by the government as a mark of diſtinction on particular perſons.
Soubah, Soubahdar,	Or Suba, The viceroy of the Deckan, or of Bengal.
Sunnuds,	See Saneds.

T.

Tank,	A pond, or pool of water.
Tanka,	The revenue appropriated by the Mogul for maintaining a fleet at Surat.
Tankſal,	A mint for coinage.

Telinga,

Telinga, Telingas,	The Carnatic country; and soldiers raised there, or sepoys, sometimes called Tellingas.
Tom-Toms,	Drums.
Topasses,	A tawney race of foot soldiers, descended from Portuguese marrying natives; and called Topasses; because they wear hats.
Tunkahs,	Assignments upon lands; or rents assigned to the company.
Tuzsaconna, Ginanah,	Wardrobe and seraglio.

V.

Vakeel, or Vaqueel,	An English agent or resident at the Nabob's court: also an agent or minister for the Moors.
Vizerut,	The grant for the Vizirship.

Z

Zemin,	Ground.
Zemindary,	An officer to take care of the rents arising from the public lands.
Zentoo,	See Gentoo.

A VOYAGE TO THE EAST-INDIES.

BOOK I.
The Author's voyage from ENGLAND *to* BOMBAY.

CHAP. I.

Voyage from the Downs *to* Johanna. *Account of some sea-fish: the flying-fish; bonitos; albacore; dorado; shark; sucking-fish; pilot-fish; yellow-tails. Account of some sea-birds; the tropic-birds; albatrosses; noddies; and boobies. Account of a water-spout.*

T was in the ftation of a covenant fervant, and writer to the Eaft-India company, that, in the month of March 1750, I embarked on board one of the company's fhip's, named the Lord Anfon, Charles Foulis, commander, bound for Bombay and China; at the former of which places, I was to be left under the difpofition of that prefidency.

VOL. I. B BY

By such as are on the point of commencing travellers, on the sea, especially upon a voyage, in which so long intervals occur between land and land, the following general hint will not, I hope, be thought impertinent. They will then certainly find their account, in framing, before they are embarked, a list of such necessaries, as they may probably want in the course of the passage, concerning which, they will do well to take the advice of such as have been the like voyage before, and who, by their own knowledge and experience, will be best qualified to inform them, not only of the most material requisites, but even of sundry little items, which to name here might seem trifling, and of which the miss however is serious, when out at sea, where it is not often easy to repair one's improvidence.

Another caution, too, as trite a repetition as it may appear, I am induced not to omit re-inculcating, for having observed it commonly neglected: and that is, for such as have reason to apprehend the sea-sickness, not to go on board with a full stomach: not that even, by this means, such as are liable to it, will wholly escape it; but so much is certain, that they will be affected in a less violent degree. And when under the influence of it, as it is necessary to eat and drink, not only to support nature, but to avoid the dangers of over-straining and reachings of an empty stomach, the lightest, and most digestible foods, are the most preferable.

On the 30th of March 1750, we sailed out of the Downs, in company with four East-Indiamen; but as there nothing occurs material to be remarked of these our consorts, some of whom soon after parted company, I shall say no more of them.

We were then soon out of sight of British land, and got into the main-ocean; and as it could

THE EAST-INDIES.

could be but tirefome to the reader unverfed in navigation, and fuperfluous for one who underftood it, to be detained by a dry uninterefting journal of winds, courfes, and the like common occurrences at fea, I fhall only offer thofe points which are of a more general nature, to the curiofity of the reader: and even then have an apology to make for the unavoidable repetition of defcriptions, with which a number of travellers, who have preceded me in this fubject, feem to have exhaufted it. All the novelty then that can poffibly be expected, in a voyage now fo common and well known, muft arife from the different points of view, in which nature prefents the fame objects to different perfons, or at leaft often, fo as to afford fome new light to be thrown upon them.

As the fifhes then form no fmall part of the entertainment, in the courfe of the paffage, I fhall begin with them, juft premifing, that befides the ufual tackle of lines, and hooks of all fizes, there are no fhips on thofe voyages, but are equipped with a competent number of harpoons or fifh-gigs. This is a long ftaff, armed at one end with a clufter of well tempered iron prongs, which being barbed hinder the fifh, on being ftruck with it, from flouncing off. The other end is heavily cafed, or wrapped round with lead, fo that when delivered from the ftriker's hand, with a line to it that runs the length of the ftaff, it ferves, by its weight, to cant the fifh upmoft, in a pofition the moft favorable to bring it on board.

THE flying-fifh, are moft generally feen within the tropics, or in the latitudes near them. Their fize is, commonly fpeaking, that of a large herring, to which they have fome refemblance. The over-proportioned fize of their fide-fins, countenance very clearly the opinion of their being affifted by them, in the fpring they make out of the water,

water, on being purfued by the larger fifhes of prey; as thofe fins continuing fpread muft naturally gather fome air. But I much doubt, whether what is called their flight is not more properly an extended leap (like that of the flying-fquirrels on fhore, to whom the expanfion of a membraneous fold, that makes part of the fkin of their hind legs, ferves for a kind of wings) and that their neceffity of replunging into the water, is not fo much owing to their fins drying, in fo fhort a fpace as 25 or 30 yards, and requiring wetting afrefh, as to the force of their fpring being fpent. There are many fifh, befides them, that take very confiderable leaps out of the water, though not of fuch a length as they do, from their fide-fins not being fo well adapted for a continuance of a motion compounded of flying and leaping. So far is certain, that they have no guidance from their fight, but are urged headlong onward by a mechanical impulfe, infomuch, that they not unfrequently fall into fhips, and efpecially in the chains, which being lower than any part of the gunnel, ftop, and receive them. They are a very welltafted fifh, and often feen in great fhoals, flying from the purfuit of the Bonitos, Albacores, and Dorados, whofe choice prey they feem to be, very few of thofe fifhes being caught, without fome of them being found in their ftomachs, and accordingly the beft baits for thofe fpecies are an imitation of the flying-fifh, which being fwung to-and-fro, reprefent their flight, fo as to deceive and bring them greedily to the hook. Nor does this fifh find enemies only in its own element; for feveral fea birds, watch hovering for its emerfion, and dart down on it, with fuch quicknefs, as to make it their prey, before its re-plunge, fo that it fuffers a fatal perfecution in both elements.

It

THE EAST-INDIES.

IT was not till about the latitude of thirty, that we faw and caught feveral Bonitos, a fifh of the fize of a middling falmon, to which it is not unlike, but rather thicker for its length. This fifh undoubtedly takes its name, from its relifhing fo well to the tafte of the Portugueze, the firft navigators on this ocean, that they called it Bonito, which anfwers in our tongue to delicious. Not that, in effect, it is remarkably fo; but very probably, was fo welcome to the firft captors of it, perhaps on the dearth of frefh meals, that they honored it with that appellation, which has continued to it ever fince. It is a very firm, and not unpleafant fifh; but rather dry, and requiring a rich fauce, to entitle it to its name: though drynefs is a reproach that in fome degree belongs, generally fpeaking, to thofe fpecies, that may properly be called ocean-fifh: to which it is no contradiction to obferve, that they are fometimes taken near the land. The Bonito feeds upon all fmall fifh, efpecially the flying-fifh, with the imitation of which they are often caught, and often ftuck with the fifh-gig.

THE Albacore, is another fifh of much the fame kind as the Bonito; but grows to a larger fize, fome being taken efpecially by the hook, from fixty to ninety pounds weight and upward. The name of this fifh too is taken from the Portugueze, importing its white color. They are rather drier eating than the Bonito. For the reft, their prey, and method of catching them is the fame, and both are at certain feafons infefted with a worm, that makes them in an agony fpring out of the water, fo high as to fall into boats, when in the way of their leap.

WITH refpect to the Dorado, it may be obferved how difficult it is, for an appellation, when once fixed, however wrongfully applied, to be shaken off, or corrected. It is no new, but certainly a just remark, that this fish is very improperly called a Dolphin, having not the least resemblance to the description, or delineation of that fish, by authors, painters, or statuaries. The Portugueze, however, gave it the name of Dorado, from its golden-like hue, which is the groundwork of a beautiful azure, that is blended with it: and, in truth, nothing can be imagined of a more lively gloss than its colors, which however, on the fish being taken, fade off sensibly in a few minutes, adding one more striking instance of the alterations produced by death in all the animated creation. This fish, which is caught exactly in the same manner as the Bonitos, or Albacores, their food being the same, is generally greatly preferred to them, in point of taste. Their size is commonly about three or four foot, and delicately shaped; except that the head seems rather too large; though the chief bone of it, on dissection, appears admirably modelled for a cut-water; and, indeed, they swim with an inconceivable rapidity.

Having however, as I conceive, very justly divested the Dorado of the appellation of Dolphin, the point is where to place it more properly: and I apprehend, that the fish now called Porpoises can only lay claim to it. Some however deny this, and insist on the dolphin being a creature of the imagination, not only on the account of the fabulous properties, attributed to it by the antients, such as taking the famous musician Arion on its back, its tameness, and likings to human society, of all which distinctions there exist at present no traces; but also in respect to the curve form, it, as preserved in paintings and statues, being different from the porpoise, which when taken, appears as straight a fish as any that swims.

Without

Without prefuming to decide the queftion, I can only fay, that it can hardly be thought, that fo many authors would have treated fo currently of a fpecies entirely non-exiftent, however fome of them might mix the falfe and marvellous in their accounts of it: and as to the form, the difference arifing from the curvature, is probably owing to its being conftantly reprefented in the point of leaping, when either the eye is deceived by the quicknefs of the tumble, or the porpoife really bends the body, in a manner anfwerable to the ufual delineation of the dolphin, which, with the fimilar projection of the fnout from the head, feem to authorize in fome degree the conjecture of the porpoife, being no other than the dolphin of the antients; at leaft, it is not fo thoroughly different from the reprefentation of it, as the dorado, the fize of which befides is much too fmall, for its having any pretenfion to pafs for it.

The fhark, which is fo common a fifh near the land in feveral parts of the lower latitudes, is not unfrequently met with in the main-fea; but then it is chiefly in calms, or very light breezes, when it will follow a fhip for a confiderable time, unlefs betrayed to the hook by its natural voracity: for it is commonly too large to be maftered by a harpoon, or fifh-gig. Any thing almoft for a bait will ferve; but it requires a ftrong hook to hold it; and thofe of the larger fize, the noofe of a running-tackle to bring them on board: where, as foon as they touch the deck, they make all fhake again with the violent flounces of their tail, capable of breaking a man's leg: yet they are prefently fubdued by a cut of the ax on it, which deprives them inftantly of all power, fo that they are foon difpatched. The common length of this fifh is from nine to fifteen feet; but I have been credibly informed, there are fome of them of twenty

twenty feet and upwards. It has no scales. The skin of it is rather rough, like shagreen, than very hard; of a deep brown, and somewhat greenish color, and whitening by degrees to the belly. One of them will generally make a meal for the whole ship's company; but then they are the ranker, in proportion to their size, and at best afford an indifferent repast: the fins only excepted, which though covered with a skin hard enough to be used as a slate to write on, when jerked, or dried in the sun, afford however when prepared, according to the Chinese cookery, a very delicate dish. They cut them out in strips, or rather filaments, which when seasoned in their manner, are stewed into a tender gristly substance, extreamly well-tasted, and is by them esteemed one of those rare provocatives to venery, that at once stimulate and strengthen.

This fish must however have been much more effectually the terror of the seas, had nature endowed it with an agility, and disposition of parts, answerable to that of its voracity, which is so especially assisted with a dreadful triple row of teeth, as sharp as razors. But, besides its not being the swiftest swimmer, its mouth, by being placed considerably within the projection of its snout, towards the belly, obliges it to turn on its back, or at least sideways to snap at its prey, which it does so heavily, that good swimmers will, with a knife, either for diversion, or for the sake of shewing their skill, attack it in its own element, and diving under the belly, where the skin is very soft, rip it open, or oblige it to sheer off. How they engender cannot be ascertained; but it is certain, that the females are not only viviparous, the young ones being found alive in their bellies, when taken, but they occasionally afford them a retreat in it, until they out-grow the size of wanting one.

THERE

THERE is alſo another ſort of them, called the bottled-noſed ſharks, of a dark blueiſh hue : but of thoſe I never ſaw any caught; and being looked on as not fit to eat, they are rarely meddled with, unleſs purely for ſport.

THIS fiſh too has, like its name-ſakes the human ſharks, on the land, its dependents, or under-ſuckers, as well as its ſcouts or guides to its prey.

THE ſucking-fiſh then aptly enough repreſents the firſt, being a ſmall fiſh, rarely above a foot long, and often much ſhorter. They faſten upon the ſhark, by the means of an oval-ſhaped membrane of a texture, admirably adapted for that purpoſe, with which they ſtick ſo cloſe to the ſkin of the ſhark, commonly on its ſides or back, as not to part with it, even when it is taken, and no ſtrength of hands can hardly ſeparate them, if pulled againſt the grain of the ſucker; but ſliding them on forward, with the grain, they eaſily enough come off; and this force of adheſion continues whilſt there is any life in them, as may be proved on applying them to a table, or any hard ſubſtance. It doubtleſs annoys the ſhark in the nature of vermin, drawing its ſuſtenance from the ſlimy oozing of its body, whilſt it can neither ſhake it off, nor come at it to deſtroy it. The gills of it are placed in an inverted poſition, opening upwards. It is of a dull muddy ſlate color, and of no uſe for food, having neither ſubſtance nor taſte.

THE other ſpecies of attendants on the ſhark, are what is called pilot-fiſh, which ſome writers have confounded with the ſucking-fiſh, though of quite a different ſpecies; being perhaps one of the beautifulleſt fiſh that ſwims : ſeldom above a foot, or a foot and a half long, ſtreaked tranſverſally with blue, and a yellowiſh brown, that have a very pleaſing effect in the water, but loſe much of their lively gloſs when taken. Theſe fiſh are ofteneſt

ſeen

seen in small shoals, swimming immediately a-head of the shark, or near him. When a bait is thrown out for the shark, they cluster to it, without attempting to nibble themselves, but by their motions to and fro, seem to guide the shark towards it, from whence they derive their appellation of pilot-fish; when in company with the shark, they rarely take the small hook themselves; but when they have lost this their consort, or follow a ship, either singly or in shoals, they will then sometimes bite, and be caught. They are esteemed, for their size, the most delicious eating that the ocean affords, having nothing of that dryness reproachable to the other fish of it, as before observed.

There are also often caught, with the hook, or harpoon, a fish, called yellow-tails, from the color of that part, from one to three or four foot long. They are very eatable, but inferior in point of taste, and beauty of color to the dorados, which they otherwise much resemble in their make.

As the above-noted species of the fish-kind are what chiefly occur in the passage, I imagined, I could not without impropriety entirely omit them; and, for the same reason, shall just make a summary mention of the sea-birds, that are most commonly observed in the track of this navigation.

Near, or within the tropics, as the term imports, are often seen what are called tropic-birds: white, of the size of a large hawk: with nothing remarkable but a length of feather, that proceeds from their tails.

Albatrosses, which are met with more frequent as you approach the land, are a very large bird, and from their size, received from the Portugueze the name of Alcatruz, or Ostriches (having no other resemblance to that bird) from which by corruption is derived Albatrofs. These are the birds, which are the most cruel enemies to the flying-fish: and their beak is so sharp, that it enables them,

them, as they dart down on the wing upon any fish, they fee on the furface of the water, to fcoop out a piece of it, when too large to carry the whole away.

The noddies and boobies, being of the fize of a large duck, plainly receive their name from their fillinefs, in fuffering themfelves to be taken by the hand, as they perch upon the yards, or other parts of the fhip: which cannot be from wearinefs, being web-footed. For the reft they are too tough, and fifhy, to be eatable.

THURSDAY the 10th of May, we faw a water-fpout, which burft very near us. Its firft appearance refembled a black fmoak, fomewhat in the fhape of an inverted pyramid. This is a body of water, collected between a cloud and the furface of the fea; but we had no occafion to fire at it, which is often done to diffipate it by the explofion. They are fometimes many minutes in falling, and irritate the water to that degree, as to produce a great ebullition and foam. If it burfts on the deck of a fhip, it will go near to fink it, with the great weight of water, with which it is pregnant: but, I believe, there are few inftances known of fuch an accident, this phenomenon being always in the day-time, and the danger eafily avoided, by forcing its difperfion, or fteering clear of it.

BESIDES that, and the common incidents of land-falls in our way, we had no remarkable occurrence, unlefs that on Thurfday the 7th of June, as one Stedman, the carpenter's mate, was about fome little jobb on one of the fhip's fides, and being carelefs in his hold, a large wave came fuddenly, and wafhed him into the fea; immediate notice of which being given to the captain, we brought to all ftanding, and threw over a large grating, and an empty cafk, of the latter of which he luckily got hold, and the boat being expeditioufly tiously hoisted out, and manned, they were just time enough to save him. Though he was allowed to be an excellent swimmer, the sea was so prodigiously rough, that he could scarce have kept a minute longer on the cask, without being washed off. We were going at the rate of seven knots, or miles, an hour, when this accident happened, which made the saving him a very hazardous point.

SATURDAY the 28th of July, we anchored happily in the road of Johanna, having been now near four months since our departure from the Downs.

CHAP. II.

The five COMRO *islands. Account of* JOHANNA. *View of it from the road. Boats come off, and their nature of dealing. Of the other four islands,* COMRO, MAYOTTA, MOHILLA, *and* ANGAZEJA. *Landing of the sick men for refreshment.* —*The town of* Johanna. *Of the founder of that government in the present family. Soil and trade. A trip into the country. The king goes on board the* ENGLISH *vessels. His subjects way of begging: their houses; diet; dress; treatment of infants; language, and religion. Their land and sea animals; their fruit. Departure from* Johanna : *and arrival at* BOMBAY.

THE view of this island to those on board-ship in the road, is of itself so extreamly pleasant, as not to need the circumstance of its being a landing-place, after so long a run, to recommend it. The hills high, and covered with evergreens down to the water's edge, and disembosoming to the sea, in a delicious valley, altogether form one of the most pleasing landscapes that can be imagined;

THE EAST-INDIES. 13

imagined; nature there luxuriating into a romantic wildneſs, with which the eye, if not more delighted, is at leaſt leſs apt to be ſatiated, than with the tame inſipid regularity of art.

The ſhip was no ſooner anchored, than ſurrounded with a number of canoes, hurrying on board with refreſhments of all ſorts, of the produce of the iſland; and it was humorous enough to mark the confuſion, and ſtrife, among the rowers, who ſhould get firſt to their market, the ſhip. They are ſometimes overſet, when the ſea is any thing high: but, without any danger to their perſons, being excellent ſwimmers, and loſe only their little cargoes of green-trade. Theſe canoes are moſt of them ballanced on each ſide with out-leagers, compoſed of two poles each, with one acroſs, to prevent their overſetting. They uſe paddles inſtead of oars; and make no diſtinction of head or ſtern. Their larger boats, called panguays, are raiſed ſome feet from the ſides with reeds and branches of trees, well bound together with ſmall-cord, and afterwards made water-proof, with a kind of bitumen, or reſinous ſubſtance. The maſt, for few have more than one, carries a ſail or two, which is made either of coconut leaves, or ſheer-graſs matted together; and in theſe boats they will venture out to ſea, for trips of three or four weeks, and ſometimes longer.

It was common, not many years ago, for the natives who came off with refreſhments to the ſhips, ſuch as freſh coconuts, plantains, fowls, goats, &c. to deal entirely by way of barter, for handkerchiefs, rags, glaſs-bottles, bits of iron, in ſhort, all ſorts of frippery, without any reſpect to money. But of late they begin to know its value; and it is only the moſt inconſiderable articles, that they will now part with, in that manner; yet

they

they still afford every thing cheap enough, not to be repined at.

Johanna is one of the five Comro islands, which take their name from the largest island Comro, the other four being distinguished by the names of Mayotta, Mohilla, Angazeja and Johanna. This last lies in the latitude of 12 degrees, fifteen minutes south: all of them opposite to the African shore, between which, and the great island of Madagascar, is formed what is called the Mozambique-channel, from Mozambique a small island belonging to the Portugueze, where they have a very considerable settlement, close upon the continent, in the latitude of 14 south.

Comro, the largest island, is not at all frequented by the Europeans; because it has no safe harbor, or roadstead to it: besides, the natives have the character of a barbarous, untractable people, that will suffer no commerce with strangers. Perhaps too, not without reason: as it was common for the Portugueze especially, in the early times of their navigating those seas, to take the advantage of the simplicity of the inhabitants, unacquainted with arms, and incapable of defence, and land parties out of their vessels, to rob, and commit all manner of outrages on the natives, not unfrequently carrying them away slaves; a procedure, which may have given them a traditional aversion to, and jealousy of all strangers in general: and very probably the revenge they might thereon take on the next comers, without distinction of the innocent, may have gained them that inhospitable character, which is to this day continued to them.

Mayotta, Mohilla, and Angazeja, are also little resorted to, on account of the superior advantages of Johanna, in the safety of its roadstead; which, joined to the more civilized disposition of

its

THE EAST-INDIES.

its inhabitants, have nearly engroſſed the cuſtom of the Europeans touching there for refreſhments.

On a ſhip's arrival, and anchoring on the weſt ſide of the iſland, where the road is; it is the common practice to pitch a tent aſhore, made of the ſails and ſpare-booms, for the reception of the ſick, who, though never ſo much diſabled with the ſcurvy, generally recover their health ſurprizingly quick; as much doubtleſs by the ſpecifically reviving influence of the earth itſelf, as even by the variety of excellent refreſhments, with which the country abounds, as oxen, goats, fowls, fruits, all admirable in their kinds, and the freſh water perfectly good. The danger is for the common ſailors, who arrive well and in health, leſt they ſhould by their intemperance, eſpecially in the raw fruits, contract, or lay foundations for diſtempers to break out when they get to ſea again.

It has been ſaid, that the lying aſhore is prejudicial, on account of the moiſt vapors diffuſed from the neighboring hills: but I rather think the unwholſomeneſs to conſiſt chiefly in the inſufficiency of the lodgment under a tent, to reſiſt the keenneſs of the night air, and the damps of the atmoſphere, riſing directly from the earth itſelf. This I ſubmit to the judgment of the phyſicians.

From the ſpot where the tents are pitched, is about a mile's walk along ſhore, to what is called the town of Johanna, to come at which you croſs over a ſmall rivulet, very near it. This town, or more properly ſpeaking, village, is compoſed of about two hundred houſes and huts together. Thoſe which being of ſtone, may perhaps deſerve the name of houſes, belong to the chief, who is honored with the title of king of Johanna, and to the principal men of the country. Their beſt buildings, at leaſt all that I ſaw, are but of one ſtory, and even thoſe very low. They ſuffer ſtrangers

gers to come in familiarly to their first apartment, all the others being reserved for their families. The house where the king resides is built of stone and mud, and does not make a figure superior to a common English alms-house, being wretchedly furnished, aukwardly hung with pieces of coarse chintz, with here and there a small trumpery looking-glass. Yet with all this inferiority of parade and state, in comparison with what is seen in more extensive and civilized dominions, the title of king is not so absolutely improper to the chief of this island, which contains, on a gross calculation, about thirty leagues in circuit, seventy-three villages, and near thirty thousand inhabitants; he having all the essentials of royalty, an unlimitted power over his subjects, both in temporals and spirituals.

The grandfather of the present king, if I may then have leave to use that term, was an Arab, or Moorish trader to Mozambique, where, on a quarrel with a Portugueze fidalgo, or gentleman, with whom he was dealing for slaves on that coast, he had the fortune to kill his adversary, and was thereon obliged instantly to fly, and put to sea in the first boat he could seize on the shore, when the first land he made was Johanna, where he took refuge. Here meeting with an hospitable reception, he remained some years in obscurity, until an Arab tranky being driven in there by stress of weather, he made himself known to his countrymen, for whom he procured all the relief the place afforded.

In the mean time he had so perfectly acquainted himself with the language and manners of the inhabitants, and was so captivated with the fertility and pleasantness of the country, that he not only relinquished every thought of returning to his own, but laid a scheme to obtain for himself the sovereignty of this; in which he was greatly coun-
tenanced

tenanced and affifted by the Arabs his countrymen, who came into his views, for the advantage they expected to reap from his fuccefs.

HE proceeded not on a plan of violence, but of infinuation, in making himfelf neceffary to the natives, whom he inftructed in the ufe of arms before unknown to them, efpecially the zagay or lance, which thofe of any confideration among them, now handle with dexterity. This then, with other methods of war which he taught them, entirely new to thefe fimple favages, proving of fingular fervice to them, againft the inhabitants of the neighboring iflands, efpecially of Mohila, with whom they had conftant bickerings, fometimes invading, and fometimes invaded, acquired him fuch a confideration and authority, that he foon availed himfelf thereof, and procured himfelf to be elected their chief or king, and invefted with a defpotic power. Yet this was not obtained but by degrees, and by great art: themfelves too being divided among one another. As foon, however, as he had carried his point, he made them repent of their credulity and confidence. For not only ftrengthening himfelf by calling in fome of his countrymen with their families, but choofing for his guards the moft bold and determined of the natives, he was prefently in a condition to eftablifh an arbitrary government. Such as endeavored to oppofe him in his pretenfions and innovations, he forced from their families, and fold for flaves to the Arabs; who, on this alteration, encreafed their refort there for trade, which they ftill continue. In fhort, he fucceeded fo entirely, as to overcome all oppofition, and to bequeath the peaceable fovereignty to his fon, who was about forty three years of age, when this his father died, and who had no farther trouble or conteftation with his fubjects, until he alfo dying, a few years ago,

ago, left two sons, of whom the eldest is at present the governing chief.

When a ship arrives, it is necessary to obtain his licence for dealing with the natives; especially for the greater articles of refreshments, such as goats and oxen, as well as for wooding, watering, and landing the men: the permission for which is however purchased at a very reasonable expence, of a few presents of some yards of scarlet cloth, a little gun-powder, a few muskets, or other European commodities.

As the soil is of itself so naturally fertile, to produce every thing they covet for food, so their constitutional indolence keeps them satisfied, without any attempts at improvement, by tillage or cultivation. The Arabs, who have also extended their controul to the neighboring islands, which are in some sort of subjection to them, find it worth their while to come to Johanna in their trankys, which are a kind of uncouth vessels, of seventy to a hundred tons, and carry back ladings of coconuts, with some cowries, a kind of shells, which are an article of trade; and perhaps a few slaves. It is from them that the Johanna-men have lately learnt the utility of money, in purchases from them, of coarse piece-goods, and other India commodities.

There are doubtless too, among the great variety of plants the earth yields here in a wanton profusion, some valuable simples, of which the power and salutary virtues remain unknown for want of a sufficient botanical enquiry; which I am induced to mention, from one of the natives there having made himself very useful, by the little skill and knowledge he has acquired in them, purely by dint of his own natural genius, without any assistance of education. This man, now much advanced in years, and known by the nick-name

of

of Purser-jack, speaks English fluently, and is readily serviceable in all intercourse with the natives: but what he is chiefly considered for among them is this, his uncommon knowledge of medicinal plants, by which he has done surprizing cures, and what is more, without fee or reward.

The second day after our arrival, having an inclination to go up into the country with another English gentleman, a passenger in the Benjamin, captain Meard, I applied to this man for a guide, who accordingly procured us two stout fellows, that understood a little broken English, as indeed many of them do, who have any dealings with the shipping.

As we set out pretty early in the morning, we made a shift to penetrate about five miles into the country before the sun began to be any ways troublesome; and this was no small stretch, considering the mountainous way we had to go. We had fowling-pieces with us, and the view of excellent sport in shooting, could we have reached the places where we might perceive the game lay: but we could not conquer the ascent of the hills, though we endeavoured to scramble up them on our hands and knees. We were therefore obliged to rest satisfied with what small birds presented themselves, in the vallies and hills that were passable. We made our breakfast on pine-apples, and the milk of cocoa nuts, which served to quench our thirst. About noon, coming to a beautiful piece of water, we seated ourselves in the shade by the banks of it, to make a second meal, as well as to enjoy the tinkling of several little springs, and natural cascades, that fell from the rocks, and according to their distance seemed to found a gradation of notes, so as to form a kind of agreeable soothing water-music.

The orange and lime-trees, which ſtood in great numbers about that ſpot of ground, bending under the weight of their fruit, diffuſed a moſt fragrant odor. There were alſo pine-apples which grew wild, of eleven and thirteen inches circumference, of a much richer flavor, than thoſe I afterwards met with in India. Our guides too made us diſtinguiſh a number of goyava, and eſpecially plumb-trees, the ſize of whoſe fruit is about that of a damaſcene, and leaves a pleaſing reliſh on the palate for ſome minutes after it is eaten. All theſe growing promiſcuouſly, and without the leaſt arrangement or order, combined with the falls of water, and the ſtupendous height of the ſurrounding hills, covered with trees and verdure, and in their various breaks and projections, exhibiting the boldeſt ſtrokes of nature, altogether compoſed what might, without exaggeration, be called a terreſtrial paradiſe, compared to which the fineſt gardens in Europe, with their ſtatues, artificial caſcades, compartments, and all the refinements of human invention, would appear poor indeed! here it was impoſſible for art to add any thing, but what would rather ſpoil than adorn the ſcenery.

It was not then without regret that we quitted ſo charming a ſpot, after having feaſted our eyes with the beauties of it; to which it may be mentioned as no inconſiderable addition, that there was no fear of wild beaſts, or of venomous creatures mixed with our pleaſure, the iſland being ſo happy as to produce none. We returned to our tent, well paid for the ſlight fatigue we had undergone in this little excurſion.

The king reſides for the moſt part about nine miles, according to their computation, up in the country, ſeldom coming down to what they call their lower town, on the ſea ſide, but when the European

European ships are lying there, and is then accompanied by a numerous retinue.

WHEN he comes on board our veſſels, which he rarely miſſes, he always expreſſes a great deſire of knowing the name of every thing that is new to him; and as he has a tolerable ſmattering of the Engliſh tongue, is very inquiſitive concerning our wars in Europe, and is eſpecially well pleaſed with the civility of our captains, who regale him with European fare, and who generally ſalute him with five guns, on his paying them a viſit, and the like number at his departure. This laſt is a ceremony he would not willingly diſpenſe with; becauſe this mark of reſpect gives him an air of importance among his ſubjects.

HIS attendants, who do not altogether ſtand ſo much upon ceremony, as their ſovereign, have a forward way of begging any thing they fancy; and put on an air of diſſatisfaction, if they are refuſed.

THEY begin, as I before obſerved, to be better acquainted with the value of gold and ſilver, and are not altogether ſo fond of baubles as they uſed to be: for if we want to purchaſe cattle, fowls, or cowries, they deſire to be paid either in ſpecie, fire-arms, or gun-powder. They have likewiſe fallen upon a method of ſolliciting thoſe who come there, particularly all paſſengers, to contribute a dollar or two, towards improving their navigation, which they carry on with the African continent; and by way of perſuaſive example, produce ſeveral liſts of perſons who have ſubſcribed to that purpoſe; ſo that they ſometimes collect thirty or forty dollars a ſhip, from thoſe who touch there: and when the captains leave the place, they generally make it a point for them to ſign, and leave with them a certificate of good uſage.

The huts of the lower fort of people, are built something after the nature of our barns: the sides are a sort of reeds tied together, and plaistered over with a mixture of clay and cow-dung; the roofs thatched with a kind of matting of coconut leaves. He is esteemed a man of rank who has a house of stone and mud.

They subsist chiefly on vegetables and milk, which they have here in great plenty and perfection. Instead of oil and vinegar to their sallads, that are of the lettice kind, they use a kind of liquid, somewhat like our treacle; being a preparation of the juice, yielded on incision from the coconut-tree, before it is thickened into the consistence of Iagree, which is a kind of coarse sugar they make from it.

Those of quality are to be distinguished by the nails of their fingers and toes, which they suffer to grow to an immoderate length; being tinged with the alhenna, a yellowish red, furnished them by a certain shrub that grows in the marshy places of the island; a practice used all over Arabia, and in most places of the Turkish dominions. They usually carry large knives, or poniards, stuck in a sash they wear round their waists; some of which have silver or agate handles; but commonly wrought wooden ones. They are most of them tall of stature, strong, and well proportioned; have long black hair, piercing eyes, lips somewhat inclining to be thick, and are in general of a color between olive and black. Their women are rather more clumsily made.

The common people have no cloathing but a piece of coarse wrapper, which goes round their loins, and often barely covers their sexual parts; with a skull cap, of any sort of stuff. Those of a superior rank have a kind of wide-sleeved shirt, which hangs down over a pair of long drawers,

and

and a waiſtcoat made thick or light, according to the ſeaſon : but few wear turbands, unleſs ſuch as are of great diſtinction.

The women are more curious in their apparel, wearing a ſhort jacket and petticoat, with a kind of looſe gown, and a veil to cover their faces. Their arms and wriſts they uſually adorn with a number of bracelets, made of glaſs, iron, copper, pewter, and ſilver, according to their reſpective ranks or circumſtances. The ſmall of their legs, their fingers and toes, are likewiſe decked with chains and rings. Their ears are ſtuck full of mock jewels, and ornaments of metal, inſomuch that the lobes of them eſpecially are greatly dilated and weighed down, which they are from their infancy taught to conſider as a beauty.

They ſuffer their children from their birth, males and females, to go ſtark naked, until from five to ſeven or eight years old : a cuſtom they have in common with the Orientals, who are not ſo much governed in it by the heat of the climate, or neceſſity, as by phyſical reaſons. They imagine that infants are conſtitutionally more apt to be hurt by heat than cold ; and that the free acceſs of the air to all parts of their bodies, is even nutrious, and more favorable to their principles of growth, than if they were ſweltered up with ſwathing clouts; which, they think, rob them of a hardineſs conducive to their health ; and, in caſe of any diſpoſition to deformity, obſtruct the free courſe of nature, always working for the beſt, and tending to clear itſelf of any imperfections. That alſo, by this method, thoſe little creatures are preſerved from the irkſome galling and chafing of cloaths, ſo often breeding their complaints and cryings ; which, if not carefully attended to, terminate through their ſtraining into ruptures, and at leaſt require abſorbent powders to imbibe the acrid

acrid sweat, to which they are then subject. How far they may be in the right, I do not presume to determine, against the European custom, probably too prevalent and established to admit of a change; yet this is certain, that it is rare to see, I will not only say, a deformed person, among them, but even one who is not admirably proportioned: and I have reason to think ruptures almost unknown to them, which are so common in Europe: some of them are, it is true, when young troubled with the navel-rupture; but this they soon recover, and is without bad consequences.

Their language is a corrupt Arabic, mixed with the Zanguebar-tongue of the opposite part of the continent, from whence it is probable the Comro islands were originally peopled. But the whiter sort of them, who are generally of the best rank, or at least the most esteemed among them, partly derive their color from the Arab mixture, and partly from their communication with the Europeans, which was formerly much more common than at present. They have adopted the jealousy of the Arabs, together with their manners and religion; though theirs is as yet no more than a gross Mahometism, adulterated with the remains of their antient superstition, especially among the lower sort.

I could not learn that the Portugueze, or any of the Romish priests, had ever made any great efforts to introduce the Christian religion; probably from a sense that there was little or no money stirring here, which is usually their primum mobile: however, they affect religion for their pretext, as they are very indifferent about being pastors to sheep that have not a golden fleece; and, to say the truth, they generally take special care, wherever they go, in quality of messengers of the glad tidings of the gospel, to be, like other

mercenary

THE EAST-INDIES.

mercenary meffengers, well paid for their trouble; as will be more amply fhewn, in the account I referve to give in its place of that fort of chriftianity, they make fuch a boaft of having propagated in India, with fo little foundation for any plea of merit in it.

THEIR manners ftill retain a great deal of the fimplicity of uncultivated nature. The mildnefs of the climate renders them indolent, and prone to venery. They often make ufe of the liberty granted them by their law of divorcing their wives, upon flight pretexts, for the fake of novelty; though they have generally two or three of them, and are confined to no number of concubines they can maintain. They are forward enough to beg any thing they like; but not thievifhly inclined. They treat the Englifh in particular, very cordially and fraternally; not purely from a principle of intereft and convenience, which however has doubtlefs fome influence; but alfo of gratitude, for the effectual affiftance they formerly received from them in their wars with the Mohilians. Being moreover affured, by a frequent intercourfe, that they have no defign of invading their country, or liberty, of which they retain a ftrong jealoufy againft other European nations, and of the Portugueze efpecially; to whofe ufurpations of the fea coaft on the continent they are no ftrangers; againft which they chiefly, and with great reafon, rely on the inacceffibility of their mountains, of which nature has formed for them an impenetrable barrier, and defence of the interior country.

ALL their woods, as I have before obferved, are clear of any wild beafts of prey; nor are they infefted with any venomous animals. They have a great number of monkies of different kinds and fizes; and a beaft about the bignefs of a common one, with a head greatly refembling that of a fox, a fox, with a lively piercing eye. Its coat is of a woolly kind, most commonly of a mouse-color; and its tail, of about three feet in length, is variegated with circles of black, within an inch of one another, from the setting-on to the top. The natives call it a Mocawk, and when taken young it soon grows very tame. They also abound with squirrels, which are generally large and shy, but neither well-shaped nor agreeably colored. Their oxen, of which they have great numbers, are of a middling size; and, like those in the East Indies, are remarkable for their difference from ours, in having a large fleshy excrescence between their neck and back, which are called the hump, and when kept in pickle for some time, are generally preferred either to tongue, or udder, tasting like firm marrow: nothing too can be imagined sweeter than their flesh. What fowls we purchased were also extremely good and fat: however, while we remained there, I had no opportunity of tasting their game, of which they are said to have great and excellent variety: but the natives are bad sportsmen, either with net or gun.

The sea also furnishes them with fish of different sorts, and in great abundance, which they are very expert at catching. They have one particular species, which is called the parrot-fish, beautified with the liveliest colors that can be imagined; is about three foot and a half in length, thick in proportion, and reckoned delicious eating. They have also some flat fish, that a good deal resemble the turbot; likewise thornbacks, mullets, and several other sorts, of which I could not learn the names.

Besides many fruits they have in common with the Indies, which it would be tiresome, and out of place to enumerate, there is one remarkable sort of sweet oranges, of a small size, not exceeding that of a common plumb or apricot; but replete
with

THE EAST-INDIES. 27

with a juice, far more deliciously flavored than the larger sort, such as are generally imported in England from Portugal, under the name of China-oranges. Doubtless too, their being gathered ripe, and fresh from the tree, is an advantage to their taste; and they may safely be eat in great numbers.

Upon the whole then, it is not easy to conceive a place more perfectly suited for refreshment, after a tedious passage at sea, than the island of Johanna; there lying no objection to it, that I could learn, except the want of proper lodgment ashore, which might be easily provided for; and its distance, which would be more convenient, if it was so much beyond midway from England, that it makes the interval from land to land, rather too long for the preservation of health, especially among the common-sailors, not so preventively provided with necessaries against the ravages of the scurvy, as the officers and passengers. To say the truth, considering how precious the lives of men ought to be held, the precautions in their favor, great as they are already, on board the Europe ships, are not so sufficient, but they might receive some beneficial addition, in which both humanity, and the safety of the voyage itself, might find an account.

Saturday, the 4th of August, early in the morning, we unmoored the ship; and on receiving nineteen head of cattle on board, hoisted in the long-boat: in the afternoon weighed anchor, with a light breeze from off the shore, and made the best of our route for our next post of destination, Bombay; where, without any material occurrence in the passage, we arrived on Tuesday the 28th of the same month, and came to an anchor in the road, saluting the fort, as customary, with nine guns, which was returned with the difference of two less in number.

BOOK

BOOK II.

Of BOMBAY.

CHAP. I.

Author waits on the governor. Situation and latitude of the island. Advice for preserving health. Former unhealthiness of the island, and its present melioration in that point accounted for. Distempers. Seasons.

ARRIVING at Bombay, I went ashore in the evening, about six o'clock, where, with the other gentlemen entertained in the same service, we waited on Mr. Wake, then governor, with our respects; who received us with great affability and politeness, inviting us to supper with him; and in the interval, we retired to find out such gentlemen, belonging to the place, for whom we had letters.

It was my good fortune to be recommended, by a director in London, to a gentleman who was nephew to the governor, and at that time resided in the factory. He saved me the trouble of enquiring after him, by sending a servant to bring me to his apartment; and who afterwards, in honor of my recommendation, did me all the good offices, so welcome and so necessary to strangers, especially on their first arrival in a place new to them, and where they must consequently want advice and directions. I mention this, not only by way of gratitude, but as a just caution for all who

may

may be in the fame cafe, of going abroad to fuch places to get provided with effectual recommendations; for it too often happens, that many reft fatisfied with either improper ones, or with fuch, as being mere matter of form, are treated fo by thofe to whom they are addreffed.

I was then foon put into a regular way of life, and had no other inconveniencies or complaints, but what one is ufually expofed to, in the change of a native climate for a foreign one. And here, though this place is pretty well known by a number of defcriptions of its origin, fituation, climate, &c. it might be deemed an imperfection in my plan, were I not to mention, at leaft fummarily, thofe particulars: as the reference to other books or accounts, would break the connection and order, required for the readers ideas, which muft be the clearer, for the whole being prefented to him at one view.

BOMBAY is an ifland, in the latitude of eighteen degrees, forty-one minutes of north latitude, near the coaft of Deckan, the high mountains of which are full in view, at a trifling diftance; and is fo fituate, as, together with the winding of other iflands along that continent, to form one of the moft commodious bays perhaps in the world; from which diftinction it received the denomination of Bombay, by corruption from the Portuguefe Buon-bahia, though now ufually written by them Bombaim. Certain it is, that the harbor is fpacious enough to contain any number of fhips; has excellent anchoring-ground; and by its circular pofition, can afford them a land-locked fhelter againft any winds, to which the mouth of it is expofed. It is alfo admirably fituated for a center of dominion and commerce, with refpect to the Malabar coaft, the Gulf of Perfia, the Red-Sea, and the whole trade of that fide of the great Indian

Peninfula,

Peninsula, and northern parts adjoining to it: to the government of which presidency they are vey properly subordinated.

CONSIDERING too that this island is situated within the tropics, the climate of it is far from intolerable on account of its heat, in any time of the year; though never susceptible of any degree of cold beyond what must be rather agreeable to an European constitution. In the very hottest season, which immediately precedes the periodical return of the rains, the refreshment of the alternate land and sea-breezes is hardly ever wanting, the calms being generally of a very short duration; so that perhaps, in the year, there may be a few days of an extraordinary sultry heat, and even those may be made supportable, by avoiding any violent exercise, by keeping especially out of the malignant unmitigated glare and action of the sun, and by a light unoppressive dyet. Great care too should be taken of not exposing one self to the dangerous effect of the night-dews, and of the too quick transition from a state of open pores, to their perspiration being shut up; which is so often the case of those, who, from an impatience of heat, venture to sleep from under cover, in the raw air of the night, pleasantly indeed, but perniciously cooled by the absence of the sun: a circumstance yet more fatal, to such as have besides been heated by any intemperance in eating and drinking.

BOMBAY, in fact, had long borne an infamous character for unhealthfulness. It was commonly called the burying-ground of the English; but this was only until an experience, bought at the expence of a number of lives, had rendered the causes of such a mortality more known, and consequently more guarded against. Among others, the principal ones doubtless were:

FIRST,

THE EAST-INDIES. 31

FIRST, the nature of the climate, and the precautions and management required by it, not being so sufficiently known, as they now are; if that knowledge was but prevalent enough, with many, for them to sacrifice their pleasures of intemperance, or the momentary relief from a present irksomeness of heat, to the preservation of their healths.

FORMERLY too, there obtained a practice esteemed very pernicious to the health of the inhabitants, employing a manure for the coconut-trees, that grow in abundance on the island, consisting of the small fry of fish, and called by the country-name Buckshaw; which was undoubtedly of great service, both to augment, and meliorate their produce: but through its quantity being superficially laid in trenches round the root, and consequently the easier to be exhaled, diffused, as it putrified, a very unwholsome vapor. There are some, however, who deny this, and insist on the ill consequences of this manure to be purely imaginary, or at least greatly exaggerated; giving for reason, that the inhabitants themselves were never sensible of any noxious quality in that method; and that if the island is now less unhealthy, the change must be sought for in other causes. But all are agreed, that the habitations in the woods, or coconut-groves, are unwholesome, from the air wanting a free current through them; and from the trees themselves, diffusing a kind of vaporous moisture, unfavorable to the lungs, a complaint common to all close-wooded countries.

THERE has also been another reason assigned, for the island having grown healthier, from the lessening of the waters, by a breach of the sea being banked off; which however does not seem to me a satisfactory one. There is still subsisting a great body of salt water on the inside of the breach, the communication of which with the sea, being

less

less free than before the breach was built, must be in proportion more apt to stagnate, and breed noxious vapors; so that this alteration by the breach cannot enter for much, if any thing, into the proposed solution, which may perhaps be better reduced into the before-mentioned one of the different diet, and manner of living of the Europeans: not however without taking into account, the place being provided with more skilful physicians than formerly, when there was less niceness in the choice of them. Surgeons, and surgeons-mates of ships, and those none of the expertest, used to be admitted almost without any, or but a superficial examination: though in so tender a point, as that of the life of subjects, always precious, and surely more so, where they are so difficult to recruit. The same negligence was also observed with respect to the gallies, and other armed vessels of the company in those parts: and to say the truth, the pay was too slender to invite into such service any capable persons. Here I cannot omit inserting, though digressively, one instance of a wanton disregard to that material point, of the truth of which I have been credibly assured. Mr. Phipps, one of the former governors, on examining the marine establishment of Bombay, wherein he proposed making retrenchments, by way of currying favor with his masters at home, which is often done, by the falsest, and most ruinous œconomy, observed the surgeons pay, rated at 42 rupees per month, which, at the usual way of reckoning of a rupee for half-a-crown, was just five guineas. " What, says he, there must be " some mistake, the figures are transposed, it must " be 24 instead of 42:" and for the sake of this, in every sense a barbarous joke, he, with a dash of his pen, curtailed the pay accordingly: but
surely

THE EAST-INDIES.

surely this was rather cutting into the quick, than paring off excrescences.

WHATEVER may be the reason, the point is certain, that the climate is no longer so fatal to the English inhabitants as it used to be, and incomparably more healthy than many other of our settlements in India.

THE most common disorders are fevers, to which muscular strong men are more subject than those of laxer fibres; and bloody fluxes, but the last make much less ravage than they used to do, where they fixed, from the superior method of treating them. New-comers too especially are liable to some cutaneous eruptions, such as the prickly heat, which is rather reckoned beneficial than otherwise; and a sort of tetters, called ring-worms, from their circular form, about the size of a shilling, which however soon submit to a gentle physicking, or even to some slight outward application.

THE Barbeers, a violent disorder that generally ended in rendering all the limbs paralytic; and the mordechin, which is a fit of violent vomiting and purging, that often proved fatal, are distempers hardly now known on the island.

IN short, this place, the name of which used to carry terror with it, in respect to its unhealthiness, is now no longer to be dreaded on that account; provided any common measure of temperance be observed, without which the tenure of health, in any climate, must be hazardous.

THE seasons however can at most be divided into three; the cool, hot, and rainy: or indeed properly enough into the dry wreather, which lasts eight months in the year; and into the wet, which continues about four months raining, but with short intermissions. The setting in of the rains, is commonly ushered in by a violent thunder-storm, generally called the Elephanta, a name which it probably receives in the Asiatic style, from the comparison of its force to that of the elephant. Yet this is a pleasing prelude to the refreshment that follows, from the rains moderating that excessive heat, which is then at its height, and naturally brings on, with the sun that raises the vapors, the relief from its intense ardor. They begin about the 28th of May, and break up about the beginning of September, after which there is never any, unless, and that but rarely, a short transient shower. This rainy season, though extremely hot, in any dry intervals, when the sun shines out for a few hours, is counted the pleasantest: yet the end of it, and some days after, are not reckoned but the sickliest time of the whole year, from the abundance of exhalations forming a kind of faint, vaporous bath, from which those who lodge in apartments the highest from the ground are proportionably less in danger, the atmosphere growing gradually clearer upwards.

During this season the country-trading vessels are laid up, especially those belonging to the black-merchants, with whom it is a kind of superstition not to send any to sea, until after a festival on the breaking up of the rains; the ceremony of which consists chiefly in throwing, by way of oblation, a consecrated coconut into the sea, gilt and ornamented. Then and not till then they look on the sea as open and navigable until the next returning rains. How this solemn anniversary foolery came to be established, I never could learn from any of the natives; it being probably one of their many traditional customs, the original of which is lost in the remoteness of their antiquity.

CHAP.

CHAP. II.

Of the government of BOMBAY: *its charter. Of the military and marine forces: militia. The piratory on that coast: measures to oppose it. Mildness and tolerancy of the* ENGLISH *government.*

THE government of this island is entirely English, subordinate to the court of directors of the united companies of merchants of England trading to the East-Indies, who appoint, by commission, a president, to whom they join a council consisting of nine persons; the whole number of which are rarely, or rather never on the spot, being employed as chiefs of the several factories subordinate to that presidency. Those of the council as are at Bombay are appointed to the posts of the greatest trust, such as accountant, warehouse-keeper, land-paymaster, marine-paymaster, and other offices for transacting the company's affairs. They are generally such as have risen by degrees from the station of writers, and take place, unless otherwise ordered from home, according to the seniority of the service.

THE president then, and such members of the council as are on the spot, being convened by his order, signified to them by the secretary, constitute a regular council, in which all matters are decided by majority of votes: though the influence of the president is generally so great, that few or no points are carried but according to his will, and dictates. For should any of the council oppose him, he has it so much in his power to make their situation uneasy to them, that they must quit the service, and repair home, where, unless the occasion of discontent is very flagrant indeed, they rarely meet with much countenance or redress;

the

the company thinking it rather more political to wink at the faults of a governor, where they are such as not to be too hurtful to their service, than to expose their affairs to the hazard of worse inconveniencies, from the dissensions of any number of absolutely co-ordinates. And to say the truth, this weight a top, though liable from human infirmity to be sometimes oppressive, serves to keep the under parts steady and fixt in their place: besides, it is easier to make one person accountable for the administration of things than a number; and since the president is he on whom the company chiefly relies, it seems but reasonable that he should have the greatest share of power.

As to the matters of a judicial nature, they were in the year 1727 settled by a royal charter, respectively obtained for the three chief presidencies of the company in India: to wit, Bombay; Fort St. George, or Madrass, on the coast of Coromandel; and Calcutta in Bengal. How this charter was received or managed in the two last places, I have had no distinct account: but as to Bombay am better informed.

At the time this charter was procured for these settlements, it was generally believed to have been sollicited by Mr. Harrison, once a governor of India, but at that time a director of the East-India company: who, in fact, meant it as a temporary expedient for preserving and extending his influence over the direction by this proof of his favor at court; though the plausible pretext alledged was the better administration of justice in those colonies. That such however could not be the true intention, must appear clearly from the neglect of all the proper and competent means for establishing it, especially with reference to Bombay; and indeed as to the two others, I never heard that there was any more care taken of them. The charter then appointing

pointing the judges of Oyer and Terminer, the mayor's court, and the court of appeals, this laſt to confiſt of purely the preſident and council, was only attended with a manuſcript book of inſtructions; which, granting it was framed by the ableſt lawyers in the kingdom, could be but a very imperfect guidance to the gentlemen nominated to the ſeveral judicial offices neceſſary to the execution thereof. Theſe gentlemen being, generally ſpeaking, ſuch as came very young out of their country, bred up entirely in a mercantile way, and utterly unacquainted with the laws of England, were in courſe liable to make great miſtakes, eſpecially in caſes of capital importance: and however their natural good ſenſe and well-meaning might make a ſhift in purely commercial caſes to decide with tolerable equity, they could not but be greatly at a loſs in thoſe of a mixed nature, or where it was neceſſary to pay a regard to the particular laws of England. No perſon had been ſent out with capacity or knowledge enough to put this new method of procedure into a proper courſe, and to aſcertain the limits of the ſeveral juriſdictions: ſo that the charter was left in a manner to execute itſelf. But this inſufficiency of judgment was not even the worſt of its conſequences: for ſeveral of the company's ſervants, named eſpecially to fill the offices of mayor and aldermen of the mayor's court, even though their juriſdiction was ſubordinate to the court of appeals, aſſumed to themſelves ſuch an authority and independence, as made the governor and council jealous of theirs being leſſened, or at leaſt checked by it. This bred ſuch feuds and diſſenſions, that ſeveral of the members of the mayor's court conceiving themſelves aggrieved, quitted the ſervice, and repaired home to the company with their complaints. All which might have been in a great meaſure prevented,

vented, if proper perfons had been appointed, and sent out by the company, to give these new powers their due digestion and form. Whereas, as it was, the want of knowledge, the inexperience and aim at independence in the appointed members of the several courts, rendered this accession of authority a dangerous tool, in the hands of perfons so disqualified for the exercise of it : so that it is scarce a doubt, but the charter had been better not obtained, than no better a provision have been made for its administration and maintenance. The neglect of such necessary precautions, are evidently fitter to give a sanction to unavoidable errors, and breed dissentions, than to promote a regular distribution of justice: for any such disposition, which could only be made by sending out persons competently learned in the law, and vested with a sufficient authority, would not only have been attended with a great expence, but might have too much interfered with the plan of government instituted by the company at home, and have broke that unity of direction, so necessary to the due subordination of their servants.

As to the military and marine force, it is considered as more immediately under the direction of the president, who is entitled general and commander in chief; though nothing material is supposed to be ordered concerning either without the concurrence of the council.

WITH respect to the military, the common men are chiefly such as the company sends out in their ships, or deserters from the several nations settled in India, Dutch, French, and Portuguese, which last are commonly known by the name of Reynols (Regnicolæ); and lastly, Topazzes, mostly black, or of a mixed breed from the Portuguese, to whom, and indeed to all the Roman-catholics in the military service, there is not the least objection made,

or

THE EAST-INDIES. 39

or moleſtation given on account of their religion, of which they have the freeſt exerciſe imaginable; nor is the leaſt expediency of changing it even mentioned to them; whereby they are ſo eaſy on that head, that they might ſafely be truſted in any war againſt thoſe of their own religion, ſuch as the French, or even againſt the Portugueſe themſelves. At leaſt I never heard of any complaint relating thereto.

THESE are formed into companies under Engliſh officers, ſo as to compoſe the preſidiary force of the iſland; and are beſides occaſionally draughted off in detachments or parties ſent upon command, either in the land-ſervice, or in re-inforcement of the ſubordinate ſettlements, or on board the armed veſſels, which conſtitute the companies marine in thoſe parts.

IN the military may alſo be included many regularly formed companies of the natives. Theſe ſoldiers are called ſepoys, who have their proper officers with the titles in the country-language, all however under the orders of the Engliſh. They uſe muſkets, at which they are indifferently expert; but they are chiefly armed in the country-manner, with ſword and target, and wear the Indian dreſs, the turbant, cabay or veſt, and long drawers. Their pay is but ſmall, comparatively to the Europeans; and yet they are on many occaſions very ſerviceable from their inurement to the climate, and diet of the country; and are rarely known to miſbehave or give way, if they are well-led, and encouraged by the example of the Europeans, with whom they are joined. Generally ſpeaking too they are very faithful to the maſters who pay them, or to uſe the expreſſion familiar to the natives, to thoſe whoſe ſalt they eat.

THERE is alſo on the iſland kept up a ſort of militia, compoſed of the land-tillers, and banda- rees,

rees, whose living depends chiefly on the cultivation of the coconut-trees; who, though not regularly disciplined, would be of good service, especially in any laborious part of military duty, and would assist in the defence of the island, against any foreign invasion, for the sake of their families there settled and from attachment to the English government, the mildness and justice of which is the more sensible to them from the comparison obvious to make of it, to the oppression of the neighboring governments.

Besides the necessary charge of a presidiary force, for the defence of the island, the company has been obliged for a number of years to keep up a military marine, for the protection of trade upon the coast, the whole length of which has, for time immemorial, been infested with pirates, and bears some resemblance to that part of the African coast, which has so long been infamous for this practice. Certain it is, that but for the constant check they were kept in by the English naval force in those parts, those seas would have swarmed with piratical vessels, and no trading one, unsufficiently armed, could have escaped them.

The coast to the northward of Bombay and Surat, was chiefly the harbor of a nest of pirates, called Sanganians, who seldom extended their cruize far beyond the latitude of their ports, and were especially troublesome to the trading vessels bound in or out of the Gulf of Persia: but they rarely attacked any ship of strength; their cruizers being of no size, nor carrying any artillery equal to such an attempt, Their object too was chiefly plunder, without making slaves of those they found on captured vessels; a rule which however they sometimes broke thorough, where there was any considerable ransom to be hoped.

THE EAST-INDIES.

ON the opposite coast, which forms the end of the Persian Gulf, were seated the Muskat-Arabs, whose first putting forth ships for cruizing was purely out of revenge against the Portuguese, whom they endeavored to harrass by all means, and even proceeded so far, as to make descents on their settlements bordering upon Surat, where they committed all sort of devastations. But having once got a relish of pillaging such enemies at sea, they began to extend their attacks indiscriminately on other nations, and among them on the English, from whom however, after receiving various defeats, they were induced to abstain in future, and little by little taking a commercial bent, they have much remitted of that piratical turn, and keep vessels of force rather upon the defensive, than for any other purpose, and therewith held the power of the famous Shah-Nadir in defiance, who had the reduction of them much at heart.

FORMERLY too the Malabar coast, which though it gives its name to the sea-shore as high as Surat, properly begins at Mount-Dilly, was also noted for the pirates that it bred, who greatly disturbed the navigation of the Indian seas. These were long ago quieted by the Portuguese armaments; and since, having been not only overpowered by the English, but discountenanced by the country-governments, who used to give them harbor and protection, are now dwindled to nothing.

To the northward of Goa, there were several petty chiefs, who carried on this piratical course; but at length came to an amicable correspondence with the English, from their dread and jealousy of the superior and growing power of Angria, their common enemy, though from different reasons.

IT was then principally on account of Angria, whose dominions stretched from the mouth of Bombay

Bombay harbor, down a great length of coaſt without a material interruption, that the company was, in its own defence, obliged to keep on foot a very expenſive maritime force. This force conſiſted chiefly of gallies built here in England, on the moſt beautiful models that can be imagined, carrying about eighteen or twenty guns, and provided with oars, which were of ſpecial ſervice in a calm. They had alſo a few grabs, being veſſels of much the ſame burthen, but built in the country, on the model of Angria's grabs, with prows, which ſeem beſt calculated for carrying chace-guns. The ſcheme of thoſe people's gunnery being chiefly to get into the wake of their enemy, and rake him fore-and-aft; a kind of quarter-maſter conducting the veſſel till he brings the maſts of his chace into one, at the inſtant of which he gives the word for firing, and commonly does the greateſt execution in the rigging, after which they have the eaſier market of the veſſel thus diſabled. Otherwiſe, they are too ſlightly built to lay along-ſide of any ſhip of the leaſt weight of metal. Their great ſtreſs lies on thoſe prow-guns, which they manage to ſpecial advantage in a calm, having armed boats to tow them a-ſtern of the veſſel they attack, and which for want of wind cannot avoid them. Of theſe armed boats called Gallevats, the company maintains alſo a competent number, for the ſervice of their marine, being not only of uſe to oppoſe them to the enemy, but for purſuit, or expeditions in ſhoal-water. For further ſtrengthening too of the naval force in thoſe parts, the company occaſionally ſtations at Bombay ſome larger built ſhips from Europe; which, for their ſuperior weight of metal, and greater difficulty of boarding, eſpecially in deep water, with any thing of a commanding gale, have nothing to fear

from

from those slight vessels; though, in a calm, they might gall and plague them sufficiently.

ALL these vessels that formed the military marine of Bombay were chiefly manned with English, or with European deserters from other nations; and according to the exigency reinforced with detachments of soldiers from the land-forces, to serve in the nature of marines. These vessels were to guard the navigation of those seas, and convoy the trade employed on collateral services; such as protecting the interest of the company, or vindicating its honor, where requisite within the bounds of that presidency's department; as in the Red Sea, Gulf of Persia, the Bar of Surat, &c.

BUT whatever care could be taken of employing these cruizers to safety and advantage, it could scarce happen otherwise, but that Angria, always alert, and who knew too well the inferiority of his strength, to attack them without great odds on his side, should now and then over-match them so with numbers, as to get the better; but as more will be said of him hereafter, I shall drop him here.

TOWARDS defraying the charges of this marine, the company required of all the trading vessels, those of the other European nations excepted, to take the passes of the Bombay-government, for which they paid so small a consideration, that I never heard the least murmuring; the merchants being duly sensible not only of the benefit their trade received from the English protection, but that this contribution was far short of the cost of it.

NOTHING however has more contributed to the population of this island, than the mildness of the government and the toleration of all religions; there not being suffered the least violence or injury to be offered, either to the natives or Europeans on that account. The Roman-catholic churches, the

Moorish

Moorish mofchs, the Gentoo pagodas, the worship of the Parsees, are all equally unmolested and tolerated. They have the free exercise of all their rites and religious ceremonies, without either the English interfering, or their clashing with one another. This toleration also makes a contract very favorable for our nation, to the rigors of the inquisition, which take place in the neighboring territories of the Portuguese, whose having rendered themselves odious on that account, was not one of the least reasons that facilitated their being driven out of the greatest part of them by the Morattoes, who are all Gentoos. Mr. Bourchier, the present governor, has greatly exerted himself, on the troubles of the government at Surat, and in the countries round about, to draw a confluence of their inhabitants, merchants, and tradesmen to settle at Bombay, where they experience quite another treatment and security than under their own governments. In truth, this gentleman's conduct cannot be too much commended for his incessant endeavors at increasing the population, and improving or inlarging the trade of the island; especially for his care of cultivating peace and friendship with those dangerous and powerful neighbors the Morattoes; who, being now masters of the contiguous island of Salsett, can at pleasure streighten the supplies of the island, and interrupt its inland communication. But of them more in its place.

CHAP.

THE EAST-INDIES. 45

CHAP. III.

Of the state of landed property on the island. ENG-
LISH, *how ill used by the* PORTUGUESE *in the cession of this island. Land-proprietors.* PARELL
*the governor's country-house. Coconut-oarts: rice-
fields. Brab-trees; toddy-birds. Cultivation improved; to what owing.*

IT is to be observed, that when the cession of
this island and harbor was first made to the
English by the Portuguese, although so far deficient
as it was, against the terms of agreement between
the two crowns; and that the island of Salsett,
which was manifestly included in the regalities of
Bombay, was unjustly withheld from us, and consequently greatly lessened the importance of an
island, which must chiefly depend for its support
on that of Salsett: the Portuguese also clogged
the surrender of even this small part of what was
our due, with the condition that the inhabitants,
late their subjects, were to enjoy their possessions
in the same manner as before we took possession.
The island was then, and still continues, divided
into three roman-catholic parishes, or Freguezias,
as they call them; which are Bombay, Mahim,
and Salvaçam; the churches of which, are governed by roman-catholic priests, of any nation but
the Portuguese, against whom the English wisely
objected, from the danger of their connection and
too close correspondence with the priests of their
own nation, in the neighboring Portuguese dominions, of whom we had repeated reasons to
be jealous. The bulk then of the land-proprietors
were roman-catholic Mestizos and Canarins. The
first are a mixed breed of the natives and Portuguese: the other purely aborigines of the country,
converted

converted to what the Portuguese call the Faith. The other land-owners were Moors, Gentoos, and Parsees; but these last are of moderner date, having since purchased on the island. However, to all these the article of security to their property has been inviolably kept, and the right of inheritance is regulated according to the respective laws and customs of the several denominations of cast or religion. The land is chiefly employed in coconut-groves, or oarts; rice-fields, and onion-grounds, which are reckoned of an excellent sort on this island.

The company have also acquired a considerable landed estate, either by purchases, confiscations for crimes, or treasons, and seizures for debt; for which estate there is a particular officer, under the title of super-intendant appointed to administer.

There are two very pleasant gardens belonging to the company, cultivated after the European manner: the one a little way out of the gates, open to any of the English gentlemen who like to walk there; the other much larger and finer, at about five miles distance from the town, at a place called Parell, where the governor has a very agreeable country-house, which was originally a Romish chapel belonging to the jesuits, but confiscated about the year 1719, for some foul practices against the English interest. It is now converted into a pleasant mansion-house, and what with the additional buildings, and improvements of the gardens, affords a spacious and commodious habitation. There is an avenue to it of a hedge and trees near a mile long; and, though near the seaside, is sheltered from the air of it by a hill between. Here the governor may spend most part of the heats; the air being cooler and fresher than in town; and nothing is wanting that may make a country-retirement agreeable.

As

As to the oarts, or coconut-groves, they make the moſt conſiderable part of the landed property; being planted wherever the ſituation and ſoil is favorable to them. When a number of theſe groves lie contiguous to each other, they form what is called the woods, through which there is a due ſpace left for roads and pathways, where one is pleaſantly defended from the ſun at all hours in the day. They are alſo thick-ſet with houſes belonging to the reſpective proprietors, as well as with huts of the poorer ſort of people. I have before remarked, that they are however reckoned unwholeſome for want of a free ventilation.

As to the coconut-tree itſelf, not all the minute deſcriptions of it, which I have met with in many authors, ſeem to me to come up to the reality of its wonderful proprieties and uſe. Nothing is ſo unpromiſing as the aſpect of this tree; nor none yields a produce more profitable, or more variouſly beneficial to mankind: it has ſome reſemblance to the palm-tree; perhaps, one of its ſpecies: the leaves of it ſerve for thatching, the huſk of the fruit for making cordage, and even the largeſt cables for ſhips. The kernel of it is dried, and yields an oil much wanted for ſeveral uſes, and makes a conſiderable branch of traffic under the name of Copra. Arrack, a coarſe ſort of ſugar called Jagree, and vinegar are alſo extracted from it, beſides many other particulars too tedious to enumerate. The cultivation of it is extremely eaſy, by means of channels conveying water to the roots, and by a manure laid round them, of which I have ſpoke already. An owner then of two hundred of theſe trees is reckoned to have a competency to ſubſiſt on.

As to the rice-fields, they differ in value, according to the fineneſs and quantity of rice they produce. The growth of this grain has a particularity

cularity not unworth mentioning; which is, that as it loves a watry soil, so to whatever height the water rises, wherever it is planted, the growth of the rice keeps measure with it, even to that of twelve or fourteen foot, the summit of the stalk always appearing above the surface. It is also remarked, that the eating of new rice affects the eyes. The fact is certain, though I cannot assume to give the physical reason for it.

There are also here and there intersperfed a few brab-trees, or rather wild palm-trees; (the word brab being derived from *Brabo*, which in Portuguese signifies wild) that bear an insipid kind of fruit, about the bigness of a common pear: but the chief profit from them is the toddy, or liquor drawn from them by incisions at the top, of which the arrack that is made is reckoned better than that from the coconut-trees. They are generally near the sea-side, as they delight most in a sandy soil. It is on this tree that the toddy-birds, so called from their attachment to that tree, make their exquisitely curious nests, wrought out of the thinnest reeds and filaments of branches, with an inimitable mechanism. The birds themselves are of no value either for plumage, song, or the table, and are about the bigness of a partridge.

This island is however a strong instance of the benefits of a good government, and a numerous population, by not a spot of it remaining uncultivated: so that though it is far from producing sufficient for the consumption of the inhabitants; and notwithstanding its many disadvantages of situation and soil, it yields, in proportion to its bigness, incomparably more than the adjacent island of Salsett; whether under the government of the Portuguese, or, as it now is, under that of the Morattoes.

CHAP.

CHAP. IV.

Of the fortifications, public works, and buildings of BOMBAY. *The castle might have been better situated: the town walled round: out-forts: the breach:* ENGLISH *church. Private buildings and* GENTOO *pagodas. Malabar hill. Story of a* GENTOO GIOGHY. *Rock of purification.*

WHEN the English first took possession of this island, they found in that part of it, which chiefly commands the harbor, an old fortified house, the residence of the Portuguese governor; and though this house might have served for other valuable uses, they were tempted to make it the centre house of the castle which they built round it. It is however impossible to conceive, in every sense, a more incommodious structure; and the same, or perhaps less cost, than the reparations and additions have stood in to the company, would have built a much better mansion new from the ground. Yet the false œconomy of preserving this old piece of building, which need not to have been demolished or thrown away, had such effect, that it hindered the English not only from consulting a more commanding situation to the harbor; which is that of Mendham's Point; but made them blind to the disadvantage of the fort built round it; being overlooked by an eminence near it, called Dungharee Point, on which there is only a small untenable little fort, of no defence, and which serves now for the town prison, for debtors, or criminals.

THE castle however itself deserved a better situation; being a regular quadrangle, well-built of strong hard stone. In one of the bastions of it that faces Dungharee Point, there is a large tank or cistern hollowed, which contains a great quan-

VOL. I.   E   tity

tity of water, that is conftantly replenifhed by the ftationary rains. There is alfo a well within the fort: but the water is not extremely good, and liable to be dried up in the heats. It is alfo to be obferved, that the water in general on the ifland is not reckoned the beft; and has been given for a reafon why the Gentoo merchants were not fo forward to fettle on it. Water being a point of great confequence with them; for as they drink no fpirituous liquors, they are very curious and difcerning in the tafte and qualities of waters.

Some years after, as the town grew more populous, it was judged expedient to add the fecurity of a wall round it; and even then, they neglected to take in, as they might have done by a fmall extenfion, that dangerous poft of Dungharee, which evidently now commands both town and caftle. The curtains however between the baftions, were of little more ftrength or fubftance than a common garden wall : but there has lately been added at a great expence a ditch that encompaffes the wall, and can be flooded at pleafure, by letting in the fea, at which the ditch terminates on two fides, fo that the town is thoroughly furrounded with water. It is now one of the ftrongeft places by much that the company have in India; and, confidering the commodioufnefs of its harbor, might not be improperly made their capital place of arms, in the fame nature as Batavia ferves the Dutch: efpecially if the envious Portuguefe had not detained us from that fertile large ifland of Salfett, which would have compleatly ferved for a granary to it. Inftead of which, their fupine indolent government fuffered the Jefuits, who are better known in India by the appellation of Paulifts, from their head church and convent of St. Paul's in Goa, to get by degrees, and with their ufual arts and management of the laity, by much the greateft part of that

ifland

island into their own hands; and which they kept wretchedly fortified, so that it fell an easy conquest to the Morattoes, and at the same time we lost an useful barrier between us and that rapacious people.

At proper posts, round the island, there are disposed several little out-forts and redoubts; as at Mazagam, Sion, Suree, and Worlee: none of which are capable of making any long defence. The fort of Mahim is by much the most considerable, next to that of Bombay; being situate at the opposite extremity lengthways of the island. It commands the pass of Bandurah; a fort which almost fronts it on the opposite shore of Salsett, from which it is divided by an arm of the sea, that is however capable only of receiving small craft, that does not bring in great business to the custom-house established there.

The breach is the work that next claims mention, and is the most considerable for the cost of it. About two miles out of town, towards the middle of the island, the sea had so gained upon it with its irruption, that it almost divided the island in two, and made the roads impassable. It did not then only take up a large expence to drain off a great quantity of this water, but to make a causeway that should bankoff this inundation. This causeway is above a quarter of a mile in length, and of a considerable breadth: but there is one gross fault remarked in it, that being bending near its middle, the architect has opposed to the sea a re-entering angle instead of a saliant one. Perhaps he had his reasons, but at least they do not appear. In the mean time, there still lies within the breach a considerable body of water, that has a free communication with the sea, as appears by its ebbing and flowing, and probably is but the wholesomer for it. Though it is not unlikely that this subterraneous intercourse may, in procefs of time, undermine and blow up the caufe-way. After all then I am far from convinced, that the benefits accruing from the breach are equal to the expence of it; which, I am affured, could not be much lefs than a hundred thoufand pounds.

The only Englifh church at Bombay, and which is full fufficient for any poffible congregation of them at it, is a building extremely neat, commodious, and airy; being fituate on what is called the Green; a fpacious area that continues from the fort thereto, and is pleafantly laid out in walks planted with trees, round which are moftly the houfes of the Englifh inhabitants.

These are generally but ground-floored after the roman fafhion, and moftly with a court-yard before and behind, in which are the offices and out-houfes. They are fubftantially built with ftone, lime, and fmooth plaiftered on the out-fide. They are often kept white-wafhed, which has a neat air; but very offenfive to the eyes from the glare of the fun. Few of them have glafs windows to any apartment, the fafhes being generally paned with a kind of tranfparent oifter-fhells fquare-cut; which have the fingular property of tranfmitting the light full fufficiently, at the fame time that they exclude the violence of its glare, and have befides a cool look. The flooring is generally compofed of a kind of loam or ftucco, called Chunam, being a lime made of burnt fhells; which, if well tempered, as they have a peculiar art of it, is extremely hard and lafting, and takes fo fmooth a polifh, that one may literally fee one's face in it: but where terraffes are made of it, unlefs the chunam is duly prepared, and which is very expenfive, is apt to crack with the violence of the fun's heat. There have been alfo fome attempts to paint the ftucco walls in apartments: but they have

The West side of Bombay Green

have never succeeded, being presently spoiled, and discolored by the saline particles of the lime, for which hitherto there has been found no cure.

AND here I cannot omit mentioning an use made at Surat of this manner of terrassing, for I saw no such thing at Bombay; some having, instead of gravel walks in their gardens, stucco ones, a little raised above the garden-beds: so that they must be dry to walk on immediately after the most violent rain: but then, what with their whiteness and polish, they must have a very disagreeable effect on the eye, in a sun-shiny day; besides their being so slippery.

THE houses of the black merchants, as they are called; though some are far from deserving the appellation of black; are for the most part extremely ill built, and incommodious; the window-lights small, and the apartments ill distributed. Some however, make a better appearance, if only a story high: but not the best of them are without a certain meanness in the manner, and clumsiness in the execution that may be observed, comparatively, and without any partiality to the European architecture, even the most ordinary.

THERE is yet a convenience most of those houses either of the English or natives have; which are small ranges of pillars that support a pent-house or shed, forming what is called, in the Portuguese lingua-franca, *Verandas*, either round, or on particular sides of the house, which afford a pleasing shelter against the sun, and keep the inner apartments cool and refreshed by the draught of air under them. Such colonnades might methinks even in England not be unserviceable to summer-houses especially; which being so heated by a constant sun in the middle of the day, as to be hardly tolerable, cannot be supposed to be cooled fast enough even in the evening to allow of their being a refreshing retreat. It is under these Verandas that the owners, especially the natives, generally enjoy the fresh air, and often transact their business or receive visitants.

Most however of the best houses are within the walls of the town; which may be about a mile in circuit.

As for the pagodas of the Gentoos, there is not one of them worth mentioning in regard to their appearance; being low mean buildings; commonly admitting the light only at the door, facing which is placed the principal idol, made after the various imaginations they have of the subaltern deities they worship, of which more will be said in its place. They fancy, it seems, that a dark gloomy place inspires a kind of religious horror and reverence. They are remarkably fond of having those pagodas among trees, and near the side of a tank, or pond, for the sake of their ablutions; which they do, not like the Mahometans, so much practice as a religious ceremony, as purity for cleanliness; and I might add, for the voluptuousness of them in those hot countries. These tanks, or ponds, are often very expensive works, being generally square, and surrounded with stone-steps, that are very commodious to the bathers. The most remarkable pagoda on the island is on Malabar-hill, which is something more than two miles distance out of town, and is a kind of promontory that stretching into the sea, forms, together with a small island called Old Woman's Island, what is called Back Bay, the entry of which is shut up by a ledge of rocks running from the one to the other. On this hill, which is far from an high one, and of easy ascent, about a mile from that ascent, after passing a plain a-top of it, on a gentle declivity to the sea-side, stands the Gentoo pagoda, with a large tank or pond a few feet from it, and is of

fresh

THE EAST-INDIES.

fresh water, formed by the draining of the rains, though not many yards from the sea, with which it is near on a level, on the side that is open to it, all but where the pagoda stands between a part of it and the shore. The other three sides are surrounded with trees that form an amphitheatre, on the slopes of the hill towards it, than which no prospect that I ever saw, or can conceive, forms a more agreeably wild landscape. The trees open to all the force of the winds, follow the general law, and take a strong bent to the opposite point from them, but with such regularity, that one would think they had been trimmed or pruned to that figure they exhibit. These trees give one the idea of the temple-groves, so often pictured in the antients. A little beyond that spot, towards the extremity of the hill, was built a very small pagoda, of no manner of appearance, or worth mentioning, but for the sake of the founder of it, an itinerant Gioghi or Gentoo vagrant priest, who not twenty years ago was at the expence of it, out of the alms and voluntary donations collected from those of his religion on the island. And as there is something in his history that characterises them, I shall summarily insert it here, as I received it from a Gentoo who knew him, and hope I shall be forgiven the digression.

This man, when he first came on the island, might be about five and thirty years of age; tall, strait, and well-made. By his account, and a very probable one, considering their profession of vagrancy, he had been all over Tartary, Thibet, and on the borders of China. At length he took Bombay in his rounds, and here, though according to his institution, which is strictly that of the old Gymnosophist of India, so plainly and so truly mentioned in antient history, he ought to have gone stark-naked; yet, out of deference to our manners,

manners, when he took his station up on this hill, he just covered those parts which the common ideas of decency oblige to conceal, not so much, but that might plainly be seen a brass ring passed through the prepuce, which does to those of his profeſſion, the same office as a padlock or girdle of chaſtity is ſuppoſed to do to the Italian women. His hair too, which was twice the length of his body, that is to ſay, reaching down to his heels, and thence to the crown of his head again, was wreathed in rolls round, and roſe in a kind of ſpire of a ruſſet color, into which it was ſun-burnt from its original black. This man, on his arrival at Bombay, addreſſed himſelf ſolemnly to the Gentoos, and to them only, for money towards founding the ſmall pagoda I have mentioned; nor indeed did I hear it ſuggeſted that he applied it to any other uſe. But his ſcheme for exciting their devotion was ſomething extraordinary. He preached to them from the midſt of a great fire which ſurrounded him, and had ſomething of a miraculous air, though there was nothing but what was very natural in it. He had a platform of earth made of the elevation of about two foot, and about twelve or fourteen foot ſquare. Round this was ſet a pile of wood, which, being lighted, made him appear as if preaching from amidſt the flames, though they never touched him; but muſt have been unſupportable to any except himſelf, who had been from his childhood inured by degrees to bear ſuch a heat. This device had its effect, for it produced to him a collection, at ſeveral times, to the amount of what he required.

And here I cannot quit Malabar-hill, without mentioning another particularity of it. At the very extreme point of it, there is a rock on the deſcent to the ſea, flat a-top, in which there is a natural crevice, that communicates with a hollow

that

THE EAST-INDIES. 57

that terminates at an exterior opening towards the fea. This place is ufed by the Gentoos, as a purification of their fins, which they fay is effected by their going in at the opening, and emerging out of the crevice; which to me feemed too narrow for perfons of any corpulence to fqueeze through; though I have been credibly affured, that feveral very fat perfons have atchieved it. However, this ceremony is of fuch repute, in the neighboring countries, that there is a tradition, which I do not pretend to warrant, that the famous Conajee Angria ventured by ftealth, one night, on the ifland, on purpofe to perform this ceremony, and got off undifcovered.

CHAP. V.

Of the iflands adjacent to BOMBAY. OLD WOMAN's *ifland*. HENARA *and* CANARA. BUTCHER's *ifland*. CARANJA. ELEPHANTA, *and its famous cave*. SALSETT.—*The ceffion of* BOMBAY *farther explained. Queen* CATHERINE's *dower liquidated*. JAPAN-TRADE *loft by it*. Salfett *conquered by the* MORATTOES. *Inconveniencies of that change of mafters to* Bombay. *Ruins of* Canara. *Diftrefs of the* PORTUGUESE, *forced to feek refuge on* Bombay.

THE firft ifland occurring to notice, and ftretching from Bombay, from which it is only feparated by the fea at flood, and eafy to walk over to on the ebb, is called Old Woman's ifland, though for what reafon I know not. It is a very narrow ftrip of land, about two miles long, terminating at the end in a fmall eminence, or hillock,

upon

upon which a look-out-houſe is kept for importing veſſels. Near the middle of this iſland are three tombs, kept conſtantly white-waſhed to ſerve for land-marks, and direction into the harbor. From the end of the iſland ſhoots forth a dangerous ledge of rocks, to ſuch as do not give them what the ſailors call a good birth, by ſteering wide of them. For the reſt, it produces nothing remarkable, and yields only a ſcanty foddering for a few cattle; on which account it is rented out at a ſmall rate, not exceeding, I think, five and twenty pounds, or two hundred rupees per annum.

At the mouth of the harbor lie two ſmall fortified rocks, called Henara, and Canara, which you leave on the right hand as you enter the harbor. Theſe were in the hands formerly of Angria, and the Siddees, or Moors, which laſt have been long diſpoſſeſt of them. In the poſſeſſion of an enemy they are very diſadvantageous to us, for their overlooking our harbor; but I fancy they muſt fall ſooner or later into the hands of the Morattoes, who have lately ſwallowed up moſt of the neighboring country, and to whom ſuch a ſeizure can make but a trifling comparative acceſſion of power.

Over againſt our caſtle, at the diſtance of three miles, lies Butcher's iſland, ſo called from cattle being kept there for the uſe of Bombay. It belongs to the Engliſh, who keep an enſign's guard there, with a fort, not of much more defence than a good pigeon-houſe; though in the hands of an enemy it would ſerve to ſtreighten the harbor greatly. It is very ſmall, its utmoſt length not being two miles, and in breadth no where ſcarce one.

About three miles from thence lies the iſland of Caranja, in ſize inconſiderable, and lately belonging to the Portugueſe; but fell with many other of their neighboring places, under the power

of

of the Morattoes. It affords nothing but a little rice, fowls, goats, and garden-ftuff for the Bombay market.

Two miles from Butcher's ifland, and ftill fronting the fort, lies the fmall but famous ifland of Elephanta. It can at moft be about three miles in compafs, and confifts of almoft all hill; at the foot of which as you land, you fee juft above the fhore on your right hand, an elephant, coarfely cut out in ftone, of the natural bignefs, and at fome little diftance not impoffible to be taken for a real elephant, from the ftone being naturally of the color of that beaft. It ftands on a platform of ftones of the fame color. On the back of this elephant was placed ftanding another young one, appearing to have been all of the fame ftone, but has been long broken down. Of the meaning, or hiftory of this image, there is no tradition old enough to give any account.

RETURNING then to the foot of the hill, you afcend an eafy flant, which about half way up the hill brings you to the opening or portal of a large cavern hewn out of the folid rock, into a magnificent temple; for fuch furely it may be termed, confidering the immenfe workmanfhip of fuch an excavation, and feems to me a far more bold attempt than that of the pyramids of Egypt. There is a fair entrance into this fubterraneous temple, which is an oblong fquare, in length about eighty or ninety foot, by forty broad. The roof is nothing but the rock cut flat a-top, and in which I could not difcern any thing that did not fhew it to be all of one piece. It is about ten foot high, and fupported towards the middle at equidiftance from the fides, and from one another, with two regular rows of pillars of a fingular order. They are very maffive, fhort in proportion to their thicknefs, and their capital bears fome refemblance to a

round

round cufhion, preffed by the fuper-incumbent mountain, with which they are alfo of one piece. At the further end of this temple are three gigantic figures, the face of one of which is at leaft five foot in length, and of a proportionable breadth: but thefe reprefentations have no reference or connection either to any known hiftory, or to the mythology of the Gentoos. They had alfo continued in a tolerable ftate of prefervation and wholenefs, confidering the remotenefs of their antiquity, until the arrival of the Portuguefe, who made themfelves mafters of this place, and in the blind fury of their bigotry, not fuffering any idols but their own, they muft have been at even fome pains to maim and deface them, as they now remain, confidering the hardnefs of the ftone. It is faid, they even brought field-pieces to the demolition of images, which fo greatly deferved to be fpared for the unequalled curiofity of them. Of this queen Catherine of Portugal was it feems fo fenfible, that fhe could not conceive that any traveller could return from that fide of India, without vifiting the wonders of this cavern; of which too the fight appeared to me to exceed all the defcriptions I had ever read of them. About two thirds of the way up this temple, on each fide, and fronting each other, are two doors or out-lets, into fmaller grots or excavations, and freely open to the air. Near and about the door-way, on the right hand, are alfo feveral mutilated images, fingle and in groupes. In one of the laft I remarked a kind of refemblance to the ftory of Solomon dividing the child, there ftanding a figure with a drawn fword, holding in one hand an infant with the head downwards, which it appears in act to cleave through the middle. The out-let of the other on the left hand, is into an area of about twenty feet in length, and twelve in breadth, at the upper end

of

of which, as you turn to the right, prefents itfelf a colonnade covered a-top, of ten or twelve foot deep, and in length anfwering to the breadth of the area; this joins to an apartment of the moft regular architecture, an oblong fquare, with a door in perfect fymmetry; and the whole executed in quite a different tafte and manner from the oldeft or beft Gentoo buildings any where extant. I took particular notice of fome painting round the cornifhes, not for any thing curious in the defign, but for the beauty and frefhnefs of the coloring, which muft have lafted for fome thoufands of years, on fuppofing it, as there is all reafon fo to do, cotemporary with the building itfelf. The floor of this apartment is generally full of water, its pavement or ground-work not permitting it to drain off or be foaked up. For it is to be obferved, that even the cavern itfelf is not vifitable after the rains, until the ground of it has had time to dry into a competent hardnefs.

In the mean time it feems to me fomewhat furprizing, that fo admirable, fo ftupendous a work as this which one would think almoft above the reach of human performance, cannot by any books or tradition, that ever I could hear of, be traced up to its authors, no not even by conjecture. For to give that name to the ridiculous opinion of its having been executed by Alexander's order, would be doing it too much honor. In the firft place, it is clear both by hiftory and tradition, that the Macedonian conqueror never penetrated fo far into India. Or was it even true that he did, What likelihood is there that he fhould employ his army, or any body of men, on a little ifland not three miles in circuit, without a drop of frefh water on it, and quite wide of his route, to hew fuch a temple out of the middle of a mountain, the bare excavation of which out of a folid rock muft have

taken

taken a number of years? To say nothing of the chizzeling it into the regular form of pillars, and the rest of the architecture which it to this day exhibits. Besides, there is not in the images, or sculptures, to be found the least shadow of allusion to the history, manners, or worship of the Macedonians; and what is yet more unaccountable, no not even of the Gentoos. The likeliest conjecture then that occurs is, that the religion of these last must have undergone some revolution (though this they strictly deny) and that this temple must be the work of the old Aborigines of the country. This conjecture is confirmed by the present Gentoos not retaining, that ever I could learn, any veneration for this place, or any regard for it, but on account of its undoubted antiquity. Perhaps, if a proper enquiry was to be made, there might be found among some of the Bramins of the continent, who are the depositories of the antientest histories, as well as of oral traditions, some accounts whereby to ascertain the epoch and origin of this next-to-miraculous work, so as to satisfy the curiosity of the lovers of antiquity, and who could never have a more noble object. In the mean time, it were to be wished, that some good draughtsman would oblige the public with accurate drawings and dimensions taken on the spot, examining withal the continuity of the rock thus excavated, the hardness of it, and calculating the time, and numbers of men it must have taken up to bring it into its form. For certainly there is to be found in it wherewithal to exercise worthily the pencil of a Cornelius le Brun, whose justness cannot enough be commended; and it is impossible for mere verbal description to give an adequate idea of it.

This place being so near Bombay, affords the English inhabitants there, not only an easy opportunity of gratifying their curiosity, in visiting

THE EAST-INDIES. 63

so remarkable a spot, but occasionally of a very agreeable party of pleasure. Sometimes in their way thither they dine at Butcher's island, on account of the conveniency of the officer's house to receive them. Others again prefer carrying their provisions with them, and dine in the cave itself, than which, in the most sultry days of the heats, there cannot be imagined a cooler and more pleasant retreat. For though the air be almost on fire, you are no sooner entered the cave, than you are refreshed with a sensible coolness. The three openings abovementioned not only furnishing sufficient light, but a thorough draught of air, that does not so much convey freshness into the cave, as it receives it from its constant temperature, preserved to it by its impenetrability to the sun, from the thickness of the mountainous mass above it: and even the light that comes into it through the portals, has lost by the way all the force of those fiery-particles, to which it gives so great an activity. For it is observed in India, as well as in all hot countries, that the exclusion of light, is in some measure an exclusion of heat, and that but darkening an apartment only, sensibly cools it. This rule admits of no exception, except in places where the soil and situation are of such a nature, as to continue the heat, even after the actual presence of the sun is withdrawn; as in Gombroon on the coast of Persia for example, where a high massive hill behind it, to which it is a kind of focal point, and the bituminous quality of the earth, are circumstances that do not allow of the air's cooling between the sun-set and sun-rise.

But, asking pardon for this digression, and resuming my present subject, I am to observe, that for the rest, this island contains nothing more that is worthy of notice. There are not above two or three huts upon it; which is not surprizing, considering the little land there is to cultivate, and that there is no water on it, but what may be saved from the rains. The growth of the hill itself is only underwood, and grafs; which, in the dry feafon, are often fet on fire, and will continue burning for three or four days; attended with this benefit, of fertilizing any cultivable fpots on it, and of the falts being wafhed down by the rains into the lower grounds; a practice that is much followed in all thofe countries, which they call burning the land.

To the northward of the ifland of Bombay, and in one place, at Sion, only divided from it by a narrow pafs fordable at low water, lies the comparatively great and fertile ifland of Salfett; our being defrauded of which is a lofs can never enough be regretted, and is at this day fo bitterly felt by the company, and in coarfe fo detrimentally to the Englifh intereft.

It is in length about twenty-fix miles, and on a medium breadth of eight or nine. The foil very rich, and improvable by cultivation into the bearing of every thing producible between the tropics. It is every where well-watered, but was employed by the Portuguefe chiefly to raife rice, with which it ufed to furnifh Goa, and was called its granary. There is alfo great ftore of almoft all manner of game on it, both of the fur and feather. In fhort, I cannot eafily conceive that there can be a more agreeable fpot in the univerfe. But it was effentially neceffary to Bombay, which, with its number of inhabitants, cannot well fubfift without its fupplies of all manner of provifions.

Nothing could be harder than to disjoin it from the regality of Bombay, to which it ftood formally annexed, and was confequently comprehended in the treaty of ceffion. In lieu of accomplifhing which, in breach of all the rules of good faith,

THE EAST-INDIES. 65

faith, they put us off with a place that had no merit in it, but the bare harbor, and its being the nominal feat of government; which however, under the Portuguese, could raise it to no consideration beyond that of a poor fishing-place. And even this single island of Bombay, thus amputated of its vital member, they did not yield up, not till after they had obliged the English commander, sent out by the king with forces to take possession of it, to winter on a small wretched island down the coast, called Anjadiva, where he lost the best part of his men through sickness, want of provisions, and inconvenience of lodgment. At length however the English, wearied out with a fruitless insistence, were weak enough to compound for a part, since the whole of their due was thus perfidiously withheld from them; and being admitted to the possession of Bombay, that too was clogged with the restrictions relating to private property, which I have before-mentioned, and which might have been thought no more than reasonable, if the other part of the dominion annexed to it had been thrown in.

Thus this part of the dower of queen Catharine of Portugal, to whom her barrenness can never be mentioned as a reproach, but only as a misfortune both to her and the nation, was almost shrunk to nothing; for the improvement of the English afterwards cannot be taken into the reckoning. Every one knows what was the fate of Tangiers on the coast of Barbary, soon after demolished and given up, on account of the expence of it not answering the ends of keeping it, for which reason only, the Portuguese were probably induced to part with it to us. Even too the sum collaterally paid for the dower of the queen, was by that good-natured king employed in an armament appropriated to the protection and defence of Portugal itself,

itself, against the designs of the Spaniards upon it, who were at that time looked upon in no other light than a revolted province. But there was still a worse consequence attended that inauspicious alliance, which has not been at least generally remarked, and that is, that we undoubtedly lost the trade of Japan by it; and this will not appear a forced or far-fetched inference, to those who shall combine with it, the circumstance of the Portuguese being about that time expelled Japan, with all the detestation and resentment of which that nation was capable, and for which it was so justifiable, after their priests being the cause of the massacre of above forty thousand revolted Japanese, besides numbers executed with tortures, in cold blood, to whom the church of Rome has given the appellation of martyrs; though nothing is more certain, that this extermination of the Christians took place purely upon a political, and by no means a religious account, which was only the accessary motive. Whilst the Portuguese or Romish priests contented themselves with preaching the tenets of their religion, however opposite they were, or repugnant to the established one of the country; they had all the liberty, nay all the encouragement imaginable. But when that nation, always jealous of foreigners, and now wise in time, discovered that under the pretext of propagating their doctrine, they formed parties in the state, and even intermeddled with the succession which they caballed to make it fall on one of their favorers; when the Japanese, I say, were informed, by the indiscreet confession of one of the Spanish commanders (for Portugal was then annexed to Spain) that the way his master had made use of to subdue many nations, was to send missionaries before, whose business it was to form a sufficient party among their converts, to join with such forces as should be sent to subdue

the

the reſt; no wonder that thus forewarned as they were, that fierce, ſuſpicious people took the alarm, and were determined to get rid at any rate of ſuch dangerous innovators, and proceeded to the extremities they did, on finding that nothing leſs than ſuch extremities were neceſſary. But even then the Engliſh were not involved in that proſcription and expulſion. They remained upon toleration, and at leaſt upon as good a footing as the Dutch themſelves. But theſe laſt; in purſuit of their ſcheme of engroſſing this trade, made no ſcruple of availing themſelves of ſo favorable a conjuncture, as that of our alliance by marriage with the king of Portugal, whom the Japaneſe conſidered with reaſon as their bittereſt and perpetual enemy. They inſinuated then to the emperor the danger to him from this connection, and gave ſuch plauſible colors to it, and drew ſuch probable inferences from it, that alarmed his jealouſy; upon which he lumped concluſions againſt us, and forbad the return of any of our ſhips there, on pain of death, a prohibition which has not been repealed to this day.

All theſe conſiderations on which I have the more inſiſted, as they ſet the injuſtice done us in the detention of the iſland of Salſett in the ſtronger light, evince the truth of that general remark, of the Engliſh being ſo liable to be overreached in their negotiations, treaties, and compacts.

However, it was ſome alleviation of the damage we ſuſtained, that at leaſt this iſland, whilſt in the hands of the Portugueſe, formed a barrier to us, againſt the invaſions of the Morattoes; and whilſt we were at peace with that crown, and there appeared no probability but of its continuance, Bombay enjoyed, in ſome meaſure, the advantages of that iſland's produce, and ſupplies of proviſions, which was alſo a mutual benefit.

But ſuch was the ſupine indolence, and blindneſs of the Portugueſe government to its own intereſt, that notwithſtanding it was ſo inflexibly reſolute in keeping poſſeſſion of this iſland, which was ſo much our due, from us, I ſay, who were their friends and allies, it took no ſort of care to defend it againſt their conſtant and natural enemies the Morattoes; yet nothing was eaſier than to ſecure it. Thoſe people had not then the leaſt maritime force, and the iſland could only be attacked by land at one very narrow paſs, fordable at ebb only, which was called the paſs of Tannah. Here they had only a miſerable redoubt, of no awe, or ſtrength. At length, however, on the appearance of an approaching rupture with the Morattoes, they began to ſee the expediency of fortifying this important poſt; and with an abſurdity hardly to be believed, they began the conſtruction of a fort, that would have indeed effectually anſwered the deſign, if the Morattoes could be ſuppoſed ſuch ideots as to ſuffer them to finiſh it, when they had not provided even the ſhadow of a force to cover the building, or repel any interruption of it. Accordingly the Morattoes very quietly let them go on with the fortification, of which themſelves were ſure of reaping the benefit. For before it was finiſhed, and well-nigh finiſhed it was, they poured their troops into the iſland, and eaſily took a fort, the walls of which were in ſome places open, and the batteries yet unmounted with cannon; after which they had not the leaſt oppoſition worth mentioning to encounter on the reſt of this iſland: the fort of Bandurah, or rather a fortified houſe of the Jeſuits, over-againſt Mahim, not holding out two days. In ſhort, this great and noble iſland fell as eaſy a prey to the Morattoes as themſelves could have

THE EAST-INDIES. 69

have wifhed: by which means Bombay is now become a frontier open to their incurfion, or invafion, upon the leaft mifunderftanding; which can hardly be avoided, fooner or later, with a people naturally unftable, ignorant of their own interefts, or at leaft, and at beft very indifferent to commercial ones, preferring, like moft of the Orientals, a momentary prefent profit, either to a lafting one, or to a much greater one, if at any diftance of time. Befides, that without any actual hoftility, they may greatly ftreighten and diftrefs Bombay, both by non-concurrence to its fupplies from Salfett, and by interrupting their inland communication with the continent, of which the pafs of Tannah is as it were the key. And with refpect to thefe people, it is not now, as formerly, when the Europeans could over-awe them with their artillery, and fuperior fkill of war, a fuperiority, which though ftill preferved, is not however equal to the advantage that is on their fide of infinitely fuperior numbers, who are befides no longer to be frightened with the noife of powder, and in the ufe of which themfelves are fo greatly improved, as to practice mines, and mortars, in which if they do not as yet equal the Europeans, they have however learnt not to be fo much afraid of them, as they at firft were, when lefs acquainted with them. Befides, when the Portuguefe firft made their fettlements in thofe parts by force, the country-powers were all difunited, and too much at variance among themfelves, as well as too conftantly kept in check by the Mogul government, to act effectually againft thofe invaders, and oppofe their fortifying in their country. But the cafe is now greatly reverfed with them, in all thefe points.

SALSETT, then fubjected to their dominion, reduces the tenure of Bombay itfelf to very precarious terms, and confequently leffens its value, in propor-

proportion as it leſſens its ſecurity. Though for the preſent perhaps, the Gentoo government may be rightly ſenſible of the advantages it derives from Bombay being in the hands of the Engliſh ; advantages which it knows itſelf too well to hope the continuance of them, upon taking it from them ; yet ſuch is the natural fickleneſs of thoſe people, ſuch the ſpirit of rapine and plunder, and the greedineſs for immediate profit, conſtitutional to them, that there is no ſolid dependence to be placed on their ſentiments from one day to another. Nor could all the fortifications of Bombay be ſuppoſed capable of holding out againſt them, if they are once bent on a conqueſt of it ; eſpecially as they look upon it as an annexion to Salſett that is wanting to compleat their conqueſt of the coaſt ; and beſides, as originally belonging to themſelves, in quality of the natural lords of the whole country.

They can with eaſe bring from an hundred to two hundred thouſand men into the field, moſt of them horſe, inured to the climate, and not un-furniſhed with fire-arms and artillery. They are at home, and capable of being conſtantly ſupplied with freſh recruits. Imagine then if Bombay could expect to hold out long againſt them, if they ſhould be in earneſt to reduce it. How far in the right they were, I will not pretend to ſay ; but when they firſt heard of the ditch projected round the town-wall, and of its dimenſions, they affected at leaſt to hold it very cheap. " Let them alone " (ſaid they) it is not at preſent worth our while " to break with the Engliſh ; but whenever that " ſhall be the caſe, we can fill their ditch up in " one night's time with our ſlippers." I ſuppoſe, that at that time they had no idea of its being a wet one ; though that would not much increaſe the difficulties of the ſiege.

Thus

THUS by the fatal relinquishment of our undoubted right, to a nation that made so ill an use of it, we have in Salsett lost all that could render Bombay essentially valuable. The extent of it, the fertility, the excellence of its waters, every thing in short that could be acquired, should have drawn to us a confluence of the greatest merchants in the neighboring countries, and from Surat especially, who were strongly invited by that mildness and liberty in our government, of which they were, one may say, eye-witnesses. Their sole objection was the smallness of the island, and the indifferent water: whereas in Salsett there was room enough to spread themselves, and the water as before observed excellent. In short, by the addition of Salsett, Bombay might have been easily made as considerable to the English as Batavia to the Dutch, with all their advantages of the neighboring spice-islands; as this harbor is so near Surat, the center of the Indian trade, and every way commodious for commanding the navigation of the Indian seas.

IN even the unimproved, and tradeless condition of that island, under the Portuguese government, its revenue was, upon a tolerably just estimate, computed at near five lacks of rupees, or sixty thousand pounds sterling per annum; which, to reckon at the rate Bombay has been with all its disadvantages improved by the English, is not, moderately speaking, the fourth part of what it would have produced to us, to say nothing of the inestimable benefit it would in all probability have been in other respects, and especially that of our then having every thing necessary within ourselves.

FOR the rest, except the abundant riches of nature, there is nothing remarkable in it but the ruins of a place called Canara, being excavations of rocks, supposed cotemporary with that of Elephanta,

phanta, and are much more numerous, but none of them approaching to it in bigness or workmanship.

The mountains of it are pretty high, and there is a tradition that they emerged together with the subjacent land out of the sea, by a violent earthquake: to confirm which it is pretended, that there was on the top of the highest hill, not many years ago, found a stone-anchor, such as was antiently used for the vessels of that country; but I cannot say, that I ever heard this story was founded on any good authority.

If any one however should hereafter attempt a survey or description of Elephanta, it will doubtless be also worth his while to pass over to Salsett, and take a view of Canara, as it may probably furnish him with lights, and conjectures, by the comparison of both.

When this island was lost to the Portuguese, and consequently the jesuits, who were owners of much the largest part of the land, were the greatest sufferers, none were however less pitied even by the Portuguese themselves, especially by those from whose families their arts had extorted their possessions. Their insolence too was as boundless as their avarice, which last has prevented the island from being fortified, whilst it was yet time from their backwardness to contribute their quota of the charges. Thus the more they had to lose, the less were they willing to pay towards securing it.

It was a melancholy sight on the loss of Salsett, to see the many families forced to seek refuge on Bombay, and among them some Portuguese Hidalgos, or noblemen, reduced of a sudden from very florishing circumstances to utter beggary. However, they found relief from the usual generosity of the English, notwithstanding the just mat-

ter

ter of complaint they had againſt their nation, eſpecially on the occaſion of that very iſland, the loſs of which through ſuch ſcandalous negligence brought ſo great a danger home to their own doors: they found, at Bombay, an hoſpitable refuge, and all the friendly entertainment and conſolation they could wiſh. One of them was extremely pitied by the Engliſh, a gentleman called John de Souza Ferras, who was before that time poſſeſſor of a very conſiderable eſtate in Salſett, and who had greatly endeared himſelf to the Engliſh by his kind and generous reception of them at his houſe whenever the occaſion offered. He continues I believe to this day, if alive, at Bombay, very much careſſed and eſteemed by the Engliſh gentlemen who were acquainted with him in his proſperity.

BOOK

BOOK III.

Of the MORATTOES, *and* ANGRIA.

CHAP. I.

Of the MORATTOES. *Derivation of their name. Aborigines* GENTOOS: *conduct of the* MOGULS *towards them.—Rise of the* SAHA *or* SOW-RAJAHS. *—Disposition of the* Morattoes. *Proficients in engineering; nature of their troops. Curious in their arms.—Situation of* BOMBAY *with respect to them. Opinion of the wealth of* Bombay. *Rapaciousness of the* Morattoes: *frank acquiescence in their character of perfidiousness: not sanguinary: their usage of captives in war. The fort of* RAREE, *the residence of the* Saha, *or* MAR-RAJAH: *his subjects credulous in astrology. Story of the* Mar-Rajah *and a reputed sorceress. Description of the* Morattoes *persons and dress. Their women; and the charge against them of poisoning their husbands groundless.*

AFTER speaking of the islands, there remains to add some account of the continent bordering upon Bombay, to which one may say it is, in some measure, contiguous; since by the means of the two forts at Sion, and Tannah, one may pass to it without taking boat: but as all that is necessary to be mentioned of it is included in the description to be here given of the Morattoes, who are lords of all the neighboring parts of it, there is no need of making a separate article of it.

THE

THE EAST-INDIES. 75

THE name of Morattoes, or Marattas, is, I have reafon to think, a derivation, in their country-language, or by corruption, from Mar-Rajah the chief, or rather, to fpeak more juftly, the king of that powerful tribe, having all the diftinction and effence of fovereign power centering in his perfon. But this name of Morattoes is purely local, and confined to their own country; for all over India, and no farther off than Surat, they are more currently known by the appellation of Ghenims, unlefs their late fpread of conqueft fhould have more generalized it than it was before. As to the word Ghenim, if I am not greatly miftaken, it imports as much as free-booter, and is beftowed not only on the Morattoes, but all thofe mountaineer tribes of the Gentoos, who commonly make a war rather of pillage or plunder, than a regular one for glory or conqueft.

BUT to give fome idea of this people at prefent fo powerful, that they have brought near all Indoftan under their fubjection, and give laws even to the Mogul government, it will be neceffary to trace them fummarily to their origin.

IT is then to be obferved, that when the Mongul-Tartars, whence the title of Mogul is apparently derived, founded their fovereignty upon the expulfion of the Pattan-Moors, and in proportion as they extended their conquefts over the country, many of the Aborigines Gentoos, who were incapable of making head againft them in the field, or plains, and unwilling to fubmit to the yoke from the fworn enemies to the Gentoo-worfhip, who, wherever they penetrated by force of arms, made it a point of religion to deftroy their temples and idols, with all the fury of bigot-zeal, they retired for fhelter to the numerous mountains of Indoftan, and there burrowed in inacceffible faftneffes; upon which Aurengzeb gave them the humorous nickname

name of mountain-rats. But then, as thefe Gentoos were fplit into various tribes, under chiefs of different families, whofe difunion had already facilitated the invafion of the country, firft to the Pattans, and then to the Moguls; the diffenfions and jealoufies ftill continued in force enough to hinder them from uniting againft the common enemy. Of this the Moguls, in the flourifhing ftate of their empire, knew perfectly well how to take the advantage, and put in practice that great ftate maxim of dividing in order to govern. What then by courting fome, by menacing others, and by awing all of them with ftanding armies, which if they could not penetrate into their ftrong holds, or abfolutely conquer them, could ftill ftraiten and diftrefs them, they brought feveral of their Rajahs under a kind of tributary fubjection, and had art and intereft enough to oppofe them againft each other. Some of them even came occafionally to court, and not only paid perfonal homage to the Mogul, but did military duty and fervice round the court, while they ftill referved their refpective dominions in the mountains. While the Moguls continued this practice of fowing diffenfions among thofe warlike tribes, and of employing occafionally and aptly the ways of rigor, or of compliance, to intimidate or footh powers, which were impenetrable for their armies to deftroy, that empire enjoyed a tolerable ftate of peace and fecurity. But as foon as the government began to relax on that capital point, having fallen into the hands of a fucceffion of indolent princes, engroffed by the pleafures of their feraglio's, and weakened by the contempt into which their negligence plunged them; the Rajahs perceived the change, and lifted their heads upon it. They could eafily have recovered the dominion of the whole country out of the Mogul's hands, if they had not ftill perfifted in fuch

their

their difunion, that they could not agree among themfelves who fhould poffefs the empire. They had rather fee it in its nominal fubjection to the Tartar family, than any one of their own nation affume it over the reft; and each minding only to incroach upon it for his own particular benefit, the whole ftate of Indoftan remained and ftill remains a common prey to their feveral incurfions, and devaftations, which is the only point wherein thefe Rajahs agree.

It was towards the latter end of Aurengzeb's days, that one of thofe Rajahs, called Sevajee, or rather Sow-rajah, took the advantage of that monarch's declining as well in judgment as in years, fet up openly the ftandard of revolt, and bearded him with the pillage twice repeated of Surat, the capital town of trade of his whole dominions. Nay, fo fecure was he of his point in it, fo affured of the negligence and fupinenefs of the government, that he intimated to the town the day he had prefixed for entering and plundering it, and was as good as his word; not having met with the leaft oppofition, unlefs in the Englifh and Dutch factories, whofe pofture of defence faved them from fharing the common fate.

By this exploit, and other fuccefsful enterprifes on the Mogul dominions, he acquired fuch ftrength and reputation, as enabled him to give a certain confiftence, and regular form of government to that affemblage of free-booters, which he had collected out of the mountains of Deckan, and whom the temptation of pillage had united under his ftandard. Mafter then, by continual encroachments every way round him, of a confiderable and populous body of dominion, he affumed the title now continued to his fucceffors of Mar-rajah, or Arch-rajah, and appeared in a condition to give laws to the Mogul empire; at the worft he was affured of

there

there being no human poſſibility of coming at or driving him out of his inacceſſible retreats in the mountains. Yet, it is obſervable, that all the time he was acting thus in open defiance to the Mogul emperor, he never profeſſedly threw off a nominal ſubmiſſion to his throne. He had even the aſſurance to ſtyle himſelf his general in Deckan. Theſe meaſures he doubtleſs kept out of regard to the jealouſy of the other Rajahs, who had not yet ſo openly renounced their vaſſalage, and who differed from him however in nothing but their appearances more, while they claimed in fact as abſolute an independence.

His ſucceſſors purſued invariably his ſyſtem of politics and activity: and as their dominions encreaſed, they ſet on foot more numerous and more regular armies, under able generals: ſo that from a ſet of banditti or free-booters they aſſumed a more national form, without departing in the leaſt from their original ſpirit of rapine and plunder. One would otherwiſe naturally think, that as faſt as they formed their ſtate into order and conſiſtence, they would encourage trade, which is every where, by civilized nations, conſidered as one of its chief ſupports: but, hitherto at leaſt, they have given no indication of a commercial turn: on the contrary, wherever their arms have penetrated, or their influence extended, they have deſtroyed all trade and manufactures. On the coaſt, a little to the ſouthward of Bombay, there exiſted not long ſince ſome very conſiderable manufactures, which were annihilated by the oppreſſion and harraſſments exerciſed on the artizans, inſomuch that there is not the footſtep of them left. At preſent they ſeem to have placed their whole dependence on the ſword: nor do they want for great caution, conduct, and policy in the extention of their dominions. They ſeem in no hurry for puſhing their conqueſt,

THE EAST-INDIES. 79

conqueft, but patiently wait for their beft time and opportunity: and even where they meet with a repulfe, they yield with great fupplenefs to the force of the conjecture; they retreat with as good a grace as if they had fucceeded, and prepare their meafures cooly to return afrefh as opportunity may favor them.

They have encouraged deferters from the European nations, from whom they learnt the art of engineering, as far as the fkill or knowledge of thofe deferters reached; the Indians in general being ready imitators to a certain point, or ftandard, at which they commonly ftop, not being curious of perfection in any thing. It has however been obferved, that though they gave fuch deferters a pretty high pay, compared to the fmall one with which they fatisfy their own natives, fhould they fave or hoard up any fum, which by the by they rarely do, they do not fuffer them to quit the country, unlefs at the hazard of a dangerous efcape, or unlefs they purchafe their freedom with a delivery of all they are worth. But, in truth, and confiftently enough with fuch treatment, no Europeans take fervice among them, except fuch as are of defperate fortunes, or have committed crimes that obliged them to feek refuge there. When fuch Europeans have exhaufted their ftrength, and power of fervice, they are fuffered to languifh in mifery and poverty, neglected and defpifed by thofe their employers.

By this means however the Morattoes have been rendered capable of forming regular fieges, with which they were before utterly unacquainted. Thus, when they took Baffaim from the Portuguefe, a place ftrongly fortified, at leaft fuppofed fo againft any attempts of theirs, which is fituate on the coaft on the continent a few miles to the northward of Bombay, they erected regular batteries,

teries, threw in bomb-shells, and proceeded by sap and mine, until the town saw itself forced to surrender.

YET with all this, their troops * are fitter for a war of incursion, than for regular campaigns. They are chiefly composed of land-tillers, called Corumbees, with whom their seed-time and harvest are essential points to be consulted, and adjusted to their expeditions; for their manner of government admitting no importations, or material supplies from without, they would run the hazard of a famine on any deficiency of cultivation. Thus they are equally bred to agriculture and arms, and perhaps are not the worse soldiers for this alteration. Their pay is extremely small, and that generally not furnished in money, but in rice, tobacco, salt, pieces of apparel, and other necessaries of life, which are there at a cheap rate. And indeed otherwise their bringing such numerous armies into the field could not be accounted for, considering their exclusion of trade.

THEIR horses, on which they chiefly rely, are a small but hardy breed, like that of the mountains of Scotland, inured to fatigue, and of secure footing for the rugged roads among the hills, and a very small matter of forage serves them.

FOR arms, a great many of them have muskets, but generally indifferent ones, and most of them match-locks. These they use chiefly in bush-fighting, where when they have made a discharge, they retreat in a hurry to their main body: but their chief dependence is on their swords and targets. Their swords are, generally speaking, of an admirable temper, and they are well trained up to the exercise of them; so that on all occasions in

---

* See vol. II. introduction, p. xi.

battle, they quit their musket, and betake themselves to them with great success. They are so curious in the blades, that they hold the European broad swords in great contempt, especially the common-sale ones, that are sent out by our ships. When the Derby, captain Ansell, was so scandalously taken by a few of Angria's grabs, whose marines are exactly the same as the Morattoes, and often some of their subjects; there fell into Angria's hands, among a great quantity of other valuable military stores, some chests of sword blades, on examining of which Angria said, that the English swords were only fit to cut butter with.

As to their targets, they are exactly round, convexing almost to a point on the out-side, light, and covered with so smooth and hard a varnish or lacquer, that if tolerably good, they will easily turn a pistol-ball, and at some little distance a musket one.

THEY also have among them excellent slingers, and archers; but of these they make lately less account since the introduction of fire-arms; though, considering their imperfection in the management of these last, it is a query whether they are much gainers by the change.

As to the rest of their dress, nothing can be imagined meaner. A roll of coarse muslin round their heads, to which they give the name of puckery, or turbant, or perhaps a bit of cloth, or striped callico, or cuttance-cap; a lungee or clout, barely to cover their nakedness, and a pamree or loose mantle to throw over their shoulders, or to lye on upon the ground, composes the whole of their wardrobe. This however is only to be understood of their common men, though the officers do not much out-figure them: so that nothing can present a more despicable appearance than these troops, together with their little ill-favored horses, the furniture of which is in a ftile anfwerable to the reft.

THEN their diet is extremely portable; they require no great magazines of provifions, no ovens, or embarraffment of waggons. A little rice, and a leathern flafk for water, which they call a Metarrah, are all that is requifite, fo that every foldier may eafily carry his own allowance: nor do the officers fare more fumptuoufly, nothing being fo plain as their food, efpecially during their expeditions, which they conduct with amazing rapidity, and not too without great ftratagem and cunning.

AGAINST fuch numbers, with the advantage of being in their own country, it is not very probable, that any force we could afford from Europe fhould materially or ultimately prevail. Otherwife nothing could be more for the Englifh intereft, than endeavoring to reconquer the ifland of Salfett from them, for reafons too obvious to need a recapitulation here: but it is now only mentioned to explode a propofal, I am told was once made of fuch an attempt. The fituation of Bombay is however now rendered fo precarious, that there is no fuch thing as either quarrelling with the Morattoes to advantage, or trufting to them with fafety, nor indeed feeing any end of this dilemma.

IF they were a people capable of hearing reafon on their true permanent interefts, in contradiftinction to their momentary ones, they might eafily fee that Bombay, in the hands of the Englifh, is a greater advantage to them, than if it was in their own; as it is a great inlet of trade into all their dominions that lye round it, by means of the feveral creeks and rivers that communicate with that harbor, a trade which themfelves for many reafons could not expect to invite or bring into them. They are alfo well affured, that the

Englifh

THE EAST-INDIES. 83

English court no settlements but on account of their commerce, always beneficial to the countries round about, and never dangerous to them, from its not being attended with the spirit of conquest, even their forts being rather mere warehouses than curbs upon the natives. These are arguments too, of the force of which they will sometimes own themselves convinced, and perhaps really are so at the time, but then there is no dependence on their continuance in that mind. A change of their ministers, a fancy that shall take them in the head, that Bombay would afford a good present pillage, or a scheme of humoring their troops, who are never better pleased than with a promise of plunder; any of these, or the like motives, are sufficient to make them break of a sudden through all their resolutions, and ties of a greater interest; and what is more, though known to themselves to be so.

THE principal men among them, though probably better informed themselves, cannot root out of the minds of the bulk of that people in general, a strong notion, that Bombay incloses great riches, an idea which they do not fail of annexing to trade, and which, such is their constitutional indisposition towards it, they are not yet tempted to introduce, or improve in their own dominions. This false opinion however they have of the advantage accruing to the company from the possession of Bombay, though it is far from paying its own charges, and is only kept for the convenience of its other settlements and factories, has such an influence, that they think no demands too exorbitant for purchasing their toleration and tranquility.

As an instance of this way of thinking in those people, may be produced the terms on which Samboo or Sambajee Angria insisted, when certain overtures of peace were set on foot between him and the government of Bombay. After some preface on the prodigious advantages of the English trade on that coast, which must in course enable them to afford what he demanded, he confined himself however to no larger a sum than twelve lacks of rupees, or about one hundred and fifty thousand pounds per annum, which he required in consideration of his desistence from his hostilities, and non-interruption of our navigation. I do not know that he ever sunk his demand afterwards; but only that the English government treated his proposal with the contempt it deserved, and made a jest of it. Nor was this indeed worth mentioning, but to shew the popular opinion in those parts of the wealth of the English, which inspires the country-government less with respect, than with a desire of plundering them.

Nor can this unfavorable disposition of the Morattoes towards foreign merchants be much wondered at, when it is equally and more so towards those of their own country. For the few that are induced to live under their government, for the sake of the gain to be made on the traffic of the absolutely necessaries of life, are obliged to conceal, as they would murder, their being in good circumstances. Towards which they affect all the appearances of poverty, in their houses, dress, and all externals, to avoid being pointed out as a prey to their rapacious government, which is sure ultimately not to spare any rich subjects, though they will sometimes leave them quietly for a long time to gather wealth, which they look on as so much in bank for themselves, whenever they please to call it in: and in this point they make no distinction of any rank or condition, but that of the great military officers, whose property is more respected for obvious reasons of state. They are their instruments of oppression, whom it is not so safe to disoblige or discourage. But, though they are Gentoos,

THE EAST-INDIES. 85

toos, whom one would in courfe think awed by their priefts or bramins, they fpare them no more than the reft, when they are reputed rich, and will, without ftanding upon any ceremony with them, ufe menaces, and even tortures, to fqueeze money out of them. This fhews they are either not overloaded with religious fcruples, or that they look on the temporalities of their priefts, as making no part of the facrednefs of the function, and that they are not difqualified for officiating their fpiritual duties by their want of worldly wealth.

As this rapacioufnefs is chiefly the characteriftic of the Gentoo government, whereas that of the Moors or Moguls is much more temperate and juft, it is often the reafon why thofe of their fubjects, who can efcape the dangerous repute of being rich, bury their wealth in fecret places, unknown often to their neareft relations, and even to their heirs, when by chance they died fuddenly, or at a diftance from their homes. Befides, fuch is their tenacioufnefs of thefe treafures, that when fome, in confequence of their falling under the fufpicion of wealth, have been expofed to violent tortures, they have had the conftancy to hold out, and keep the fecret of their hoards, though in all other points they were known to be the arranteft cowards. In the mean time, by unexaggerated accounts, it is amazing to reflect what immenfe treafures have been buried and loft on folely this principle of prefervation; for it is an utter fable, that they are looked upon as ufeful to them in the other life. A proof of which is, that the fame fort of people are never known to bury their treafures under a free government, where they are not afraid of being pillaged, and where they can fafely leave them to their heirs. I have heard it averred, that the fums of money thus interred in the courfe of paft ages, at leaft equal thofe in prefent circulation all over Indoſtan. Perhaps this eſtimate is hyperbolical, though there are not wanting good reaſons to countenance it.

So much is certain, that the Gentoo merchants, eſpecially the Banyans, and even the Bramins or Gentoo-prieſts, prefer living under a Mooriſh government, or indeed any government to that of the Gentoos; being at leaſt ſure that they can no where meet with leſs ſafety, or more oppreſſive exactions. Surat is one inſtance of this, which is crowded with Gentoo merchants, and mechanics of all ſorts; where, though they are ſome times expoſed to the avarice and vexations of bad governors, they are only tranſient and partial ſtorms: whereas the Gentoo government is one continued and univerſal ſyſtem of violence and injuſtice.

Such are the people now the immediate neighbors of Bombay, in whoſe character nevertheleſs there is ſomething paradoxical. For though too perfidious to be ever ſafely truſted, at leaſt they do not, like a polite neighboring nation in Europe, affect a parade of ſincerity or good faith. They do not deſire to be taken to be more honeſt than they are, and would be the firſt to laugh at thoſe who ſhould repoſe any confidence in them. They make no profeſſions of friendſhip beyond words of common courſe, or ſet formularies of compliments, which they do not expect ſhould be taken for more than they are worth. They never ſet forth any pompous manifeſts, decked with the falſe colors of eloquence, of their good intentions to the peace of mankind, at the inſtant that they are taking all the meaſures in their power to diſturb it. They conſider themſelves always in a ſtate of war, open or underſtood, with thoſe powers whoſe dominions they covet; and conſequently think, that all feints, ſtratagems or advantages are fair, as from enemy to enemy.

TREACHE-

THE EAST-INDIES. 87

TREACHEROUS as they conftitutionally are, they yet are not accufable of that common attendant on treachery, cruelty. They are not accounted fanguinary. They do not ufually rob and murther, unlefs where this laft is abfolutely neceffary to the firft, and then doubtlefs they do not ftick at it. What prifoners they make in war they feldom detain, but get rid of them as foon as poffible, to fave the charges and trouble of keeping them; unlefs where any ranfom is in view, and then they will not fcruple ufing the harfheft means towards extorting what they expect from them. Slaves they rarely make, unlefs they fhould have a view of a market for them; for they would make money of any thing: but though flaves are often bought in India, there is no fettled vend for fuch as are taken in war. It is chiefly in times of famine that parents are fometimes driven to difpofe of their children to the Europeans, or Moors, for I never could learn that the Gentoos dealt in them: neither can the Gentoos keep a flave under their roof of any religion but their own, on account of the profanation their law attributes to it. Befides, fervice is fo extremely cheap among thofe people, that there are always numbers of domeftics to be found, ready to ferve for bare victuals and raiment.

SLAVERY being out of the queftion in the incurfions of thofe people, whofe fole object is prefent plunder, they are the lefs a terror to the neighboring countries, and efpecially to the poor land-tillers and peafants, who generally keep nothing in their huts worth carrying away, and thus are abundantly defended from loffes by having nothing to lofe.

EVEN in their plundering of towns, unlefs actuated by fome extraordinary motive of refentment, they obferve a certain moderation. Thus, for example,

ample, when they pillaged Surat, besides their respecting the lives of the unresisting inhabitants, and the saving the houses from fire, they were far from rigorously ransacking it; it being a maxim with them (to use their own phrase) not to pluck up a beard by the roots, but to shave it, so that it may grow again, to serve another opportunity.

Upon the whole, they may be pronounced a sort of a civilized nation of banditti, who, it is not impossible, though at present it does not seem very probable, may in process of time be brought to adopt more social maxims of government, and rise into dignity and rank with the other lawful or regular powers.

The Mar-rajah, the sovereign of these people, generally keeps his court, or more properly speaking, considering their purely military constitution, his head quarters, at the fort of Raree, in the mountains of Deckan; and if reports do not bely it, this must be the most compleatly impregnable place in the universe. It is represented as a fortified mound of rocks, extremely high, and so steep, as but by one narrow pathway, to be accessible to human footing; with this advantage, that the enclosure of it is large enough, independent of the stores accumulated there, to grow grain sufficient for the maintenance of its garrison, which were it but a handful of men, could with pleasure defend it against the greatest armies that could be brought to take it; not to mention that the passes and defiles leading to it among the mountains, are so rugged and narrow, that the Morattoes must be all asleep, to suffer any armies to penetrate to that fortress.

Here the Mar-rajah principally resides, with a kind of military court, composed of his generals and officers, and keeps all the state of a sovereign prince,

THE EAST-INDIES.

prince, with all the infignia of royalty about him; one of which, peculiar to the Rajah's of Indoftan, is their long veft, which only differs from that of other common ones, in the make towards the bottom, being floped into a peek downwards on each fide.

At this court, both the fovereign and the courtiers are fo entirely engroffed with their attention to military operations, that having that fuper-addition to the natural indolence of the orientalifts in general with refpect to arts and fciences, they appear entirely incurious of the European manufactures, or rarities, whether of nature or art. In vain then would be fhewn to them any of thofe exquifite pieces of workmanfhip, which are produced by our artifts. They would indeed, out of civility, praife them with an air of carelefs indifference, and their natural covetoufnefs would perhaps not fuffer them to be forry for being prefented with them; but they would much rather receive the equivalent in fheer money, diamonds, or precious ftones, of which the currency is to the full as regularly fettled. This tafteleffnefs too is fo thoroughly rooted in them, that though no people are fonder of decking out their women with rich jewels, yet they would prefer thofe of their own workmen's comparative coarfe and clumfy fetting, to thofe of a Robertfon or a Lacam, and that not from any laudable partiality towards their own country-men, but purely from the want of a relifh for perfection, which makes them contented with what they have a habit of daily feeing. Thus a watch of the moft beautiful and niceft make, is only valuable to them according to the metal it contains; and a painting of Raphael's or Titian's would move them no more than it would a horfe.

In the profound ignorance in which they are bred, and in which their parts that are naturally

extremely

extremely lively remain immerſed, or receive at the hands of tradition a wrong direction, it is not ſurprizing, that they ſhould be liable to take ſtrong impreſſions of ſuch groſs errors and prejudices, as thoſe in favor of judicial aſtrology, of which it is but ſo lately that the politeſt courts in Europe have ſhaken off the yoke. Theſe people in general are ſcrupulouſly addicted to believe in that vain ſcience, and religiouſly obſerve the good or bad days, indicated to them by their aſtrologers, who are chiefly Bramins, and whom they conſult on all occaſions; but this folly is no more than they have in common with the reſt of the Orientaliſts. Their credulity extends yet farther, to the opinion they have of wizards, and ſorcereſſes, of whom they tell many ſtories that they firmly believe. One of them, which I had from a Gentoo who came from that country, and very gravely aſſured me of the truth of it, I take leave to relate, not moſt certainly as either believing or expecting it to be believed, but purely as a ſpecimen of the genius of invention of thoſe people, with reſpect to any thing that favors their credulity.

THE preſent Mar-rajah being informed of the great reputation of a certain woman in his dominions for ſorcery, and fortune-telling, ſent for her to court, with an intention to put her to death, on what particular provocation was not ſaid, but firſt had the curioſity to ſee her. The woman accordingly appeared before him: ſhe was then about forty, very corpulent, and not of an ill preſence. He aſked her ſternly, if ſhe knew why he had ſent for her? "Yes, anſwered ſhe (with the utmoſt in‑
"trepidity and unconcern) you have ſent for me
"to take away my life; but before you proceed
"to that, I hope you will, for your own ſake, per‑
"mit me to give you a ſalutary warning." Curioſity, or perhaps the apprehenſion natural to that

prejudice

prejudice which admits of the poffibility of witchcraft, moving the Rajah's affent to it, fhe ordered two fowls to be produced, the one a cock, the other a hen. The cock was fet down on the ground, full of life and fpirits; then taking the hen, fhe defired the Rajah to mark the confequence. At thefe words fhe wrung the neck of the hen off, when at the fame time the cock, though untouched by any one, imitating all the convulfions and agonies of its death, accompanied the hen in it. " This, Sir, (faid fhe to the Rajah determinately) " remember to be a type of your fate and mine." The Rajah ftruck with this, not only defifted from his intention, but intreated her to be near his perfon, fettled a confiderable penfion on her, ordered her a palankin and attendance, and in fhort treated her thence-forwards like a perfon, with whofe life his own was wound up.

As to the perfons of the Morattoes, they are generally a clean-limbed, ftrait people, it being very rare to fee any deformed perfons among them. Some of them are mufcular large-bodied men; but their vegetable diet, and their not being trained up to a proper exercife of their bodily ftrength, makes them not fo robuft; which laft I the rather believe, becaufe it is certain, that even in this hot climate, there are often to be found, as at Surat, porters who will carry a weight equal to what any European can; however, it is certain, that the Morattoes are in battle eafily over-borne, not only by the Europeans, but by the Mogul's troops, with neither of whom they have any chance, without a great fuperiority of numbers, or from the flight and dexterity with which they handle their fwords.

THEIR complexions are of all fhades, from the deep-black to the light-brown; but it is obferved, they are fairer in proportion of their diftance from the fea-fide, and of their birth among the mountains

tains the fartheft remote from it. Their features are generally regular, and even delicate. Befides fhaving their heads, of which they religioufly preferve in the middle of it a lock at full length, fo as to tie up, and hang down behind, the Morattoes are diftinguifhed from the Moors, by two favorite curls they wear on each fide juft above the ear, which appearing from under their turbants, gives them a kind of effeminate look.

THEIR women are generally very handfome, whilft the bloom of youth continues; but that foon fading, there are few who preferve the charms of their fhape and fkin till thirty, at which they are commonly paft child-bearing. They are reckoned very faithful and affectionate to their hufbands, who do not appear to be infected with the oriental taint of jealoufy. In this country, however, the barbarous cuftom ftill continues, as indeed none are fo tenacious of old cuftoms as the Gentoos, of women burning, or being buried (for there is one tribe that buries their dead) with their hufbands: what is more, the higher the rank of the hufband is, the greater is the incumbence on the wife, to follow him in this manner; and the Rajahs efpecially have feveral of their wives burned with them: the ceremony of which, being fo amply defcribed in many authors, acquits me of entering into any further account of it here; befides that, I never was myfelf an eye-witnefs to it. Yet I believe, that the ftory of this cuftom, attributed to the Bramins devifing it, to put a ftop to the frequency of the womens poifoning their hufbands on every flight quarrel, to be an over-refinement of conjecture, as falfe as it is injurious to the women of this country; no fuch practice being either attefted by creditable tradition, or warranted by the behavior of the other Indian women not fubjected to this cuftom, and who are generally of a mould of mind
much

much too soft and tender to incur even the suspicion of such a detestable barbarity. I rather attribute it to the strength of passion, always the greatest in the weakest minds, from the greater power of all impressions on them, and of which the Bramins knew how to take the advantage, not only for the sake of paying their court to the leading men of the country, whose vanity, and that sort of jealousy founded upon it, were thus flattered at the expence of a sex, in those parts perfectly enslaved to them, and never enough considered by them; but also for the sake of the dreadful power of religious persuasion it armed them with, to establish a ceremony that is never but attended with signal emolument to themselves, and that inspires an awe or veneration for them the conductors of it.

The Morattoes, as Gentoos, agree in this, as they do in most other points in religion and manners, with the rest of the Gentoo nations, of which in its place will be given a more particular account. In the mean time, from what has been said, the situation specifically of Bombay with respect to these people, and to what is to be hoped or feared from them, may not be insufficiently collected.

CHAP. II.

Of ANGRIA, and his SUCCESSORS.

CONAGEE ANGRIA, the father of the present Angrias, having made so remarkable a figure in the history of those parts, and especially relatively to the English interest in them, for having been the first founder of a very considerable piratical state; and so many fabulous stories having been imposed on the public concerning his birth,
first

first rise, and progress, I shall in my second volume give the best and most authentic account I could obtain concerning him, and his dominions *. However, I shall here observe, that Angria, who had found means to dispossess other petty chiefs of their forts, and lands, through the acquiescence of the Morattoes, and his own enterprizing genius; having collaterally acquired vessels of greater force, ventured at length to break with our flag, and took some English vessels trading upon that coast, plundered the cargoes, and made the men prisoners, subject to a ransom.

This naturally alarmed the government of Bombay, which accordingly expostulated with him on his piratical procedure; to which he made no further answer, than that disclaiming the title of pirate, he assumed that of admiral to the Mar-rajah, to whom he insisted that the sovereignty of those seas belonged, and that he was determined to maintain it, against all such as should refuse to acknowledge, or not take his passes. And as one may well imagine these were terms to which the English government could not stoop, he went on with his usual depredations.

This obliged the East-India company to keep a constant marine on foot to hold him in check, and to protect the trade and navigation of those seas, an incumbence which greatly inflamed the charges of that presidency. Angria however made a shift to support himself by cruizing indistinctly on all nations, and by picking up such stragglers as ventured on the coast without convoy. Yet he took care never to venture below mount Dilly, or far to the northward, for fear of being intercepted and cut off his port by the English force that was employed

---

* See vol. II. p. 211—228.

to watch his motions: about 1731 he died, not in a very advanced age, being about sixty.

HE was a well-set corpulent man, rather blacker than commonly the Deckaners are; full faced, with a sparkling eye, and stern countenance. He was very severe in his commands, and exact in punishing; otherwise liberal to his officers and soldiers, with whom he affected a sort of military frankness, not to say familiarity. He was too, like the Morattoes, very careless of keeping faith, and excused the not making any peace with him, on which it was foreknown that no reliance could be had.

AFTER his death, the succession devolved on his son, Sambagee Angria, who retained force enough to do the English a great deal of mischief, and accordingly took their trading ships, both of the country, and from Europe, and even occasionally the armed vessels, when he could surprize and overpower them. He died in 1745, and was succeeded by his son Tulagree, who was dispossessed by the English in 1756, as will be particularly related in my second volume.

IT has been however proposed as a doubt, whether the English have acted for their interest, in their joining to ruin an enemy, it is true, but an enemy, in whose place another power far superior in strength is substituted, and whom there is no more safety in trusting than Angria himself.

THIS argument would be very just, if the Morattoes were not already, by their neighborhood to Bombay, in condition to do us so much mischief by land, that the consideration of what they can ever do against us by sea is absorbed in it. It may not then be unreasonable to think, that it is better to have this nation only to deal with, on the best terms of friendship that can be procured, than to continue in a constant state of hostility with a petty pirate, from whom no peace could ever be hoped,

and

and who was unfuppreffible, without a greater land force than we could conveniently bring againſt him; ſince even granted, that the Morattoes could raiſe a marine ſuperior to that of Angria, a breach with them by ſea could not be more fatal than the one at land, which would of courſe be implied in it. For certainly Bombay, according to all human appearance, ceaſes to be tenable, that inſtant the Morattoes determinately reſolve the conqueſt of it; which will not appear a hazarded conjecture to thoſe, who know the extent of the Morattoes power, eſpecially now their arms are at liberty, and free from any awe of the Mogul's. But, beſides, even allowing that the fortifications of Bombay were able to hold out againſt ſuch forces as they could eaſily bring againſt them, if they convert but their deſign into a ſcheme of blocking up the paſſes, of harraſſing the iſland with incurſions, and ſtraitening it for proviſions, they can only with a little more time, but with leſs danger and no inconvenience to themſelves who are at home, render the tenure of it impracticable, or at leaſt uſeleſs to us. If they can poſſibly however be brought to know their own intereſt; or knowing it, to adhere to it, this can never be the caſe.

BOOK

BOOK IV.

Of the MOGUL *government.*

CHAP. I.

Of SURAT : *its situation : disturbances there. History of* MAHMUD ALLY. *Character of the* BANYANS. *Style of the* MOGUL *governors. Shipbuilding : navigation : buildings and streets of* Surat : *provisions : odd names given to spirituous liquors. Account of the practice of champing : bathing : jugglers : toleration of religions : manufactures : commodious method of sale. Singular method of securing the caravans. Intercourse between* Surat *and* BOMBAY *by land. Opium : story of its paradoxical operation :* PATNA *sends the best to market : story of an* ENGLISH *gentleman dying of having sucked a poppy. Of the use of bang.— Of the* PARSEES.—*Of the* MOGUL *government, and its declension. Religion of* TARTARY *is deism. Of seraglios, and the* MOORS *taste of beauty. Buildings and gardens of the* Moguls. *Dancing-girls. Dress of the* Moors : *manners : slaves : diet : equipage and carriages. Luxury of the Orientalists.*

SURAT has hitherto been so closely connected with our government at Bombay, that some account of it falls naturally within my plan, especially as it serves for introduction to an attempt of some definition of the Mogul government, in which the English are so much concerned,

cerned, and which for many years paſt has been a kind of political paradox.

Surat is ſituate on the continent a little to the northward of Bombay, about ſixteen miles up the river Tappee, on the right-hand ſide as you go up. The river itſelf is nothing remarkable; but the city on the banks of it is perhaps one of the greateſt inſtances in the known world, of the power of trade to bring in ſo little a time wealth, arts and population, to any ſpot where it can be brought to ſettle.

It is not later than the middle of the laſt century, that this place was the repair of a few merchants, who under the ſhelter of an old inſignificant caſtle, formed up a town, which in the proceſs of a few years, became one of the moſt conſiderable in the world, not only for trade but ſize, being almoſt as large, and as populous as London within the walls, and contains many good houſes, according to the Indian architecture. A wall was ſoon, after its taking the form of a town, built round it, to defend it from the inſults of the Morattoes, who had twice pillaged it; but a wall that could only be meant of uſe againſt the ſudden incurſion of ſuch free-booters, and by no means capable of ſtanding any thing like a regular ſiege. The caſtle too, which is by the river-ſide, and which you paſs in your way up to the city, appears a ſtrange huddle of building, fortified with cannon mounted here and there without order and meaning, and without an attempt at any thing like military architecture.

In this city, before the Eaſt India company became by the royal grant inveſted with the poſſeſſion of Bombay, was the preſidency of their affairs on that coaſt: for which purpoſe they had a factory eſtabliſhed there with ſeveral great privileges allowed them by the Mogul government; and even after

The East View of Surat Castle

The South View of Surat Castle.

The West View of Surat Castle

THE EAST-INDIES.

after the seat of the presidency was transferred to Bombay, they continued a factory here, at one of the best houses in the city; which yet not being spacious enough to contain their effects, they hired another house at some distance from it, and nearer the water-side, which was called the new factory.

IN the mean time this city florished, and grew the center, and indeed the only staple of India; it being much more frequented for the sake of the vent goods of all sorts met with there, from whence they were distributed particularly to the inland provinces, than for either the natural productions, and manufactures of the country, though they also made a considerable part of its commerce. In short, there was hardly any article of merchandize that can be named, but what was to be found at all times here, almost as readily as in London itself. The company carries on annually a large investment of piece goods, especially of the coarse ones Byrampauts, Chelloes, and others for the Guinea market; but the English interest and influence seem of late years to have greatly declined, amidst the confusion and embroils of the country, a circumstance every where fatal to trade, and to that security and credit which are the life of it.

WHILE the Mogul government was in vigor, there was such a shew of justice, as induced the merchants of all religions and denominations to take shelter under it. The Gentoos especially resorted to it, and took up their abode there, not only on the account of trade, but for preferring a Moorish form of government to the living under Gentoos, who had none at all. And it must be owned, great care was taken that no very flagrant acts of oppression should be committed; so that in what sometimes happened, at least appearances were kept, and were mostly owing to the merchants

chants themselves, who on personal pique, or jealousy of trade, would find means to set the government upon one another's backs, which was not averse to interfere in their quarrels, being sure to be the only gainer by them.

As an instance of this, it may not be improper to relate the fate of Mahmud Ally, the grandson of that great and truly royal merchant Abdulgafour, of whom captain Hamilton observes, " that he " drove a trade equal to the East India company " (that is greatly exaggerated) for he had known " him fit out in a year above twenty sail of ships, " between 300 and 800 tons, and none of them " had less of his own stock than 20,000 pounds, " and some of them had 25,000, and after that " foreign stock was sent away, it behoved him to " have as much more of an inland-stock for the " following year's market. When he died, he " left his estate to two grandsons, his own son, " who was his only child, dying before him. But " the court had a fling at him, and got above a " million sterling of their estate."

One of the brothers dying, the remains of that fortune centered in Mahmud Ally, who, even after that great stroke of court-extortion, had still enough left to carry on a trade, not indeed equal to his grand-father, but however far superior to any other private person in Surat. He had also a fort of his own, called Otway, by the river-side, where he kept all his ware-houses, magazines, and stores for building ships, compactly and within himself.

But it happened unfortunately for him, that Lolldass Vituldass, a Banyan, and actually at that time head-broker to the East India company, with whose trade that of Mahmud Ally interfered, and perhaps inflamed by other personal piques and emulation, projected his ruin, and effected it.

LOLLDASS

LOLLDASS knew very well, that the Moorish governor of Surat would readily seize any occasion of destroying Mahmud Ally, not only for the sake of gratifying his avarice by the plunder of his estate, but for that of removing out of his way a man greatly obnoxious for his power to protect the merchants, being a preponderant weight in their scale, when joining them to withstand the oppressions of the government: a circumstance which had given equally umbrage to the preceding governor Sorab Cawn, who, before he was removed, had also marked him out for his prey.

THE Mogul's court was then immersed in that supine indolence, which had invited the Persian invasion by Shaw Nadir, more commonly known in Europe by the name of Thamas Kouli-Cawn; so that the Nabobs, and governors of cities, lived in a sort of contumacy or independence on his commands. But what was worse yet, especially for Surat, that rule of good policy had been omitted with respect to its government, which had always before established, that the governor of the town should be separate from, and utterly unconnected with the governor of the castle, who was even ordered not to stir out of the castle while his government lasted, unless perhaps once a year to repair in ceremony, and with all proper precautions to pay his devotions at the head-mosch. To this check was also added another, which was an universal practice over the whole empire. The Mogul used to keep a residentiary, or at least send occasionally an authorized minister, under the title of Vocaneveefs, whose business was to inspect and report to him the conduct of his governors, and prefects of provinces, to whom this person was not only unsubordinate, but an awe and terror.

ALL these wise dispositions were however, at this time of universal negligence, laid aside: and the governor

governor of the castle was not only nearly related to Teg-beg Cawn, the governor of the town, but absolutely at his disposal; so that every thing was done in a concert between them, which opened the door to the oppression that followed.

LOLLDASS taking advantage of these circumstances, and himself being rendered desperate by the declension of his own, easily found means to suggest to a governor, already greedy of embracing such an overture, the design of destroying a man obnoxious to them both.

ACCORDINGLY he took such an advantage of a storm originally raised against the whole body of merchants themselves, that the issue of it was Mahmud Ally's perishing in it: for having stood on his defence against the new governor Teg-beg Cawn, and being deserted by that party of the Gentoo merchants especially, over whom, to their afterwards great and vain regret, the influence that Lolldass had still retained, though himself was on the point of bankruptcy, had prevailed, he fell defenceless, in consequence of a confederacy of them, at which himself had been the head, for their mutual protection and security, by such a turn as could hardly be imagined things could take, and which for the rarity of it, besides the importance of its consequences, it may not be disagreeable to the reader, to see a summary account.

MAHMUD ALLY, on having certain intimation, that Sorab Cawn, the Mogul governor of the town, and with whom himself had formerly close connections and dealings, was projecting a general extortion from himself, and all the merchants of Surat, took care to spread the alarm, and invited the merchants to join him, and make a common cause against the governor; engaging himself to bear principally the charges of the contest. This league was accordingly formed, and was so succesful,

that

that Sorab Cawn was not only expelled his government, but Teg-beg Cawn, by the intereſt of the governor of the caſtle, ſubſtituted in his room, againſt all the rules of good policy, againſt the conſtitution of the ſtate, and eſpecially againſt the inclination of Mahmud Ally. For Teg-beg Cawn had been in that poſt before; but had been revoked for his oppreſſions, and had never thereafter afforded the leaſt room to hope, that he had changed his tyrannical or avaritious temper, and was beſides particularly deteſted by Mahmud Ally; who now found too late, that he had been hurried farther than what he had originally intended, which was the depreſſion, rather than the deſtruction of Sorab Cawn, who was beſides conſiderably his debtor, and began to repent of the exceſſes into which this affair had led him, eſpecially too, as thoſe very merchants, whoſe intereſt was a common one with him, had not only conſtrued his promiſes of bearing the charges of the oppoſition in an unlimited ſenſe, but had paid him ſo little regard, as without conſulting him, or indeed the dictates of common ſenſe, to ſet up a man for governor, againſt whom he had ſuch juſt objections, of a public beſides a private nature.

In this mood of repentance, for a conduct which only ſelf-defence could juſtify, or ſucceſs ſave from the charge and conſequences of open rebellion, againſt a governor appointed by royal authority, he began to relent, and incline, if not towards a reſtoration of Sorab Cawn, at leaſt to wiſh to preſerve him from falling into the hands of his enemies, who would probably have given him no quarter. The intereſt he had in his not being plundered, utterly ruined, and ultimately murdered, who was not only the lawful governor, but alſo his debtor, joined to conſiderations of former friendſhip, engaged him to give this very governor Sorab Cawn, of whose expulsion he had been the original promoter, refuge in his castle of Otway, with four others of his retinue, and by this means procured their escape.

THIS however was deemed by the enemies of Sorab Cawn, and especially by Lolldafs, who had a great hand in setting Teg-beg Cawn up, as a perfidious desertion of the league formed by himself: and this advantage he improved, so as to inflame both the new governor and all his partizans to such a pitch, that they laid siege to the castle of Otway, forced it to surrender, and, in razing it to the ground, implicitly destroyed the capital fortress of the liberty of Surat.

SOON after which, on a kind of forced visit to Teg-beg Cawn, Mahmud Ally was seized, made a prisoner, and barbarously murdered one night in the apartment where he was confined, by the governor's ruffians. Then the remains of his estate were plundered, and his two sons left entirely at the discretion, mercy, and charity of this assassin of their fathers.

NOR did Lolldafs long survive the success of his schemes; for when he saw the tragical issue of it, which went probably beyond his intentions, in the same manner as Mahmud Ally had himself been hurried along by the force of conjectures, further than he had meant in his opposition to Sorab Cawn; when he saw the fatal catastrophe of this great and beloved merchant, and all eyes turned upon him, as imputing it to him, that, joined to the disorders of his own affairs, it was thought broke his heart; he dying soon after suddenly, without any other cause visibly assignable for it, and left his sons in bankrupt circumstances.

WITHOUT taking on me to justify or condemn Mahmud Ally, having only related the facts on the best authorities I could procure, I shall only add

add that his death, which happened in the year 1732, was the epoch of the declenfion of the Surat trade, and the beginning of all the diforders, embroils, and confufion that followed, in which the Englifh were not exempt from their fhare of fuffering, and into a fpecification of which, it could be but little interefting, and very tedious to enter here *.

I HAVE before obferved, that the Gentoos were extremely numerous here; efpecially that tribe or caft of the Banyans, who are conftitutionally or profeffedly merchants. I have often read, often heard them reprefented as a tricking, artful fet of people, full of low cunning, that made it difficult to deal with them: but this can, I think, only be underftood, if it be at all true, of the petty, under-dealers among them: for thofe of them who are properly merchants, in the extenfive fenfe of that word, are in general the faireft, openeft dealers in the world; and thofe of Surat were efpecially famous for the fimplicity and franknefs of their tranfactions. For example, on a fhip's importing there, nothing more was to be done, than for the commander, or fupracargoe, to bring his mufters or famples on fhore, together with his invoice; and the confiderable merchants reforting to him, would immediately ftrike a bargain for the whole cargoe, if the affortment fuited them, with no other trouble than fettling the per centage upon the items of the invoice. In this manner many a cargoe, from five to ten, twenty, thirty thoufand pounds and upwards, has been fold in half an hour's time with very few words, and the amount paid down upon the nail, either in ready money,

---

* See vol. II. p. 320, for the reduction of Surat, by the Englifh in 1759.

or by barter, according as the vender and purchaser agreed, with as much good faith, at least, as is ever observed among the European merchants of the most established character of probity. Then their readiness at running all the hazards of trade was even proverbial, insomuch, that it has not been unjustly observed of them, that if their personal equalled their commercial courage, they would incontestably be the bravest people on the earth. But that is far from the case: one would rather think, by them, that the one excluded the other.

Those Banyans have indeed one constitutional advantage over the European merchants; but then it is such, that these last cannot fairly complain of it, which is their invincible phlegm and coolness in the course of their transactions. Whether you offer them shamefully less than their goods are worth, or fly into passions at their under-rating yours, there is no such thing as provoking them into the least show of passion or indecency. They calmly suffer you to evaporate your resentment without interrupting you, and waiting patiently till your fit of drunkenness is off, for they look on it in no other light, they return cooly to the same point, as if nothing had stirred them from it; and if they depart from it, you may depend that it is not in the least out of any consideration for what you shall have said to them in your fury, but purely for their own ends, and in consequence of their own inward representations to themselves. In that they have, in this point, the same advantage over the Europeans, that a cool gamester has over a passionate one.

But besides the number of Gentoo inhabitants of Surat, its suburbs, and neighboring villages, employed purely in trade, money-changing, brokership, and manufactures, they are often employed in posts under the Moorish government, as collectors,

THE EAST-INDIES. 107

lectors, surveyors of the customs, and other offices of trust; especially where accomptantship is required, in which they generally excel the Moors, who are bred more in the military way: and it has been observed, that none are more rigorous exacters over the Gentoos, nor readier to abet, or even set on foot any vexation, or extortion from them, than these Gentoos themselves. One would imagine oppression was their element, and that they could not breathe out of it.

THE governor of Surat keeps his seat of administration at what is called the Durbar, where he is generally present himself, and gives his orders. It is here that all actions criminal and civil are brought before him, and summarily dispatched in the Eastern manner. One piece of state too he observes, that I have no where before seen mentioned, and that is, that he never on any thing material speaks to his attendants, but writes, in the Persian language, his orders upon little slips of paper, that lie by him ready for that purpose, and when written, are called Hookums, and must be obeyed without reply. These are afterwards brought him, like a return of a judicial procefs, and being strung, serve as a kind of record of his acts of the day.

THE Morattoes are however now grown so predominant, and their influence is so far spread into that city itself, that unless the Mogul government should resume its ascendancy, of which there is very little likelihood, the government of it already so precarious, must soon become entirely dependent on them, when it is a question whether even their own clear interest in the preservation of the trade of it, will prevail over that constitutional indifference of theirs to it, and that passion for present pillage, which have been already set forth.

AT Surat too they excel in the art of ship-building. If their models were as fine as those of the English,

English, of whom especially they prefer the imitation, there would be no exaggeration in averring, that they build incomparably the best ships in the world for duration, and that of any size, even to a thousand tons and upwards. But their naval, like their other architecture, has always something clumsy, unfinished, and un-artist-like in it; otherwise the reign of their ships is much longer than that of the European-built ones: it is not uncommon for one of them to last a century, and that not so much owing to the commonly summer seas in those parts, as to the solidity of their workmanship, and the nature of the wood they employ.

As to the first, their bottom and sides are composed of planks let in to one another, in the nature as I apprehend of what is called rabbit-work; so that the seams are impenetrable: and the knees, or crooked timbers, are generally of the natural growth into that form, without being forced or warped by fire, especially where particular care is taken of their construction, and their expence not spared.

And as to the wood, it is a sort, called teak, to the full as durable as oak, and has, besides this property, that it is not so apt in an engagement with cannon-shot to fly in splinters, which usually do more mischief to the men than the balls themselves. They have also a peculiar way of preserving their ships-bottoms, by occasionally rubbing into them an oil, they call wood-oil, which the planks imbibe, and serves greatly to nourish and keep them from decay.

They do not launch their ships as we do from slips; but by digging canals from the water to where the stocks, or what they call craddles are, from which they are, as it were, dropped into the stream that is brought up to them.

I AM

I am also sensible, that Surat is not the only place by many in India, where ships are built, but none as yet are comparable to them. Pegu is also a noted place for ship-building; but I never learnt that they were as yet there come into that way of rabbit-work bottoms, which renders the Surat ships so strong: though I have otherwise seen very fine vessels of the built of that country.

The masting generally used in the country-ships, are Pohoon-masts, chiefly from the Malabar coast; but for the cordage, what is worth any thing must come from Europe: their coyr-ropes, made of the fibres of coconut-husks, being for either running or standing-rigging, more harsh and untractable than what is produced from hemp. I have, however, seen very serviceable and large coyr-cables, which, in opposition to the Europe ones, last much longer in salt-water, fresh being apt to rot them.

Their anchors are mostly European, our iron being much better, and better worked. As to sails, they are very well supplied by the country-manufacture of cotton into a sail-cloth called dungaree, which, though not so strong or lasting as canvass, Holland's duck, or vitry, is, while in use, more pliant, and less apt to split than they are. And for pitch they have the gum of a tree, which is called damar, not at all inferior to the other.

Their navigators are very indifferent artists; formerly they used to get Europeans to command their ships; but lately they make a shift to do without them, having trained up to it some of the natives, who may just serve in those parts, where they seldom put to sea but in the fair season, and where consequently they rarely meet with storms to try their skill. Their common sailors are rather better in their class, though wanting the vigor, expertness, and patience of fatigue, in the Europeans. Yet, where some of our ships have been

too

too far weakened in their crews, by sickness or other casualties, they have been obliged to borrow the assistance of these black sailors, or lascars, to bring them home. The public has here seen some of them miserable objects about the streets of London, begging charity, and exposed to all the distresses incident to persons so far remote from their native country, friendless, and abandoned, for want of knowing the laws and customs here, which joined to the thoughtlessness one would think natural to those of their rank on that element, rendered them a prey to all the little low designing people, among whom their station of life and misfortune had cast them away.

As to the buildings of Surat, there are some very good houses in their style of building, which is partly Gentoo, and partly Morisque. Those of the greatest note are so contrived, that the gateway is defensible against any sudden irruption of a few armed men : a circumstance of no small import, in a city, where often the withstanding the first brunt of any persons sent by the government to oppress, or destroy the owner, is attended with future security, by the alarm raising a party to relieve, or oppose his proceedings. The private apartments lye backwards, for the greater security of the women, of whom the Moors especially are remarkably jealous. They are very fond of having one room, at least in particular, where a fountain is kept playing in the midst of it, by the noise of which they are lulled to sleep, and refreshed by the coolness it diffuses through the apartment ; but which is attended with a damp, of which I would not advise an European to make the experiment. Besides, the common convenience of eastern sophas, which are so commodious for their manner of sitting crofs-legged, they all like European looking-glasses, which are what they chiefly hang

their

their rooms with. Another ornament too they have, which has not an ill effect upon the eye, and that is the beams of the chamber-cieling, curiously inlaid with ivory and mother-of-pearl, like the hand-fcrutores that come from thence, in florifhes and fcroll-work, agreeable to the Morifque tafte. They have generally a kind of faloon, which they call a Diwan, entirely open on one fide to the garden, where they have fountains playing, which joined to the variegated flower-beds in front of it, of which they are very curious, add to the pleafantnefs and airinefs of the profpect. In summer, when the heats are moft intenfe, though never fo intolerable as in many other places, nor unwholfome that ever I could learn, they have country-receffes a little way out of town, where they refide, or go in parties to enjoy themfelves in their gardens and frefcades, by the fide of the waters with which they are furnifhed. The Englifh company has efpecially a very pleafant garden, kept for the ufe and recreation of the gentlemen of the factory; though lately the incurfions of the Morattoes to the very gates of the city, and the conftant alarms of the country round, have made thofe rural receffes too unfafe to confift with a fatisfactory enjoyment of them.

THE ftreets of Surat are irregularly laid out; but have one propriety which renders them agreeable to the walkers, in the heat of the day, and that is, a competent width of them being left at bottom, the ftories of the houfes are carried up fo projecting over one another, that the uppermoft apartments on each fide of the ftreet are fo clofe to one another, that one may with eafe converfe from them ; a way of building, that whilft it overfhades the ftreet, does not exclude a free ventilation, which is rather attracted by it. The fhops however, though in this great trading city, where every ry thing almost that can be asked for is to be found, have a very mean appearance, the dealers keeping their goods chiefly in warehouses, and selling by samples.

As to the living in Surat, I mean for provisions, I cannot imagine that there is in the world a better place, while the communication especially with the country is open. For to say nothing of the abundance of every article which an unbounded importation throws into the market there, the natural productions of the soil are excellent in their kind, and thereby atone for their perhaps being less cheap, as to the quantity, than at some other places of India, as at Bengal especially, where the cattle and poultry are bought at a very low rate, and yet turn out dear by the time they are properly fed for the table. Here then all manner of eatables are at a reasonable price, ready for immediate use, and as good as can any where be found. The wheat of Surat is famous all over India, for its singular whiteness, substance, and taste; and nothing can exceed their sallads and roots. There are also many kinds of wild fowl and game to be had at an easy rate.

As to wines and spirituous liquors, the Europeans depend chiefly on importation for them, few relishing the distillery of the country, which however produces various strong spirits, to which they give names that would seem odd; such as spirit of mutton, spirit of deer, spirit of goat; but for the reason they annex to it, which is their throwing into the still, according to the liquor they propose, a joint of mutton, a haunch of venison, a quarter of a goat, which give respectively their names to the distillation. This they imagine, how justly I do not pretend to know, super-adds to the liquor a certain mellowness and softness, that corrects the fieriness of the spirit.

AMONG

THE EAST-INDIES.

AMONG the articles of luxury, which they have in common with other parts of the East, and especially the Mahometans, they have public hummums for bathing, cupping, rubbing and sweating; of which there needs no particular description, being so generally well known. But the practice of champing, which by the best intelligence I could gather is derived from the Chinese, may not be unworthy particularizing, as it is so little known to the modern Europeans; though on my mentioning it here in England, I have been assured, the antients practised something very like it, by the description which a friend pointed out to me: but I leave the reader to judge of the fitness of the quotation.

Percurrit agili corpus arte tractatrix
Manumque doctam spargit omnibus membris.
Mart. Lib. III. Epig. 82.

SENECA too, at the end of his sixty-sixth letter, inveighs against it as a point of luxury crept in among the Romans; which however proves that it was not unknown to them. His words are, *An potius optem ut malacissandos articulos exoletis meis porrigam? ut muliercula, aut aliquis in mulierculam ex viro versus digitulos meos ducat?* "Should I ra-
" ther wish to hold out my joints to be softened
" and suppled by some superannuated chamber-
" minion; or suffer a woman, or a man effeminat-
" ed into one, to stretch my fingers?" But whether he is right or wrong in his stoical conception of it, the Orientalists annex no idea of indecency or immodesty to it, and the manner of it is this: after the ceremony of sweating, bathing, rubbing, &c. is gone through, and which is not always previously used, since many are frequently champed at home, the person that chooses it, lies at his length

length on a couch, bed, or fopha, where the operator handles his limbs as if he was kneading dough, or pats them gently with his hands an edge, and chafes or rubs them, concluding with cracking all the joints of the wrift and fingers, and if you will allow them that of the neck, being extremely dextrous at this work.. All this, they pretend, not only fupples the joints, but procures a brifker circulation to the fluids apt to ftagnate, or loiter through the veins, from the heat of the climate, which is perhaps the beft excufe for this practice. The fenfations it excites in fome are furprifing, by its inducing a kind of pleafing langor or delirium, under which they are ready to faint away, and fometimes actually do fo. Both Moors and Gentoos are however extremely fond of this practice, and it is fo common, that it would be hard to find a barbar-native who is not fkilled in it, as one of the effentials of that profeffion; of which fome particulars are alfo different from the European. For they fhave conftantly with the grain, with great eafe and dexterity, and have all one uniform fet of materials, a round glafs, with a handle ftuck in their girdle like a dagger, which they put in your hands whilft you are fhaving: a little copper tumbler not bigger than a common tea-cup, and fome inftruments for picking the ears, and paring the nails, hung on a wire like a bunch of keys, or in a tweezer-cafe. In fhort, one muft do the Orientalifts in general the juftice to allow, that none are more ftudious of the cleanlinefs and fupplenefs of the body than they are; which they perhaps not abfurdly conceive, conduces even to the pleafure of the mind, and if even matter of fenfuality, is furely the moft excufably fuch.

The Gentoo women, and thofe of the beft fafhion, make no fcruple of going to the river-fide,

and

and bathing publicly and indifferently in the fight of the men. They go into the water indeed with their cloaths on; but the wetting them soon makes them cleave so close to their bodies, that they express very clearly the fashion and turn of the limbs; a circumstance which probably gave the Grecian artists the first notion of employing in statuary a wet drapery, as exhibiting nearest the justness of nudity, without its indecency. But when they come out of the water, and change their wet for dry cloaths, 'it is then that the eye of the most curious spectator is at fault; for they have so dextrous a knack at shifting, that though it is done so openly, not the least glimpse of any thing immodest can be perceived.

As to public diversions, or entertainments, I could not learn there were any, except the dancing-girls, and the jugglers.

As to the dancing-girls, they form a distinct branch of the community; of which more shall be said in its place.

THE jugglers, or sleight-of-hand-men, greatly excel whatever I have seen or heard of them in Europe. Their tricks and deceptions in short are so amazing, that I confess I have not the courage to relate what I have myself been eye-witness to, or been credibly assured of, for fear of being taxed with running into that marvellous of which travellers are so fond. One story, however, I cannot help relating, though digressively on this occasion, as I think it does honor to humanity, and not the less, for being found in so low and despicable a class.

A LONG-BOAT with men going up from an English ship, to Calcutta, a fortified settlement we have on the banks of the Ganges in Bengal, stopped short of it a considerable way, waiting for the return of the tide, and went on shore to a moorish village,

village, where juſt at that time were ſome of theſe jugglers ſhewing, to a mob gathered round them, their various tricks; one of which, and no juggle, was the firing a piſtol loaded with powder down one of their throats. On the arrival of the ſailors, this was to be repeated, for they had before done it, but their powder having been conſumed, one of the ſailors innocently offered the man ſome he had about him. It was accepted, and the effect of it was, that being much ſtronger than what they uſed for this purpoſe, it killed the man upon the ſpot. As he was a Mahometan, and the whole village was ſo, the mob inſtantly roſe, and were preparing to maſſacre all the ſailors there, in revenge for the Muſſulman's blood, and would infallibly have done ſo, but for the humane interpoſition of the jugglers themſelves, who declared, that however ſorry they might be for the death of their brother, it was by no means imputable to the Engliſh, who were evidently clear of any malicious deſign in it. This alone appeaſed the populace, and the ſailors were ſuffered to return quietly to their boat.

There is one particular branch of the art of theſe jugglers, I cannot paſs by, too well atteſted to doubt of it, and of which thoſe who practiſe it never refuſe giving the cleareſt proof; which is their incantation of ſnakes; I ſay incantation, though no doubt it is to be naturally accounted for, however incapable I am of it. When a ſnake lurking in an houſe has bit any perſon, one of theſe men being ſent for, will, with an inſtrument ſomething reſembling a flageolet, play certain tunes upon it, the ſound of which operates ſo powerfully on the ſnake, that he comes out of his hole, forced as it were, and with apparent reluctance preſents itſelf to thoſe ready to kill him. I am fully aware of the ridicule this will meet with from many; but prefer

even

even the certainty of incurring it, to the fuppref-
fion of what I tried myfelf to difbelieve till convinced of it. In the mean time this incredulity,
often indeed well founded, but when too general
has this ill effect, that it prevents examinations,
which might iffue in very valuable difcoveries.

At Surat, all religions are tolerated; than which
nothing can be more political, efpecially in a place
of fuch univerfal trade. The Moors, who are the
mafters, feem to relax of that rigor and fondnefs
for making of profelytes, they have in moft other
parts where their religion prevails. They are fo
little curious of encouraging apoftates, that there
are very rare inftances of any, and thofe, generally fpeaking, live and die neglected and miferable.
If they take an European into their fervice, as they
fometimes do, in quality of gunners, for they
think all Europeans are born engineers, they never
trouble their heads with what religion they are of,
or moleft them about it.

The inhabitants in and about Surat are commonly very induftrious, and have on foot a number of manufactures, which it would be too tedious to fpecify; but the moft confiderable is that
of their atlaffes, or fattins flowered with gold or
filver, which have a rich fubftantial look, though
otherwife in a very indifferent tafte. The flowers
ill fancied, and without air, and the red color
which is moftly ufed, for the ground, dull and un-
fightly.

Some fhawls are manufactured there; but few
and not of the fineft fort, thofe coming from the
province of Cachemire on the borders of Tartary,
being made of a peculiar kind of filky hair, that
produces from the loom a cloth beautifully bordered at both ends, with a narrow flowered felvage,
about two yards and a half long, and a yard and
a half wide, which without farther trouble of mak-

ing up, serves the natives for a wrapper or mantle; and, according to the price, which is from ten pounds and upwards to fifteen shillings, joins to exquisite fineness, a substance that renders them extreamly warm, and so pliant, that the fine ones are easily drawn through a common ring for the fingers.

The manufacturers have a commodious way, when their work has not been bespoke, as it commonly is by the wholesale merchants, to make a quick sale of it: they repair to the Bazar, or market-place, where they stand and hold up the piece ready finished, to any chapman that shall offer their price, much in the same manner as our farmers stand in rows at a country-market, with samples of grain in their hands, and they rarely return without disposing of them, as there are a number of petty dealers attend the market for the purchasing of them, thus at the first hand, and vend them afterwards in quantities to the greater merchants. This custom will be hardly thought a bad one, as it is a continual incentive to industry, by shewing it an easy and assured vent of its produce, and besides, frees the poor manufacturers from the tyranny of the wholesale dealers.

Surat too being the only sea-port of very considerable note, and unpossessed by the Europeans, in the whole immense dominions of the Mogul, it is easily imaginable that the inland trade, especially to Delly and Agra, the capital residences of that court, which are about a month's journey from Surat, must employ a number of caravans, or caffilahs, for the distribution of the imports. But unfortunately the roads, never perfectly safe, on account of the independent Rajahs, are lately grown much less so, from the troubles and convulsions of the whole country.

Formerly

FORMERLY the security of them was provided for by a very singular expedient. The whole caravan at setting out was put under the protection of one single person, a boy, but oftenest a woman, hired and selected from a cast sacred for that purpose among the Gentoos, from whose free-booter's tribes all the danger of the journey arises. When any of these met with the caravans, on a design to pillage them, it was the duty of this single guard to interpose, and protest against the violence, with a solemn threat to kill him or herself in case they persisted: which threat was always attended with the execution, if the robbers proceeded further; and the sure consequence was, their incurring thereby all the guilt of sacrilege, and the penalty both of a civil and religious excommunication never to be taken off, being thereby for ever degraded, detested, and renounced by their own tribes. I do not however believe that this custom still subsists: whether the race of those faithful suicides is extinguished; or what is most probable, that the Gentoos have made their religion yield to their ruling passion for plunder, and brought this custom into disuse, from their ceasing by common consent to respect it.

BETWIXT Surat and Bombay there is a constant intercourse preserved, not only by sea, the distance being but small, but by Pattamars, or foot-messengers, over land, which are used in the same way throughout India, and hired at a moderate rate, who carry letters to and fro. They are very expeditious in their journeys, and commonly use opium, which they think fortifies them, and by this means will keep on running, and dozing as it were at the same time with their eyes open, and without feeling the fatigues of the way.

AND here having mentioned opium, I shall take the liberty of a small digression thereon, that I may not

not return to it again. It is not then only the Pattamars, who take opium in the intention of strengthening their powers for service, but most of the hard laboring people of Surat, and especially the Hamalls or porters, who make a livelihood of carrying goods to and from the warehouses, and will endure such loads, as few of the stoutest Europeans can undertake. I have been credibly assured, that some of these fellows will take at one doze three copper gorze weight of this drug, without danger; which is considerably above an ounce weight, and pretend that it greatly enables them to work and carry burthens.

MANY of the rich and great contract a habit of it, but with different views; considering it not only as a high point of sensuality, from the pleasing deliriums they experience from it, but as a specific for procuring a priapism that serves to spin out the venereal congress, as long as they please, by taking a competent dose of it, usually in a vehicle of milk, boiled away from a large to a small quantity; and when they have a mind to check or put an end to its operation, they do it by swallowing a spoonful or two of lime-juice, or of any equivalent acid. By this means, however, it commonly happens that the users of it, by forcing nature, wear out its springs, and bring on themselves prematurely all the inconveniences of old age: but this is a consideration that weighs little with the generality of the Orientalists, always more actuated by any present favorite objects, than by a providential regard for remote ones.

IF you would believe them too, there is a kind of paradoxical mixture of effects in the operation of this drug, causing at once a seeming heaviness of the head, and visible sleepiness of the eye, and yet withal a great watchfulness; in confirmation of of which, the following story passes current at Surat.

That one of its town-governors, on receiving a visit from a Gentoo-rajah, with whom he was in friendly correspondence, at a garden just out of the city-walls, they met with each their guards and attendants, and without any of that treachery, which is not uncommon among them, intended on either side. As they were walking together in the garden, the governor took notice of the Rajah's guards, who were squatted down in their manner, under an open guard-room, with their heads leaning, or rather nodding upon their naked swords, and to all appearance dozing, or fast asleep. The governor then smiling remarked to the Rajah, that he had a very just opinion of his good faith, since he would venture himself to this interview with guards in such a condition, from the opium he knew it was their custom to take. " That, says the Rajah, is your mistake, and to
" prove it to you, if you have any body near you,
" of whom you do not care what becomes, bid him
" as softly as he pleases, pluck a flower out of any
" of their turbants." The governor, who either had such a person at hand, or did not apprehend the consequence, ordered one he pitched upon, to do what the Rajah had mentioned ; in proceeding to which, with all the caution recommended, and addressing himself to him, who seemed the most overcome with sleep, the Rajah's guard felt it, and without more ceremony, at one stroke cut off his arm, and the rest were instantly alert, and on foot: and thus the governor was satisfied of their vigilance, at the expence indeed of a servant, whose being guilty enough to deserve an exposure to such a trial, or innocent, was probably no great matter of consequence under that perfectly arbitrary government.

Opium

OPIUM is also considered by these people as such a specific inspirer of courage, or rather heedlessness of danger, that the commanders make no scruple of allowing it their soldiers, especially when employed on any very perilous or desperate enterprize.

THE best in the world is said to come from Patna, on the river Ganges, where at least the greatest traffic of it is made, and from thence exported all over India; though in some parts of it, especially on the Malay-coast, it is prohibited under pain of death, from the madness, and the murderous effects of that madness, it has on the inhabitants; and yet the gain attending this article, makes it be smuggled into those countries, in spite of all the laws and precautions against it.

THE soil about the Ganges is accounted the best for producing the strongest sort of opium; of which one instance occurs to me, too remarkable to suppress the mention of it. A Nabob or viceroy of those parts having invited an English factory to an entertainment, a young gentleman, a writer in the company's service, sauntering about the garden, plucked a poppy, and sucked the head of it, probably not apprehending any greater force in it, than those plants have in England. The consequence was his falling into a profound sleep, of which the Nabob being apprized, and in much concern, eagerly enquired of the particular bed out of which the poppy was gathered by him, and on being told it, with great expression of sorrow, apologized for his having supposed that the nature of the poppies was in general too well known to have needed any warning, especially as the taste was so far from tempting, but that this peculiar sort, on which the English gentleman was so unfortunate to pitch, admitted of no human remedy or counter-poison, so that nothing could save him, as effectually it turned out, for that sleep was his last.

BANG

THE EAST-INDIES. 125

BANG is alſo greatly uſed at Surat, as well as all over the Eaſt, an intoxicating herb, of which it may be needleſs to ſay more after ſo many writers, who have fully deſcribed it: and it is hard to ſay what pleaſure can be found in the uſe of it, being very diſagreeable to the taſte, and violent in its o-peration, which produces a temporary madneſs, that in ſome, when deſignedly taken for that pur-poſe, ends in running what they call a-muck, fu-riouſly killing every one they meet, without diſtinc-tion, until themſelves are knocked on the head, like mad dogs. But by all accounts this practice is much rarer in India than it formerly was.

BUT, to reſume my more immediate ſubject; I am to obſerve, that the intercourſe between Bom-bay and Surat is not without great reaſon kept up, from the conſtant attention which is to be had to the company's inveſtment, in the country-manu-factures that is carried on there, and to the ſale of the ſtaple-goods ſent out from England to that ſide of India, of which Surat is the capital mart, though lately greatly declined through the embroils of the country.

THE manufactures peculiar to that province of Guzarat, are chiefly carried on by the induſtry of the Parſees, or the race of Perſian refugees, who, ſome centuries ago, fled from the face of the Ma-hometan perſecution, then invaders and conquer-ors of the Perſian dominions. They were brought to theſe parts where they and their race have ever ſince continued *, in three veſſels, in which they embarked with the utmoſt precipitation and con-fuſion, and committed themſelves to the wind and weather, to be carried into whatever country would receive them. By tradition, and according to all probability, as being the moſt obnoxious to

---

* Except a few who have lately ſettled at Bombay.

the

the conquerors, there were among them some of the principal men of the country. Nowrojee-Rustumjee, who was here in England, and whose family was in the greatest consideration among those people, deduced his descent from those kings of Persia, whose dynasty was destroyed by the Mahometan invasion, when the last prince of it, Izdigerdes, a descendant from Cosroes, the son of Hormisdas, was dethroned and slain about the year 650. But whether his pretensions were just or not, or whether the rank of those fugitives was in general as high as their posterity assert it was; when they arrived at the country where Surat stands, they were hospitably received by the Gentoo inhabitants, who compassionated their distress, and were perhaps themselves alarmed with reason, as it proved afterwards at the progress of the Mahometans, which had thus fallen, like a storm, on a country not very distant from them.

I know there are several fabulous traditions of these refugees having landed where they first saw a fire, which they looked on as a propitious landmark to them, and that the Gentoos made a covenant with them, that they should conform to their customs, especially as to their abstaining from all animal food. But I never could learn, that these points of their history were attested by any authentic testimonials, or credited by the principal persons among them. The sole article of any consequence imposed on them was, that they should not kill any cows, or beasts of that species, which the Parsees their descendants to this day avoid, as looking upon themselves to be bound and concluded by that agreement of their ancestors; and even at Bombay, where they have the full liberty of acting as they please in that respect, I could never learn that they departed from this restriction. They also, in many other respects, adopted the

manners

THE EAST-INDIES.

manners and cuftoms of the Gentoos, rather from imitation than any neceffity; though otherwife they have kept their race unmixt. The wretched remnant of the Parfees who ftaid behind in Perfia, and weathered out the ftorm, acknowledge thefe Parfees for their brethren: but there does not appear to have been any farther correfpondence, or connection eftablifhed between them. The truth is, that the Guzarat-Parfees feem to have entirely forgot their original country; and from a long habituation, continued through fo many generations, to confider India as their proper country; even though from the laws of it, admitting no mixture by profelytifm, or intermarriage, they muft for ever remain a ftranger race. They are generally fairer than the native Indians, efpecially the coafters; though moftly and at beft of a fallow yellowifh hue; but the women, thofe of them who are kept up and not employed in hard work, are tolerably clear fkinned. They are moft of them an induftrious people, and the neceffity probably that obliged their anceftors on their firft arrival to betake themfelves to labor for a livelihood in a ftrange country, has fo far propagated its influence on the fpirit and manners of their defcendants, that they are the chief fupporters of the Surat manufactures, and of agriculture. Numbers of them are alfo employed in fhip-building, and in the diftillery-trade; which laft commonly flourifhes or fickens according as the Moorifh governors of Surat, for the time being, are fuperftitious obfervers or not, of the Mahometan law; which however, rather advifes againft the drinking of fpirituous liquors, than it formally condemns it, feveral paffages of the alcoran feeming rather levelled againft the abufe than the ufe of them, though expreffed in fuch a manner, as if the law-giver had known human nature well enough

to

to think it eafier totally to abftain from a pleafure, than to be moderate in it.

For the reft, none, or but inconfiderably few of the Parfees, either meddle at all with the government, or with the military ; fubmitting quietly to the power that is uppermoft, whether Gentoo or Moorifh, and confequently for their ufefulnefs and inoffenfivenefs, generally meet with protection from both.

At prefent the Moorifh government, at leaft nominally, prevails at Surat, though greatly declined and over-awed by their neighbors the Morattoes, with whom it is obliged to temporize and keep fuch meafures as nearly refemble a fubmiffion. Nor is it likely but things may foon end in that, unlefs the Moors, who are too much outnumbered by the Gentoos to have any hopes of fucceeding againft them, fhould be enabled by foreign affiftance to re-affume their former afcendancy, and once more drive the Gentoos back into their mountains and faftneffes.

As matters now ftand, the Moorifh fovereign of Indoftan, fo known by the title of Mogul, or rather as it fhould be Mongul, is no more than a phantom on the throne, ever fince the invafion and retreat of Shah Nadir; reigning precarioufly, and at the pleafure of the principal Gentoo-Rajahs, who raife, depofe, and even murder him, juft as their intereft or humor prompts them. The name of the Mogul-fovereignty would foon ceafe to exift, if they could agree among themfelves whom to fubftitute; and this very indetermination may not improbably be the occafion of their lofing the ground they have won, efpecially if fome of the Mahometan neighboring powers fhould be tempted either to reftore the authority of the Moguls, or to plant themfelves in his place; and either of thefe events

events is especially to be apprehended from the north-east Tartars, bordering upon Indostan, who are now greatly recruited in numbers since the exhaustment of those countries by the draughts out of them, of those swarms with which the two great conquerors, Ginghis Cawn and Tamerlane, subdued almost all Asia, carrying havock and desolation wherever their arms penetrated, and terror to remoter parts, and even to Europe itself. But, as a summary account of these mighty leaders may give a clearer notion of some points necessary to account for the present constitution and position of Indostan, I hope it will not be thought out of place, or impertinent to my subject.

GINGHIS CAWN, about the year 1200, after collecting under his standard an innumerable army of these north-east Tartars, which he had the influence to unite under him, though out of various tribes and nations before then utterly discordant, and living much like the savages of America, not only brought into subjection the great kingdom of China, and the nations bordering upon it, on the outside of the famous wall of that country, but extended his conquests to a great part of Asia, then and now possessed by the Mahometans, to whom he professed himself a greater enemy than to the Christians, whom he rather favored. As to himself, he was undoubtedly of that religion, which is called the religion of the great and learned of China, who hold no other object of worship but purely the *Thein*, or sovereign Being. This made him indifferent to all religions, and of course a tolerant; for as to the Mahometans he prosecuted them more on a political account, than for any particular aversion he had to their tenets. His sons however, after his decease, soon found that a conformity to the Mahometan system, would greatly advance their temporal scheme of settling

in

in the government of thofe rich countries, fo preferable to the mountains and wilds of Tartary. Accordingly moſt of them adopted the muſſulman faith, and made it their ſtate-religion, to ſatisfy this new ſubject, though for the reſt they acted as being far from bigots to it; as for inſtance, when Holagu Cawn, a grandſon of Ginghis Cawn, purſuing his conqueſts over Perſia, Syria, and Meſopotamia, at length took Bagdad by ſtorm, and without reſpect to the ſacredneſs of character among the Mahometans, of the line of the Caliphs, he exterminated the laſt of it in the perſon of Motazem, whom he put to death in the moſt ignominious manner, by having him dragged about the ſtreets of Bagdad till he expired. Even though Motazem appeared before him in the quality of a ſupplicant, and in the hopes of aſſwaging his wrath, had on his ſhoulders the very cloak Mahomet had once worn, and given, in a tranſport of applauſe, to Caab a poet, on his reading ſome Arabian verſes to him. He had beſides in his hands the ſtaff of that prophet; but that holy trumpery availed him nothing, for the Tartar-general ordered the cloak and ſtaff to be taken from him, and to be burnt in a pan, the aſhes to be thrown into the Tygris, not out of any contempt, as he pretended, but to hinder thoſe precious relics from falling thereafter into profane hands. This Motazem was at once the laſt of the Abbaſſid line, and of the caliphs of the Mahometans, whoſe authority had been long confined to purely ſpirituals, after having been for more than three centuries ſtripped of their temporal power; for one of them, in the year 935, having unadviſedly wholly truſted it to the chief of the military, a Turk called Rayk, who thenceforwards knew how to keep it, and transferred it to his ſucceſſors in his office, long famous in Aſia, under

the

THE EAST-INDIES. 129

the title of Emir-al-omrah, commander of the commanders, and afterwards by that of fultan, who governed both the ftate and the caliphs defpotically, till they and the caliphate itfelf fell under the fuperior ftrength of the Tartar invaders.

But this Tartar-family foon after experienced the fate that ufually attends the partition of an empire. For the defcendants of Ginghis Cawn quarrelling among themfelves, with all that inveteracy which ufually attends difcord among relations, the whole race in a little time, either fell by one another's fwords, or by the other Mahometan powers refuming courage and ftrength by their divifions, fo that at prefent not even a remnant of that family exifts in any ftate of power, except one branch of it, in the Crim or Precopian Tartary, which traces up a very dubious original to Ginghis Cawn, and is now a precarious tributary dependent on the Ottoman Porte, under the title of Khan or Cawn of Tartary. In fhort, in lefs than two centuries there was a clear ftage, as to any material oppofition from the princes of that race, even in Tartary itfelf, for Tamerlane to affume the fupreme authority, who treading exactly in his fteps, over-ran the greateft part of Afia, with a great army of Tartars, and in 1402, gave that celebrated defeat to Bajazet whom he took prifoner. But as if it had been fatal for thofe of that country to make conquefts with more eafe than they could preferve them, in fcarce more than a century, all his defcendants, from the very fame error of partition, and its confequences, were extinguifhed except that branch of it, which had penetrated into Indoftan, and conquered it from the Pattans. Thefe were alfo Mahometans, of the race of thofe Sarracens, who, after they had fpread their conquefts over Afia and Africa, had not neglected the rich provinces of India. For a party of Arabs,

Vol. I. K and

and that not a very numerous one, had some centuries before Tamerlane and his sons invasion, made a descent at Massulipatnam on the coast of Coromandel, where, meeting with no resistance from an effeminate unwarlike people, they soon penetrated into the heart of Indostan, and planted and maintained their seat of empire where it now is, about Agra and Dehli, till they were driven out by the superior force of the Tartars. Whilst the Gentoo Rajahs, through their wonted disunion and indolence, saw the change with indifference, or at least without materially taking part on either side.

The Pattans however being thus dispossessed, those of them who escaped the sword, or would not submit to the conqueror, fled to the mountains that lye towards the borders of Persia, where, only sollicitous to preserve their lives and independence, they formed a separate state, never thoroughly subdued by the Moguls, and yet never in a condition to dispute the field with them, but always troublesome, especially on their associating with other tribes of the Gentoo mountaineers, as the Rashpoots, Coolies, and Warrells, and occasionally exercising their depredations on the adjacent countries, without its being possible for the Moguls to come at them to extirpate them, especially since themselves soon became enervated by the deliciousness of those fruitful plains.

Nay the Pattans themselves seem so convinced, that the climate and soil of those provinces only serve to rob them of that hardiness they contract in the hills to which they are confined, that they have hitherto given no indications of a desire to exchange them for more pleasing abodes, or a more accessible situation. This it was that enabled them to brave even the victorious army of Nadir-shaw, whom they very quietly suffered to penetrate into Indostan, and waited his return when loaded with the
spoils

spoils of that country. Then it was that by their harrassment of his troops in the streights and defiles of the mountains, they shewed him they were so much masters of the passes, as to force him to come to a composition with him for way-leave, that had all the air of a ransom.

WHAT then between these unsubdued Pattans and the independant Gentoo-Rajahs, and both inaccessibly fortified in their mountains, it is evident, that the Mogul government had constantly a hard task to keep up a tolerably secure footing. Nor was it without at least as much art as strength, that it preserved its power, and especially with the Gentoos, whom as the most numerous, and being besides the Aborigines of the country, it had most reason to apprehend. Either then from a despair of totally reducing them, or from a growing indolence, the Mogul successors to Tamerlane applied themselves to the winning over at least to some show of homage and submission, the powerfullest of the Gentoo-Rajahs. And this they chiefly effectuated by their great toleration and easiness in point of religion.

IT has before been observed, that the governing theology in proper Tartary, was the same as it is in China, and perhaps derived from China, so that the Mahometan religion professed by the Moguls, in imitation of Tamerlane the founder of their dynasty, was rather matter of political conformity, than of persuasion, so that it did not cost them much to relax on this article. Even Aurengzeb himself, who was so strict an observer of his law, is no exception to this, since it is well known, that he made his pretences to superior zeal and austerity, serve to the ends of acquiring and establishing his usurpation over his father, and over his brothers, whom he over-reached by purely these arts of dissimulation, by which he recom-

mended

mended himself to the Mahometan zealots in the army. All the Moguls then since Tamerlane took the party of toleration, the easier for that deism, which made all religions at bottom indifferent to them, whilst they amused those of all religions with a favorable disposition towards them. Even some Roman-catholic priests, who had occasionally been caressed, and some even invited to that court, were the bubbles of this easiness in the Moguls, to listen to them, and even to permit their sons, and princes of their blood to give them hopes of being proselytes to them.

They would then, no doubt, for any scruples of their own to the contrary, have with respect to the Gentoos, acted the same part, as the Tartar princes had done with respect to the Mahometans. They would have politically embraced the Gentoo religion: but as one of its fundamentals is, the rejection of all proselytes to it, they could not, even had their persuasion been real, have paid them that compliment: all they could do, and that they did, was to appear entirely averse to any persecution on a religious account, and for the rest they continued Mahometans at large, in respect to the neighboring Mahometan powers, whom a throwing off entirely the appearances of that religion would have scandalized, and indisposed against them, to no purpose.

Here I am sensible that the procedure of the Mogul-moors in destroying the temples and idols of the Gentoos, in many parts of the country, seems to contradict the idea I have attempted to give, on the best information I could get, of the Moguls spirit of toleration. For the fact is certainly true; though these outrages were never that I could learn committed, but in the heat of war, and in consequence of the provocations that attend it: besides that, some of their generals were hurried

THE EAST-INDIES. 133

ried on by their private zeal, fo as to lofe fight of the general fyftem of the court-policy ; and what is more convincing yet is, that the Gentoo-Rajahs themfelves always looked on thofe feverities as particular cafes of exception, or at leaft never appeared to formally refent them.

BUT whilft the Moguls thus aimed at making their government the more eafy, and fupportable to that infinite number of Gentoos, by indulging them in the free exercife of their religion, they did not alfo negleƈt the policy of keeping up the divifions and jealoufies among the moft powerful Rajahs from whom they had moft to apprehend: and in this they fucceeded to their wifh, and might probably long have continued the tranquillity of their government, but for the relaxation and indolence into which the latter Moguls fell. Inftead then of keeping a ftriƈt hand over the emirs, or great officers of the court, known by the title of omrahs, which is only the plural of emir, they fuffered them to encroach on the royal authority, and themfelves became fubjeƈted to that emir, who had obtained moft influence and intereft with the military. And here again the Mogul was only defended from utter depofition by the jealoufies, and not the loyalty, of the great emirs among themfelves, whofe objeƈt of competition was, which of them fhould get poffeffion of the Mogul's perfon, and reign under the fhelter of a title, beyond which, and his feraglio or haram, they left him fcarce any fign of power. Some, even of the emirs, who were invefted with the government of the greater provinces, not only fortified themfelves in them, and afferted an independence barely falved by a nominal homage, but entered into treaties with the Gentoo-Rajahs for their mutual fupport. Thus the famous Nizam-al-muluck, formerly known by the name of Chicklis-Cawn, by leaving

K 3 his

his fon in his government, and befides fecured by his confederacy with the Morattoes, durft venture his perfon to court, where his practifes were perfectly known, and for the which being known, he was but the fafer; and, though he had many potent enemies there, his competitors for power, he had influence and management enough to procure one of the higheft pofts of the ftate, and to impofe on his fovereign the hardeft of all neceffities, that of employing and trufting a traitor knowing him to be one. But even not fatisfied with his domeftic treafons, and finding the credit of his enemies at court encreafing againft him, he invited the Perfian Shah-Nadir, better perhaps known in Europe under the name of Thamas-Kouli Khawn, to invade the Mogoliftan, pointing it out to him as an eafy prey, confidering the luxurious effeminate difpofition of a court, weakened moreover by inteftine diffentions. Shah-Nadir, whofe ruling paffion was avarice and rapacioufnefs, greedily liftening to a propofal that fo much flattered it, entered into Nizam-al-muluck's fchemes, and accordingly, after taking Candahar, that capital fortrefs which is the grand inlet into that empire, invaded India, where his expedition met with that fuccefs, which has been too fully defcribed by a Perfian writer, tranflated by Mr. Frazer, to need a repetition here.

THIS event, however, fo enfeebled the Mogul government, that the Gentoo-Rajahs beginning to feel more their own ftrength, feem now greatly to prevail, and will probably keep their afcendant, unlefs, as has before been obferved, fome of the hardy nations bordering on Indoftan, fhould fupport the Moorifh intereft, and revindicate thofe rich provinces, of which the Mogul government has either loft poffeffion, or where its intereft is
vifibly

visibly declined. And in this they have the better chance to succeed, as the bulk of the Gentoos themselves prefer a Moorish to a Gentoo-government, for reasons on which I have already sufficiently touched *.

As to the Moguls themselves, or rather the principal Moorish courtiers, for the Indians vulgarly involve them all under that appellation, though numbers of them are originally from Persia, or other parts Tartary, they, generally speaking, affect great state and splendor, according to their various appointments, and posts; and none study more the luxuries of life, though in a manner and taste somewhat different from the Europeans.

THEY take care to have their seraglios, or harams, furnished with the handsomest women that can be procured for love or money. Those of Cashmire are the most preferred in the Mogolistan, as the Georgians and Circassians are over Persia and Turkey; and with reason, being much fairer than in any other province of the Mogolistan, and having besides the advantage of a delicacy in shape and make, which is chiefly in request among them. This taste they even push to such an extravagance, as to scruple no price hardly for a female slave; which to her other beauties should have that added of a plumpness covering the smallest bones that can be imagined, for in the bone they think the weight chiefly consists, and therefore those who weigh the least, are by them reckoned the rarest and most delicate pieces. Those who, among us, pass for comely majestic-dames, would not meet

---

* For a farther account of the emperors of Indostan from Tamerlane in 1398 to his descendant Mahomed Shah in 1730: the power of Nizam-al-Muluck: the conquest of Indostan by Nadir Shah in 1738; and the declension of the Great Mogul's power, see the introduction to my second volume.

with admirers among those people. As to all their women, however, when shut up in their harams, they are extreamly jealous of them, and follow the usual Asiatic method of committing them to the guard of eunuchs, mostly made such by a total abscission. The blackest Abyssinian ones too are preferred, not only on account of their color not appearing so tempting, but for their fidelity and discretion, in which they excel the slaves of all other nations. In the mean time nothing can be well imagined more cruel, or more contrary to the benevolent institutes of nature, than thus sacrificing a number of poor creatures to the caprice and jealousy of one man, who perhaps amidst three or four hundred, nay as far as a thousand and upwards, confines his embraces to a very few of them, whilst the others, in the flower of their age, and with all the violence of the melting passion, inspired and nursed by the heat of the climate, pine away with unsatisfied desires. And sometimes the rage of them is so great, as to make them seek for relief, even to the greatest hazard of their lives.

This engrossing of such numbers of women, besides being attended with such tragical events, and the injustice of rendering miserable and useless so many of that amiable sex, besides the injury done to the population of the country, has another worse consequence, and that almost all over the East where this custom so much prevails; as it inclines both the great and the meaner sort to the nefarious sin, the same effect resulting from two very different causes. For as this custom necessarily thins society of the women, that would otherwise appear on the ranks for wives; the poorer sort, from the scarcity of that sex, in the necessity of giving their passions a vent, betake themselves to their own; whilst on the other hand,

hand, the abundance of it at command of the rich, breeds a fatiety that operates the fame difpofition. So that every confideration, human and divine, feems to eftablifh the preference of the European law permitting but one wife, to the polygamy and concubinage of the Orientalifts.

In fhort, the Moguls have chiefly adopted not only the language of the Perfians, which is entirely in ufe at court; but their manners, and refinements of luxury.

Their buildings are all in the Perfian ftile; and they are, like them, fond of fine gardens, and efpecially of water, both dormant and in action from natural or artificial cafcades, the climate fupplying them with plenty of ever-greens. In the midft of the gardens, they have commonly neat, airy pavilions, contrived with fpecial regard to coolnefs, where the owners indulge themfelves in parties of pleafure with their women, in the heat of the day, and in the cool of the evening on the fides of their ponds, finely ornamented with fteps down to the water-fide, and in the middle, on every fide of the oblong fquare, which is generally the figure of them, with places for recumbence, fpread with Perfian or Turky carpets. Their gardens are commonly pretty much like the Chinefe, in a wildernefs ftile, with this particularity, that the door is generally at a corner of the wall, inftead of being in the middle, as is the European manner. By this means the avenue to the pavilion does not front it, fo as to prefent to its view the length of a gravel, or tedioufly uniform green walk; inftead of which they prefer, for the pleafure of the eye, beds of flowers, as variegated as poffible, and in all the confufion of wild nature, which are immediately fubjacent to every fide of the pavilion, to whofe corners only the walks obliquely lead, fo as not to interfect thofe flower fpots.

spots. As to statues, knots, quaint devices, or symmetrized compartments, they have happily no idea of, or taste for them.

ONE of their great diversions at these recesses, and indeed at all their public entertainments, which diversion too they have in common with the Gentoos, are the dancing-girls; for whom they send to a particular place, either of their district or town, and of whom there are never wanting a competent number for the use of the public, to which they are so devoted, that one may safely say, that those of this profession have made vows of unchastity which they religiously keep. For according to their institutes, they are bound to refuse no one for their price, which is not indeed stated, but governed by their rate of beauty and accomplishments. There are even particular sets of them appropriated to the service of the Gentoo-temples, and the use of the Bramin-priests that belong to them. But wherever they are, whether settled or ambulatory, which last is often the case, they live in a band or community, under the direction of some super-annuated female of the same profession, under whom they receive a training, as regular as in an academy, or like horses in a manage, and learn all the paces, and acts of pleasing, in which they are but too succesful. For nothing is more common, than for the princes, and chief men of those countries, to take a particular liking to one of those creatures, and to lavish immense sums upon her, notwithstanding their haram is stocked with far superior beauties of person, who are besides possessed of that of modesty, natural to women constantly sequestered from the sight of men, and which is not at least lessened in appearance to their lords, by that constitutional violence of desire to which they are subject, and which makes some of them transgress
the

the bounds of decency, on particular occasions. These dancing-girls besides are generally recruited out of the people of all casts and denominations, though not without especial regard to beauty or agreeableness; yet even the knowledge of their being so common, cannot with many out-balance their natural and acquired charms; which will not appear incredible to those, who know how much the Opera-girls in France were, and have not yet ceased to be, in fashion. Their dances however would hardly at first relish with Europeans, especially as they are accompanied with a music far from delightful, consisting of little drums they call Gum-gums, cymbals, and a sort of fife, which make a hideous din, and are played on by men, whose effeminacy, grimaces, and uncouth shrivelled features, all together, shock the eye, and torture the ear. However, by use we become reconciled to the noise, and may observe some not unpleasing airs, with which the dancers keep time: the words often express the matter of a pantomime dance, such as a lover courting his mistress, a procuress bringing a letter, and endeavoring to seduce a woman from one gallant in favor of another, a girl timorous and afraid of being caught in an intrigue. All these love-scenes, the girls execute in character-dances, and with no despicable expression, if they are good proficients in their art; for then their gestures, air, and steps are marking and well adapted. In some of their dances, even in public, modesty is not extremely respected, in the motions of their limbs, the quivering their hips, and other lascivious attitudes into which they throw themselves; without exposing any nudity, being richly dressed and bedecked with jewels in their manner. But in private parties, to which they are called, as in gardens, they give themselves a greater loose, and have dances in reserve; in which, though still

without

without any grossness in point of discovering their bodies, they are mistresses of such motions, and lewdness of looks and postures, as are perhaps more provoking. In short, there is no allurement they omit, and rarely fail of their end; some of them amassing great wealth by this means. In the neighborhood of Goa, for example, on a part of the continent bordering on the district of that island, the dancing-girls founded a village, after being driven from Goa, by the zeal of the archbishop, where they reside in a kind of body-corporate, and where the noblemen and chief inhabitants make parties of pleasure; for it is not every one's purse can afford the expence of them. Here many of these women acquire considerable fortunes by this scandalous traffic, and throw it into a common stock, for the carrying on literally trade, being concerned in shipping and the most profitable voyages, for which they have regular brokers and factors. Or at least it was so, till Goa declined so greatly within these few years it has done, from its former splendor.

Notwithstanding numberless stories of their rapaciousness, and perfidies to their gallants, there is one told of a dancing-girl, that proves there may be, even in that class, an exception to their general want of sentiments. A Portugese vice-admiral, whose name, if my memory does not fail me, was Don Antonio de Sylva Figueroa, having lavished a great part of his fortune, among other extravagances, on a celebrated Gentoo dancing-girl, by whom he had a son, a circumstance not very common in a commerce with those creatures, saw himself reduced to a condition much beneath his rank and birth. In this state he was, when, on receiving an order from the viceroy to equip a squadron for sea, he found himself utterly unable to furnish the requisite advances to which the duty of

THE EAST-INDIES.

of his poft obliged him. This naturally made him uneafy and melancholy, which being obferved by his miftrefs, who with fome difficulty wrung the caufe of it from him, fhe left him abruptly, and in a manner, that made him conclude fhe was, in the ftile of that fort of women, going to add her defertion to that of fortune, and which would not have been the leaft of his afflictions: but he was foon furprized at her return, with a cafket of jewels and gold to the amount of near three thoufand pounds, being more than he wanted, and which fhe with a very good grace obliged him to take, as a mark of her affection. This piece of generofity, for its being fo uncommon made the more noife, and reaching the ears of the late king John of Portugal, it affected him fo, that by the next fhips he fent out letters of legitimation to the admiral's fon by that dancer. I am here aware, that a ftory fimilar to this in moft of its circumftances, is faid to have happened in England, from an opera-finger to a late Duke; which however, not deftroying the credit of this, only ferves to fhew, that if vices are the growth of all climates, fo are virtues too; though the inftances are rarer, and furely rareft among thofe of that character.

The drefs of thefe women, which is various according to the different provinces, is in all however the moft gorgeous and alluring they can imagine. They are generally loaded with jewels, ftrictly fpeaking from head to toe, fince even on their toes they wear rings. Their necks are adorned with carcanets, their arms with bracelets, and their ankles with chains of gold and filver, often enriched with precious ftones. They alfo wear nofe-jewels, that at firft have an odd appearance, but to which the eye is foon reconciled. Yet they, as well as other women in that country, have a peculiar way of managing and preferving their

breafts,

breafts, which at the fame time makes no inconfiderable part of their finery: for they inclofe them in a pair of hollow cups or cafes, exactly fitted to them, made of a very light wood, linked together, and buckled at the back. Thefe at once confine the breafts fo, as that they cannot grow to any difguftfully exuberant fize; though from their fmoothnefs and pliancy, they play fo freely with every motion of the body, that they do not crufh the exquifitely tender texture of the flefh in that part, like the ftiff whalebone ftays in ufe among Europeans. Then the outfide of them is fpread with a thin gold, or filver gilt plate, alfo fet with gems according to their ability, which compofe the richeft part of their drefs, from the difplay favored by their fwelling orbicular form; but they are eafily laid afide, and refumed at pleafure.

MANY of them, efpecially thofe who are in commerce with the Moguls and Moors, ufe the embellifhment aimed at of old throughout the greateft part of the Eaft, of forming a black circle round their eye-borders, by drawing a bodkin between them, with their eyelids fhut, that both fides may receive the tint of the ftibium or powder of antimony, that fticks to the bodkin. The powder is called by them *furma*; which they pretend refrefhes and cools the eye, befides exciting its luftre, by the ambient blacknefs. It is not eafy for Europeans unaccuftomed to it, to difcern at firft that grace the Orientalifts think it adds to them; though they prefently acknowledge is has at leaft as good an effect as patches, which appeared fo ftrange to fome Mallabar merchants, that on feeing the face of Mrs. King, the chief of Anjengo's lady, ftuck with them, they condoled very ferioufly with Mr. King on his wife's diftemper, but hoped thofe breakings-out would foon wear off. Thus arbitrary is

the

the opinion of points of drefs in different, and often in the fame countries.

ANOTHER occafional ornament the dancing-girls put on, particularly on reforting to their gallants: this is a necklace of many and loofe turns, compofed of flowers ftrung together, which they call mogrees, fomething refembling Spanifh double jeffamy, but of a much ftronger and more agreeable fragrant odor, and far preferable to any perfumes, delighting at once the fight and fmell.

FOR the reft, their cloaths are much in the fame fafhion as the other women of that country. Inftead of petticoats they wear what they call a lungee, which is fimply a long piece of filk, or cotton-ftuff, that, without any trouble to make up, ferves them juft as it comes from the loom, to gird round their loins, and defcends to about mid-leg; fo that the upper part clipping clofe, marks with great juftnefs the roundnefs, and fwell about the middle, which tapering away to the legs, gives that loofe flow, to the lower part of the lungee, of which the ftatuaries are fo fond for expreffing the garb or drapery of a nymph, whilft the jewels and chains with which their other where naked legs are adorned, have fomewhat the air of bufkins. From the girdle upwards to the neck they have no covering, but one of the ends of the lungee purpofely left untucked-in, that is flung carelefsly over their fhoulders, and a very fmall jacket, fo cut, as to leave room for the breaft-cafes before-mentioned, and ties in a fmall knot beforehand juft above the girdle. On their head they wear nothing but jewels or flowers; and their long black hair is generally braided.

I HAVE before obferved, that the younger ones receive a regular training from the elder and fuperannuated, under whom they ftudy in form all the art of pleafing, which they underftand by tradition and perfonal experience too well, not to know how

to

to pafs it for nature, in the imitation and refinement of which, without fuffering it to be feen, their art fpecifically confifts. Befides, they have nothing of that naufeous boldenfs which characterifes the European proftitutes, their ftyle of feduction being all foftnefs and gentlenefs: their careffes are not only well-managed, but well-timed, with ftrict regard to keep meafures in the cloying minutes of fatiety.

I HAVE dwelt the more particularly on this article of Afiatic luxury, as it enters for fo much into all the entertainments publick or private, of the perfonages in thofe parts.

THE drefs of the Moors themfelves is extremely becoming; having, like the greateft part of the Afiatics, adopted that purely and originally Indian manner of wearing turbants, of fine muflin, the circumvolutions of which form a covering to the head at once light, and cool, from the air eafily penetrating the folds of it; at the fame time that they defend it from the rays of the fun, the heat of which acting in a ftreight line, as cold likewife does, is rebated by the obliquities of the wreathing, which admits of an infinite variety in the manner of making up; infomuch that many tribes, profeffions, and even ranks in life, are diftinguifhed by it.

THE Turks undoubtedly took it from the Arabs and Perfians, who by certain tradition from the Indians, and that not until modernly, as appears by the defcriptions of thofe people by the antients. But that the Indian Aborigines never changed fafhion, or any other in their garb, appears clearly from what Quintus Curtius fays of them on that head, and which holds good to this day. *Corpora ufque pedes carbafo velant: Soleis pedes, capita linteis vinciunt. Lapilli ex auribus pendent; brachios quoque et lacertos auro colunt, quibus inter populares aut nobilitas*

nobilitas aut opes eminent, &c. " They cloath their
" bodies with a garment that falls as low as their
" feet: they bind their feet with fandals, their
" heads with linnen. They hang their ears with
" jewels, and deck their arms and limbs with
" gold, fuch of them efpecially as are eminent for
" birth and riches." This paffage I have not quoted
out of affectation; but to fhew how tenacious the
Indians are of their old cuftoms, as the above defcription exactly anfwers to their prefent drefs,
which has admitted of little or no variation. The
Tartar conquerors in a great part conformed to it,
as in many other particulars they found eftablifhed
in India, in like manner as their Country-men ufed
in China a policy, that did not a little contribute
to quiet their conquefts. Another point of finery
they have, which is their girdles or cumberbands on
the outfide of their long veft or cabay, generally
richly embroidered, with the two ends depending
before, bordered with gold or filver tiffue inter-
woven. In thefe they ftick, on the left-fide, their
kittarrees, or daggers, the handles of which are
either curioufly worked or fet with precious ftones.
The blade is fhort, broad, and converging to a
point, nearly in the fhape of what the ancients call
Lingula, from its refemblance to a tongue. " *Gla-*
" *diolus oblongus in fpeciem linguæ factus.*" AUL.
GELL. Their fcimetars are alfo hung carelefly before them, with the fame curiofity in the workmanfhip of their handles. Inftead however of
fandals on their feet, they wear embroidered flip-
pers, or papoofhes, which they take off within-
doors, or leave at the feet of the fophas when on
a vifit. Even the Europeans muft, on any audience at the Durbar of Surat, before they are admitted to fit in the Divan before the governor,
fubmit to pull off their fhoes; which is not quite
unreafonable,

unreasonable, as the floor is commonly spread with the richest carpets.

The Moors are also much addicted to smoaking; and the great ones among them all affect the Persian luxury in that article of cullioons, which are made like decanters of transparent glass, with enamel flowers in their proper colors, adherent to the bottom of them. These are full of water, and plugged up with a machine, that at once holds the tobacco artistly caked and lighted, and the insertion of a leathern pipe wired round, of two or three yards length, pliant and coilable like a snake, by which name it is known among the English. Through this pipe they suck in the smoak, so managed as to receive a coolness, and mildness, by passing first through the water, which it causes to gurgle, so as to form a not unpleasing noise. The poorer sort use only either a coconut shell, prepared in the same manner for smoaking through the water, which is vulgarly, from the noise it thus makes, called a hubble-bubble, or the tobacco-leaf simply rolled up, in about a finger's length, which they call a buncus, and is, I fancy, of the same make, as what the West Indians term a segar, and of this the Gentoos chiefly make use.

The Moors also give strongly into the folly of judicial astrology; which not they alone, but the Orientalists in general, including the Chinese, I suspect to have borrowed from the Indian Bramins, who in India at least are generally the almanackmakers, and constantly mark in their kalendars, what they call their good and bad days, in the observation of which they are invincibly superstitious. Nor is it impossible, that among the many points of religion, that even in the earlier ages, spread from the East westward, and especially through Egypt after the return of Osyris, who in his military expedition had penetrated into India,

that

that of the diftinction of days into aufpicious and inaufpicious, " *Dies atri, fafti, nefafti,*" might reach even the Romans, who are known to have been fo fcrupulous on that head. As to the Gentoo-Indians, they are to this day fo infatuated with this notion, that their merchants will not let a fhip fail, or care to ftrike a bargain, or, in fhort, undertake any bufinefs of importance, on thofe days that are fet down for unlucky ones.

It is alfo in refpect of a Gentoo cuftom among the head Rajahs of India, that the Mogul emperor keeps his anniverfary feaft of being publicly weighed; a folemnity which anfwers fomewhat to our keeping of birth-days.

As to the manners of the Moors and Moguls, they are nearly the fame as of the reft of the fouthern Afiatics, being greatly degenerated from the hardinefs and martial fpirit of the northern Tartars; as well from the relaxing foftnefs of the climate, as from their fliding into the Indian voluptuoufnefs and effeminacy. They are, however, from their childhood, tutored and trained up to great gravity and circumfpection in public, and efpecially to curb any paffions from breaking out into outward emotions of heat or anger, which they look on as the higheft indecency. It is perhaps from this early habit of reftraint and diffimulation, that their refentments, which might otherwife evaporate and pafs off in menaces or hard words, rankles inwardly in their bofom, till it breaks out, as they fee their time and occafion, into more fanguinary effects, and more fatal vindictivenefs. Thence the frequent plots, ambufhes, circumventions, perfidies, and deep-laid fchemes of the great men among them, to deftroy one another. Their fchool-education, which is rarely more or other than learning to read the Alcoran, and to write Arabic or Perfian, is however fupplemented by

their

their introduction into all companies, and scenes of public business, in their tenderest youth, where their fathers carry them, not without a due preparation and instruction of how they are to deport themselves; and by this means, under their watchful eye and controul, enter them early into that great university, the world. The Gentoo merchants use the same method with their children, initiating them, with the first dawn of their reason, into all the mysteries of their trade and contracts; insomuch, that it is not uncommon to see boys of ten or twelve years of age, so acute and expert, that it would not be easy to over-reach them in a bargain. In truth, their docility, sedateness, and awful regard for their parents are surprising, considering the extreme fondness of these for their children, which they temper so judiciously, as not to spoil them; their whole study being to make them consider their parents as the best and tenderest friends they can have in the world; which point once carried, the rest may be imagined to follow in course.

The Moors are also fond of having Abyssinian slaves, known in India by the name of Hobshee Coffrees. These mostly come from a certain province subject to the Negus of Ethiopia, called Innariah, to the south of his other dominions, and bordering upon what is commonly called Negroeland, in the heart of Africa, from whence they are selected, and a great traffick made of them, over all the Mogolistan and Persia: but it is chiefly from the ports of Arabia and the Red Sea, that they are brought. Nothing can be imagined more smooth or glossy, and perfectly black than their skin, in which they far surpass the negroes on the coast of Guinea, and, generally speaking, have not any thing of their thick lips, though otherwise as woolly haired as they. This species of slaves is,

however,

however, highly valued for their courage, fidelity, and shrewdnefs; in which they so far excel, as often to rise to posts of great trust and honor, and are made governors of places; when they take the title of Siddees. Such was Siddee Maffaoud, a great favorer of the English, when he commanded some years ago in Rogipore, a strong place on the coast of Deckan, near Bombay, till he was difpoffeffed by the superior force of the Morattoes; upon which he repaired to Bombay, and afterwards to Surat, where he was again put into command. Nor is this transition from servitude to power so violent as may at first be thought; since all the officers and instruments of the despotic courts of Asia are involved under the general title of slaves, of which they are even voluntarily proud, Shah Nadir himself having worn that of Thamas Kouli Cawn, or Thamas the king's slave. To do the Orientalists justice, in general they treat their slaves with great humanity, and bind them to faithful and even affectionate service, by their tendernefs and next to parental care of them. Thus the Turk and Moorish merchants breed them up to such trust-worthinefs, as to employ them as their factors and supercargoes, and suffer them not only to amass fortunes to themselves, but to bequeath them to their children, which is only matter of curtefy. The chief distinction between slaves of this sort and freemen is, that the former are not allowed to let their beards grow, which is considered as the mark of liberty, as the shaving it is held the badge of slavery; and in this point the Arabs are punctiliously exact.

As to the diet of the Moors, it is far from being despicable. Rice stewed dry they use as bread, and look on it as more wholsome, light, cooling, and natural to the climate. The infipidity of it is sufficiently corrected by the sauces with which they accompany it, and are made of fish, flesh, or fowl, generally cut or stewed so, as not to need the knife when served in, whilst the great point of them is to be high-seasoned and savory. They rarely have meat come to table in joints, and yet are very fond of a dish where the lamb or kid is roasted whole, and stuffed with raisins and pistachionuts, which then serve in lieu of bread to it. They have likewise almost as many names for their dishes as the European cookery; but the three most common ones all over India is, currees, kitcharee, and pilow. The currees are infinitely various, being a sort of fricacees, to eat with rice, made of any animals or vegetables; these last being chiefly used by the Bramins, who never eat what has had life in it; but the reigning ingredients are the pulp of the coconut for thickening, and turmeric for turning the sauce yellow, besides spices to heighten it. Kitcharee is only rice stewed, with a certain pulse they call Dholl, which they reckon very wholsome and nourishing, and is generally eat with salt-fish, butter, and pickles of various sorts, to which they give the general name of Achar. The pilow is too well known to need particularising, only it may be observed, that the addition of the bacon is an European improvement; but which, if the Moors do not admit, they supplement it with the highest spices; and the great ones, in their entertainments, make it a most costly regale, by the addition of ambergrease. I have been credibly informed, that at Fort St. George, many years ago, one dish alone was charged to the company at considerably above two hundred pounds sterling, at a treat given to a Mogul Nabob, when one Mr. Hyde was steward; a charge to which the company did not acquiesce, until it was fairly verified by examination. So much however is certainly true, that most of the Europeans soon reconcile them-

THE EAST-INDIES.

themselves to the country-diet, and many at length prefer it to their own, even in point of taste or relish, independent of its being undoubtedly more wholesome, and more adapted to the climate, than the quantities of flesh to which we are used in these colder countries, where the heat being more concentered facilitates the digestion. Few of the Moors abstain from wine or spirituous liquors; but are fonder of cordials and drams than of wine, which they do not think strong enough for them, no not even the arrac, unless treble-distilled: and, what is more unaccountable, they pretend that brandy, for example, better known on the Indian coast by the Portuguese name of Aguardiente, is cooling, when moderately taken in the very midst of any faintness, brought on by fatigue, or excessive heat of the day. They manage, however, with so much discretion and reserve in this article, that even those who have the character of the greatest drinkers among them, are never seen, in public, in the indecent disorder caused by that vice, which is not only fatal to their reputation, but sometimes precipitates their governors and great men into a dangerous abuse of their power, of which the following story may at once serve for an instance, and to characterise the genius of those Orientalists. The Nabob of the district of Ahmadavad, a prince of the Mogul's blood, not many years ago, in a drunken fit, had given an order to set fire to the great city of that name. His vizier, who saw that he was not in his senses, and yet durst not by a wise but hazardous disobedience shock the profound eastern jealousy of despotic authority, in this nice dilemma, applied for advice what to do to a Persian princess, wife to the Nabob, and not more remarkable for the exquisiteness of her beauty, than for that of her wit and good sense; being besides, not only more learned than the generality

of women in those countries, but skilled in the composition of Persian poetry, all which merit of the mind and person was not thrown away, since it had succeeded in entirely captivating and attaching her husband to her, who reposed himself principally upon her for the care of his government. Her answer upon this consultation was entirely conformable to the maxims of eastern government, and to the dictates of humanity. " The autho-
" rity of the prince, said she, is too sacred a point,
" for either you or me to take upon us to revoke
" his order. He. must then be literally obeyed.
" Find out in any corner of the town, any of the
" most detached little houses, from which there
" may be the least danger of the flames spreading.
" Set fire to them, first giving the owners time to
" escape, and paying them amply for the damage,
" and thus my husband's authority will be pre-
" served, and any material mischief prevented."
This counsel was immediately put into execution; and besides deserving to the authoress the thanks of her husband, when recovered from his intoxication, raised the reputation of that princess all over the Mogolistan.

The equipages and carriages of the Moors consist chiefly in elephants, horses, palanqueens and hackrees.

The riding on elephants is a point of state chiefly appropriated to the Mogul himself, to the princes of his blood, and the Nabobs of provinces, or the great officers of state: surely nothing can be fitter to strike an awe, or give the impressions of grandeur and pomp, than one of those enormous beasts gorgeously caparisoned, and bearing on its back a kind of canopied throne, in which the person who sits is so majestically conspicuous from such an eminence. These unweildy animals, however, are rather growing into disuse for war,
since

since the more prevailing use of fire-arms, and the discovering that with all their docility, it is impossible to break and train them to the field, so as to be sure they will not often do more mischief to their own side, especially when exasperated by wounds, to which their mass makes them a mark hard to miss.

The best horses in use come from Arabia, but chiefly from Persia, and make a considerable article of trade both by sea and land, and certainly no part of the world produces finer than either of those countries. The Moors also spare for no care or expence in their keeping, and especially for breaking them to the uses of war.

For as to the hunting or racing, though no strangers to those pleasures, they are so far considered by them as inferior points, as to have little or no share in their training.

As to the Palanqueens, they seem to me the utmost stretch of invention for humoring the constitutional indolence of those people, as surely a more lazy conveyance could not well be imagined. It consists of a bed and bedstead, with short feet, covered over head with an ample canopy; commonly of either velvet or cloth, fastened by the means of cross sticks, and silken or cotton cords to the arch of the stick or bamboo, from the ends of which arch proceed the poles which are all of one piece with it, and are carried by six, but most commonly four bearers, hired for that purpose at very low monthly wages. The person carried may very conveniently sit upright under the arch, being bolstered up in that posture, by one or two large pillows, which may occasionally serve to recline his whole length, or even sleep on them by the way. This arch of the bamboo, is prepared whilst the tree is young, by keeping it bent in such a manner, as to grow into the desired form, according to the
perfection

perfection of which, and size, it bears a less or greater price. Some of these are made very expensive according to the decorations employed on them, such as the rich stuff of which this portable couch and its canopy are made, gold or silver tassels, and feet; which last are often carved and plated over to represent couchant lions, griffins, or other figures. The ends of the poles are also incased with the like metals, generally presenting a tyger's head: but this last is a badge of authority, granted only to a few of the greatest authority and distinction: in which point they are imitated by the English; for though there are few persons of any note or eminence, but what, in our settlements, keep palanqueens, the tygers heads are reserved for the governor, and second of the council. At Calcutta in Bengal some of our gentlemen, probably disgusted with the reproachfully indolent attitude incident to this method of carriage, invented a new one, by which means the bedstead was converted into a platform, that supported a common arm-chair well fixed on it, upon which they could sit more decently and full conveniently under the canopied arch. Others contrived, still preserving the bamboo-form a-top, and at the ends, so as to be carried on the shoulders a conveyance, in all other points resembling a sedan-chair. In Bombay and Surat during the rains, they cover them with a thatch, easily put off or on, made of the leaves of brab-trees, a species of wild palm, and lined with callico, forming a snug shelter impenetrable to the violentest rain, with windows that shut or open at pleasure. In Bengal and other places they defend them, but not so effectually, with a wax or oil-cloth thrown over them. The jealousy of the Moors has also suggested them a scheme of covering the palankeens, where their women are carried; which not in the

least

THE EAST-INDIES.

leaft excluding the air, or fight from within, only hinders thofe without from feeing them; and this is effected by a various-colored filk-netting thrown loofe over the whole machine. Of the fame nature as palankeens, but of a different name, are what they call andolas, of which the couch is by the crofs-fticks faftened to a ftreight inftead of an arched bamboo, and confequently admit of no other pofture than lying at length: thefe are much cheaper, and lefs efteemed than the palankeens. Doolies are much of the fame make as the andolas; but made of the meaneft materials, being only a coyr-cott flung alfo on a ftreight bamboo, and hardly ever ufed but to carry the poorer fick. The Moors too have affixed fuch an idea of ftate to palanqueens, that in moft countries conquered by them over the Gentoos, they forbad thefe laft the ufe of them, unlefs on the day of their marriage, for which inftitution they preferve fo high a veneration, that it is proverbial with them to fay, that a man on that day is as great as a king, and confequently grudge him no enfigns of royalty.

The hackrees are a conveyance drawn by oxen, which would at firft give one an idea of flownefs, that they certainly do not deferve: for there are of them, efpecially thofe which are well trained and managed, that would maintain their rate, againft horfes in full trot, and the fmalleft are generally the fleeteft. Of thefe the Gentoos chiefly make ufe, efpecially the banyans and merchants of Surat; and though I cannot fay from knowledge that they are directly concerned in the caftrating of thofe animals, which is performed by a cruelly painful operation, not by excifion, but by the compreffion of a ligature, that intercepting the nourifhment conveyed to thofe parts, caufes them to rot off; yet it is plain, that with all their bigot veneration for that fpecies of animals, they make no fcruple of ufing them in

that

that fervice. Certainly it is more for obtaining it the moſt effectually, and for the fake of ſhow, than out of tenderneſs for them, that they keep them as ſleek, clean, and in good plight as poſſible, feeding them with balls made of the flower of gram, a kind of peaſe, and coarſe ſugar. So far they ſucceed, as to render the yoke of a pair of them far from being unſightly; the oxen of that country, eſpecially of Guzarat and Cambay, being generally white, like thoſe produced about Milan in Italy, and ſome of them as large at leaſt as our Lincolnſhire cattle; contraſting to which whiteneſs, they paint their horns with a ſhining black, and hang bells about their necks, in the ſame ſtyle, and for the ſame purpoſe, as thoſe of our carriers horſes. As to the conveyances themſelves, they are open on three ſides, covered a-top, and made to hold two people, ſitting crofs-legged in the Oriental manner, conſequently flat and without raiſed ſeats, but with a pillow at the back to ſupport or to recline on.

HERE their jealouſy has invented another method of concealing their women from ſight, by means of folding blinds, or checks let fall round the open ſides. Theſe are commonly coarſely painted, and made of the fibres of the coconut, or brab-tree leaves, ſo difpofed and loofely fown together, as to let in the air, and not hinder the ſight of thoſe within them. Theſe checks alſo, with the difference of being large and lined with ſome coarſe tranſparent ſtuffs, ferve the natives for antiporta's to their apartments, ſo commodiouſly at once for coolneſs and privacy, that ſomething of the like nature might not be a deſpicable improvement, even in Europe. Each hackrey has its driver, who ſits on the ſhaft, equipped with a goad, and who takes care of the oxen, and is called the hackrey-wallah: but, in Bengal, I am told,

the

THE EAST-INDIES. 157

the moſt eminent of the Gentoo-merchants have come into the uſe of horſes and chaiſes, in which they are ſo fond of a parade, they know they may ſafely diſplay under the Engliſh government, and which for fear of a fleecing they durſt not do, under that of the natives, as to have them richly ornamented, and even the reins garniſhed with ſilver or gilt ſtuds.

UPON the whole, it muſt be allowed, that in moſt of thoſe points, in which the luxuries of life conſiſt, thoſe Orientaliſts are little if at all inferior to the Europeans. If they have not their taſte for ſtatues, paintings, cabinets of medals, and ſuch like articles of refined curioſity, they are not at leaſt deficient in thoſe of a ſenſuality, to which the warmth of the climate ſo ſtrongly and ſo unhappily inclines them, being by this enervity and relaxation, generally ſpeaking, rendered unſuſceptible of thoſe manly virtues, and that hardineſs conſtitutional to thoſe born under the colder and rougher zones. Thence moſt probably the indolent and ſlaviſh acquieſcence of the Eaſtern nations in general, under that deteſtable form of government, deſpotiſm : where not the profuſeſt fertility of the ſoil, not the Elyzian temperature of the air in many parts, nor the choiceſt bleſſings of nature, can atone for the want of the greateſt of them, Liberty. Here an Engliſhman cannot but, in the compariſon, find freſh incentives, if that could be neceſſary, to the love of his country, in which the mildeſt laws, under the moſt admirably tempered conſtitution, ſecure to him his life, his property, and what is deareſt of all, his freedom.

CHAP.

CHAP. II.

Of the state of the Roman Catholic religion in INDIA. *Missions more political than religious. Qualifications of a Buon-Christian: quality of their concerts. Papists have borrowed several points of worship from the Orientalists, Mahometans and Heathens: points of resemblance: inquisition imitated from the Mahometans: inhumanity of the inquisition: precaution of the* ENGLISH *against* PORTUGUESE *priests: story of cardinal* TOURNON: *lying miracles of the papists: ignorance of the* Portuguese *clergy: character of the jesuits: nunneries in* India: *false pretensions to merit in the Romish missions: reason of the* English *not attempting conversions in* India.

THE numbers of Roman catholics living under the humane protection of our English government in India, where they experience all the tenderness of our truly christian spirit of toleration, furnish me with one reason for attempting to set the state of their religion in those countries in its true light. A stronger one yet occurs to me, in the expedience not only of undeceiving the public of the many false accounts imposed on it by the Roman missionaries; but of wiping off the reproach of want of zeal in the protestants, for not taking the pains that they do, in the conversion of infidels to the christian faith. To this task I shall dedicate the present chapter, which shall be followed by others, continuing some remarks I had occasion to make on the three capital divisions of worship in those parts, the Mahometan, Gentoo, and Parsee religions; in which I shall proceed, purely as a candid relator of what I could learn of them worth particularising; and not at all in the

stile

stile of a dry theological discussion, for which I confess myself entirely unqualified.

To begin with the Roman-catholic religion; it is necessary to premise, that the Portuguese, who were the first modern discoverers of the navigation to India, were also the first planters of the christian faith; such as it is, after their mode, in the countries they conquered, or into which they penetrated. Charitably then granting that the pure piety of their kings, actuated their zeal for the propagation of their faith, without worldly respects, it cannot be denied, that the conduct of their missionaries was of a nature the farthest in the world from deserving that opinion of disinterestedness. Whereever the force of the Portuguese arms prevailed, as it might easily do over nations naturally unmilitary, and at that time so unacquainted with the use and noise of fire-arms, that they were as much conquered by the ears, as by the eyes, on which last the strangeness of the European garb had not also a little effect; wherever I say the Portuguese prevailed, or gained settlement, one of their first points was to stock the place with missionaries. These, while under the sanction of a military power that awed the natives, preached a religion so new, and so hard to be understood by the natives, and so ill understood by themselves who preached it, at the same time collaterally used it as an engine for forming and securing a party among their proselytes, for advancing the Portuguese interest and power in those countries: which is exactly the same game, as had been long played by the French in America, with the Indian nations, allies to or dependent on us; with whom their missionaries insinuated themselves, where those unfair preachers on our own grounds, acted the part rather of the panders of ambition, than of the propagators of religion.

In the infancy of the Portuguese conquests, the awe they struck, the dazzling splendor of their successes, the partial preference and encouragement they shewed to all the Indian proselytes, all so far co-operated to favor conversions, that, especially on the coasts of India, they brought over if not considerable subjects, at least a number sufficient to boast of, yet nothing near so great as they represented. The truth is, that excepting a few of the best sort of the Gentoos, and those chiefly converts, less to the force of their arguments, than to certain temporal motives of advantage, of pique, or of resentment, their success chiefly lay among the lowest and refuse tribes of the Gentoos. A circumstance which alone, without any other reason of aversion, greatly impeded the progress of their mission among the higher tribes or casts, who could never be reconciled to that levelling spirit, which it is so much for the honor of the true religion to establish, by making all Christians as it were brothers. But the Bramins, and Nayrs, the nobless of the Malabar coast, could not without horror think of seeing the lowest casts, whom it was even a profanation to come within reach of their breath or touch, raised to any equality with them: whereas many of those miserable people, won by a condescension of the priests to talk familiarly with them, nay to court and bribe them to quit their native religion, in which they were so despised, and hardly treated as human creatures, listened to their arguments, and either were or pretended to be persuaded by them. And it is certainly out of these that the bulk of the new christians was formed; if the name of christian may, without prophanation, be given to such as received no better instruction than they did, consisting chiefly in the ceremony of baptism, which they were never taught to understand, in the par-

rotry

rotry of Ave-marys, and a few words learnt by rote, an Agnus Dei, or a copper crucifix hung about their necks, not forgetting a rofary, in which equipage, and with their fpecial profeffion of believing implicitly whatever the priefts believed, without knowing what, how much, or why they were to believe, they were currently pronounced *Buon-chriftianos*. Such is fuccinctly but truly the picture of by much the greateft part of the Indian converts, or of their defcendants; for it is not to be fuppofed, but that there may be fome, though a few, exceptions to this general defcription.

In the mean time, defpicable as thefe profelytes moftly were, defpicable I do not mean in quality of men with human fouls, whofe falvation is doubtlefs as precious as that of thofe of the higheft rank, in the eye of the common father of all men, but on the account of their want of apparent confcientious motives, and of the evident infufficiency of inftruction, both in point of time and manner to account for fuch a converfion; thefe profelytes, I fay, became fo many fubjects, acquired to the ftate and church, the more to be depended on, as among the Gentoos there is no fuch thing as a regrefs ever admitted into their religion, after any act of renunciation, no nor even but very rarely when the feparation has been incurred by fome involuntary tranfgreffion of thofe capital points in which their religion confifts, as fhall be more fully fhewn when I come to treat of it. Thus, when once any of thefe Gentoos had embraced the chriftian religion, they generally ftuck to it, fince they could not go back to their own, though fome afterwards turned Moors: but of this there were few examples. Though thefe converts were, as before obferved, of the loweft tribes, Cooleys, Corumbees, Pooliahs, and even Poolichees, a caft hardly fuffered to breathe the common air, being driven into the forrests and mountains out of the commerce of mankind, they did not fail of being useful to the Portuguese, who could deal by the way of arms, with the superior sort, and only wanted those of the lower for servants, mechanics, and soldiers, in which last capacity, under the name of Topasses, some did good service, and their descendants are to this day employed by our company in that quality. I have the more reason too to think, that the first converts were principally drawn out of those mean classes of the Gentoos, for that in Bombay I never could learn that any of the Christian-Indian families deduced their descent from Bramins, or Sinays, a kind of less strict Bramins, and second to them in rank. There might however easily be some without my knowing it; but I am sure they must be very few; and I was credibly informed, that even at Goa, the Portuguese metropolis, the same proportion was nearly kept. In the mean time the Portuguese of India are perfectly right to call their religion, THE FAITH, LA FEE, as being the only one, and it would be a pity there should be another like it on the face of the universe: for surely nothing can be imagined more repugnant to the true worship of God, in the beautiful simplicity of the true theology, nor more dishonorable to humanity. One would imagine, they had pillaged every other religion of every thing that was absurd, ridiculous, or detestable, to compose that monster of their own. I say nothing of what has been already made so clear, of their borrowing and adulterating, oftenest for the worse, from the ancient heathens, who themselves very probably derived many of their rites and ceremonies from the East; but shall only mention a few particulars, wherein the Orientalists challenge several points of the Roman catholic worship as originally belonging to them,

THE EAST-INDIES. 163

them, and which perhaps a chronological difcuffion of the fpecific time wherein they were adopted into that church, would more manifeftly clear up.

THE rofary, for example, is pretended to have been but an imitation introduced by fome vagrant monks, of the Tezbufh or Mahometan beads, on which thofe of that fect repeat their Bifmillah, exactly in the fame ftile as the papifts do their Paternofters, and Ave Marys; and even this cuftom comes originally from the Indian Gentoos.

THEIR mendicant friars feem but a copy, and a moft wretched one, of their mendicant Joguys, whofe abftinence from all animal food, contemplative life, aufterities and macerations, far exceed whatever their famous afcetics ever fo much attempted. From them too the Mahometans borrowed their inftitution of Faquirs, or holy beggars; fo that both Europe and Afia owe all that pefterable fwarm of vermin, the monks of both thofe religions, to a perverted imitation of the Gentoo religion in that point.

As to the matter of idols, it is great impudence in the Roman-catholics, to reproach the Gentoos with theirs; or to imagine, that the frivolous diftinction in words, between the actual worfhip of them, or of the ufing them only as helps to their memory in their devotion, can be underftood, or not rejected by them, when they fee thefe words contradicted by their actions, and the images in their churches manifeftly applied to and invoked, as if they were living reprefentatives. Can they then be blamed, if idols for idols, they prefer their own; efpecially too as they infinitely lefs nonfenfically, inftead of exhibiting them in ridiculous human forms, fuch as, for example, a woman gorgeoufly dreft like a curtezan, with a fruz bob-wig with a crown on it, and a large hoop-petticoat reaching down to her feet, tied round the neck in-

M 2   ftead

stead of the waift, and a little child in her arms, frame their images in a hieroglyphical ftyle, of which the oddity and monftroufnefs are fomewhat falved by the meaning couched under them, and by their difclaimer of attempting to reprefent the Divinity under any thing of human likenefs, further than to convey inftruction in their mythology? Thence the idol of a man with an elephant's head, of another with a number of hands, denotative of his various power, and holding fome myfterious or emblematical thing in each. All which the Bramins do not want for the fenfe to oppofe to the idols of the papifts, than whom moft certainly, fuch as they are at leaft in India, chriftianity cannot have greater enemies, fince whatever deforms the divine fimplicity of the gofpel, and by evidently worldly-interefted, abfurd, and cruel adulterations, tends to render a religion ridiculous and deteftable, muft naturally weaken its force of perfuafion, and even involve in its condemnation, though but for having the fame name as chriftians, the purer reformed. Thus, for example, the Mahometans cannot, with refpect to the proteftants, overcome that inveterate prejudice they have conceived of their being God-eaters, as they emphatically and opprobrioufly nick-name the chriftians in general, and accordingly lump conclufions againft them all. And as to the papifts endeavoring to explain away the horror created by that idea, by the word *Myftery*, a word of which too they have a perfect conception, having one in the Arab language *Gheib* (*occult*) that anfwers to it, they treat it with the utmoft fcorn and contempt, as never allowing it to enter into any definition of the Supreme Being, concerning whom they efteem all myfterious expreffions to be a prophanation of the facred fimplicity of his exiftence, and at the moft, and hardly fuffer them to be employed in
accounting

THE EAST-INDIES.

accounting for some of the fabulous visions of their prophet, as contained in the Alcoran, which however the wiser and more learned part of the Mahometans are far from either respecting or believing.

Yet candor forces me to confess, that even this scandalous conformity of the papists worship, in many points to the Gentoos, might lessen to the most ignorant and weak among them, the objection of too violent a transition; as they found in that church, so many superstitions of nearly the same nature as those to which they had been used, and from which some of them, as before remarked, had most probably been originally deduced.

It is also in justice to the papists, that I am induced to acquit them of the infamy of being the original inventors of that infernal tribunal, the Inquisition; for even that, it is not improbable they borrowed from Almamoun, one of the Arabian Caliphs, who first instituted a court of Inquisition, which however he afterwards on better advice annulled on the question which divided at that time the Mahometan sect; *whether the Alcoran was created or uncreated:* a point of about as much importance, as the famous one agitated with so much rancorous and senseless bigottry among the papists; *whether the Virgin Mary was conceived or not in original sin?* But be whose it will the invention, not imagination can reach that mixture of horror and ridicule, with which the Inquisition was set up and exercised at Goa, on the coast of Malabar, by way of aping that in Europe: only the victims of its cruelty in India, instead of the miserable Jews, of whom these could not be a sufficient number to glut its cruelty and avarice, and to furnish out a decent execution at their *Autos da Fé*, were mostly taken from out of the body of the Indian christians, who thereby stood an infinitely worse chance, than if their ancestors or they had continued,

tinued in their paganism, and consequently unexposed, and unobnoxious to the pragmaticalness of its jurisdiction. For its familiars or emissaries, in want of prey, and having their eye especially on the converts, or their descendants, especially if any of them had got rich, and would afford a handsome confiscation to that holy tribunal of theirs, the *Santa casa*, made it their business to pry into all their actions and deportments: and as these people were generally of the lowest extraction among the Gentoos, and so extreamly weak and ignorant, as to be incapable of being well-grounded in any religion, some of them might, no doubt, be tempted to retain a kind of connection with their former brethren and relations, and even occasionally assist at some of their ancient customary practices, and those most certainly not religious ones, as there was no return for them to that religion they had quitted, but which turned on the follies of divination, conjuring the sick, and the like. Yet this, or the suspicion of it, was treated as a relapse, and exposed those wretches who could only deserve pity, to the last rigors of the church-persecution: numbers of them were devoted to the flames, and piously consigned to eternal damnation, for acts of the greatest simplicity and folly, branded by the priest with the names of sorcery and apostacy; though the first is even too ridiculous to deserve a confutation of its existence at all, and the other was impossible to them, if they had even the intention of it. However, as if this tyrannical cruelty had not of itself been execrable enough, it was accompanied with that usual compliment made at the delivering over those miserable creatures to the secular power, to be burnt; which is so solemn a mockery of God and man, when the Dominicans, in whose hands that jurisdiction is, with joint-hands, and pathetic fervor, entreat that no corporal

poral harm may be done to them; at the fame that they well know the ftage and the fagots are ready prepared for their execution, and that if they were not fo, or that they were to be taken at their word, they would be the firft to cry out that their church was in danger, and not improbably excite a rebellion to reftore that very cruelty they affect to condemn, and of which themfelves are the prime inftigators and inftruments. So confummately anti-chriftianized then may this tribunal be pronounced to be, from all the manifeft motives and method of its procedure, that, if our bleffed Savior himfelf was to return on earth, into any place under the jurifdiction of the Inquifition, there is no doubt to be made, but that it would burn him for a heretic, if he ventured to preach his own pure and unfophifticated doctrine, or was to deny any of thofe points of theirs, on which they have founded the infolence of their tyranny, and the revenues of their avarice.

NOTHING however gave the neighboring Gentoo princes, and Morattoes efpecially, fo great an averfion for the Portuguefe nation, as this report of their cruelty on a religious account; for themfelves being all ftrictly and unrefervedly obfervers of toleration in their dominions, they held fuch perfecutions in the higheft horror, which had not a little fhare in the Morattoes determination to invade them as they did, and ftrip them of their territories.

IN the mean time, as the chriftian Indians were chiefly compofed of fuch as had been converted by the Portuguefe miffionaries, and numbers of them falling under the Englifh domination, the Englifh, who had fufficient caufe to be jealous of the plots and confpiracies of the priefts of that nation againft their intereft, and yet were unwilling to deprive their Roman-catholic fubjects, as for example Bombay, of the fulleſt liberty in their own way of worſhip, fell on the ſalving expedient, of an indirect application to the court of Rome, for its ſending miſſionaries of any other nation to take charge of the pariſhes under their juriſdiction, and by this means at once removed any ſuſpicion of intolerancy, and guarded againſt the danger from the ſeduction and arts of the Portugueſe prieſts. Theſe laſt were more agreeable to the chriſtian Indians in general, eſpecially as the Inquiſition had no hold over thoſe of them who were our ſubjects, and was therefore no longer an objection to the prieſts of that nation, whoſe groſs ignorance ſuited better with theirs, and whoſe diſcipline was more relaxed in points of morality, and in all points that did not affect the power of the church.

Our ſettlements were ſupplied with French, German, or Italian miſſionaries, generally of more conduct and learning than thoſe of the Portugueſe; and who were always, according to their degrees of merit, treated with regard, and even familiar friendſhip, by the Engliſh gentlemen. Certain it is too, that they live with the greateſt freedom and eaſe under our government, whoſe protection ſome of the vicars of the pariſhes do not even ſcruple to reclaim againſt any vexation or oppreſſion from the ſuperiors of their own church; as after admiſſion, they are not to be removed or replaced without the conſent of the Engliſh government. It has been ſaid, but with what truth I do not pretend to warrant, not being ſufficiently informed, that at Madraſs the Engliſh ſmarted for not having taken the ſame precaution againſt the French, their neighbors there, as they had done againſt the Portugueſe; for that the French prieſts of a fine church, they were allowed even within the walls,

had

had not a little contributed by their intelligence and connections with their countrymen at Pondicherry, to further their defigns on that our capital fettlement on the Coromandel coaft.

AMONG many inftances that might be brought to fhew, that pious frauds run through the whole of that religion, in all the nations of it, though fometimes difcountenanced by the honefter part of them, I fhall juft mention one ftory currently received in India. When cardinal Tournon, who was fpecially commiffioned by the Pope to infpect, fettle, and report to him the ftate of chriftianity in China, for which he could lay no ftrefs on the manifold falfe accounts of the jefuits, and of the religious orders there at variance with them; he touched in his way on the coaft of Coromandel, and at a particular diftrict there, under the fpiritual care of French priefts, out of curiofity called for the regifter of baptifms, an extract of which had been printed at Paris, fetting forth, that one of the fathers, as the miffionaries are called, had converted and baptifed fo many thoufands in one day, that he was forced to have two men to fupport his arms, tired with the ceremony of blefling and croffing fuch numbers. The regifter was produced, and there did not appear that on that, or any other day, more than one or two had received baptifm. On that falfification and the priefts excufing this fraud, on the old fcore of a pious intention, he duly reprimanded them, as he was in truth reckoned a man of probity. Yet he fared accordingly; for if the jefuits did not even poifon him in China, as they were clofely and perhaps falfely accufed, at leaft they were the authors of fuch indignities and ufage to him, as amounted to the fame; fince he funk and died under them, a martyr to their jealoufy and fears of his reporting nothing but what was truth of them.

But

But none were ever more induſtrious, and at the ſame time groſſer artificers of ſuch lying impoſitions and miracles than the Portugueſe prieſts. Such, for example, as of the ſhip that came in one night from the Cape of Good Hope plump into the harbor of Goa, a diſtance of ſome thouſands of miles, the devil holding the helm, and the Virgin Mary at the cond, in quality of quarter-maſter; in proof of which they ſhew you at Goa two monuments of ſtones, expreſſing the exact length of the ſhip's keel, with many of the like abſurdities; which however are matter of inquiſition to expreſs any doubt of; though ſo ridiculous, as that the relation of them would only ſurfeit the reader, or raiſe his compaſſion for ſuch credulity on one ſide, and his indignation at the coarſeneſs of the impoſtures on the other. This laſt is no wonder, conſidering the profound ignorance and impudence of the Portugueſe prieſts in general, even of thoſe who come from Europe: and as to numbers admitted into their religious orders, in India itſelf, even a Roman-catholic author, Luillier, avers, that they were often taken out of the claſs of the common ſeamen and ſoldiers, without the leaſt tincture of religion: to which I dare add, and with ſcarce the qualification of reading, and for this he notes eſpecially the Auguſtines.

The truth is, that even the prelates and dignitaries of the greateſt eminence among them, are barely tinctured with the moſt ſuperficial erudition. Their whole ſtock and fort of knowledge being juſtly enough manifeſted by their libraries, which conſiſt of nothing but books of caſuiſtry, legendary lives of ſaints, decretals with their commentaries; in ſhort, of all the rubbiſh of ſcholaſtic divinity, fitter to turn one's ſtomach againſt, than one's heart to their religion.

But

THE EAST-INDIES. 171

But what is more incredible; even the Portuguese Jesuits, to which society in France, Italy and Germany no reproach could justly be made of want of learning, or of even polite literature, are in India involved in the same gross illiteratenefs as the rest of their clergy. In short, they are profoundly ignorant of every point but one, which is the advancement of their influence and wealth by all the powers of crafty insinuation, and interested industry, for which they are so noted in Europe. Known chiefly by the name of Paulists, they observe, to all outward appearance, a more reserved and decent conduct than the other religious orders; yet, to judge by their acquisitions, seem to have better understood all the arts of legacy-hunting, and of taking in the laity for donations. Instead of their three-cornered cap, in India they generally wear a hat with enormous broad brims, always flapped round, that might well serve them for an umbrella; under which they appear abroad, with a pharisaical demureness, and dejected eyes, by way of affecting humility, or rather from not caring to look the world in the face. In short, they are as much hated and courted as in some countries in Europe, and both out of a fear of their power and vindictiveness; a fear bred by weakness, and which would vanish on their being seen in their true light.

To compleat the Indian churches mimickry of all the folly and wickedness of the European ones in that religion, they have not omitted those ecclesiastical seraglios or harams, convents of nuns, where numbers of ignorant silly girls are decoyed, and shut up, against the express will of God, so surely signified by the universal cry of Nature through all her animated works, and especially in that melting hot climate. But what gross conception the Portuguese themselves have of the chastity of these wretched recluses, may be gathered from

what

what a bigot of that nation himfelf told me; that no cucumbers, plantains (a round oblong fruit) or any thing in fhort of a fufpicious form, was fuffered to pafs their turning-box, without being firft cut in flices and difabled; left thofe fpiritual fpoufes of the Divinity fhould make a very unfpiritual ufe of them.

In feveral books of voyages, and efpecially thofe written by the priefts of that church, you feldom fail of meeting with pathetic defcants and encomiums on the ardent zeal of the miffionaries, that for the fake of propagating the gofpel quit their native countries, brave all the inconveniencies of travelling into foreign ones, and there expofe themfelves to all hardfhips, dangers, and even to martyrdom. All this is fpecious; but generally fpeaking falfe; notorioufly fo in India, where toleration is almoft univerfally practifed. If any of them have fuffered in fome parts, as they certainly have, the caufes muft be fought for not in religious but political provocation. Wherever they neftled, or could get footing, the firft ufe they were fure to make of their power and influence among their profelytes, was to put the very government, to the mildnefs of which they owed their admiffion, into danger, both from foreign and domeftic enemies, by their cabals and encroachments on the temporal power. For this it was that they were perfecuted, and not martyrized but punifhed, even to the utter extirpation out of Japan and Ethiopia of the religion they had introduced, and which thus fuffered for their crimes and exceffes, not without involving numbers of innocents in its fall: but in purely India, where they obtain fettlements, even under the Moorifh and Heathen princes, it is always their own fault, if they are not even treated with tendernefs and refpect. Every one who knows the condition of Monks in the European convents,

where

THE EAST-INDIES. 173

where they are the flaves to their fuperiors, and to the duties of a fequeftered life, having nothing but the pittance and allowance of the order, muft alfo know, that many of them can hardly change it for a worfe: whereas, when once arrived in India, and placed at the head of parifhes, in thofe delicious and fertile countries, their life then becomes a very pleafing tranfition from their former one, in every point of eafe, luxury, freedom, and fpiritual power over their black flocks efpecially; whofe ignorance and fimplicity afford them all the advantages they could wifh of gratifying their paffions, of which as mere men they are fufceptible, and as fuch commonly indulge, with the utmoft fafety, each being a kind of little pope in his diftrict: fo that it is a mere jeft to attribute any great merit to the motives of their expatiation and apoftolical labors. It is alfo not a new, though a perfectly juft obfervation, that no miffionaries hardly ever chufe any theatre for their miffions, unlefs in thofe countries where there is money or good living to be procured. They take fpecial care to fteer clear of thofe deftitute and barren places, where nothing but naked converfions are to be hoped. On fuch a choice too their merit at the court of Rome depends. If the fuccefs of their famous Xaverius had been among a poor obfcure people, inftead of the wealthy Japanefe, he had probably never been canonized, or his name found a place in the Romifh calendar.

As to the Englifh, who came later than the Portuguefe into India, they had furely reafon enough from the defpicable ftate in which in they faw the boafted converfions operated by that nation, and from the indifpofition of the foil, to receive with any hopes of fruit, the feeds of the evangelical truth: they had reafon enough, I fay, to be difcouraged from attempting, what in all moral probability

bability could promife no fuccefs, without fuch a power of miracles, as was not given to them, which they difdained to forge, and which nothing human can fupplement with efficacy againft the invincible oppofition of the united powers of climate, character, and an inveterate prejudice, yet more confirmed by the example of fuch converts, as compofe that contemptibly disfigured and corrupted chriftianity, of which the Roman-catholics have fo loudly boafted the introduction into India.

C H A P. III.

Of the MAHOMETAN *religion. How introduced into* INDOSTAN : *relaxation of zeal for* Mahomet : *character of the* KORAN. POPES, *their refemblance to the* KHALIPHS. Mahometans, *their zeal for the unity and reverence of God. Grofs conceptions fitteft for the palate of the* ARABS *in the time of* Mahomet.

THIS religion was undoubtedly introduced into Indoftan, in the ufual manner of it, by the fword; though in fome countries, more to the eaftward, as in the Moluccas, Java, Sumatra, Borneo, &c. it found its way chiefly by the infinuation of its doctrine, perfectly accommodated to the turn of thought, and fenfuality of thofe people. It was however much more rigoroufly profeffed in the provinces that now conftitute the Mogoliftan, when they were under fubjection to the Pattans, that Arab colony, which about four hundred years before Tamerlane had penetrated to Dehli, and there founded that empire, from which, after its continuance in a dynafty of thirty-one kings, they were at laft radically

THE EAST-INDIES. 175

cally expelled by Babar-Shaw, a defcendant from Tamerlane, who finifhed the conqueft of India. I have before obferved, that the Moors grew more relaxed under a feries of princes originally indifferent to all religions: but it is alfo true, that even in Arabia itfelf, the country of that founder of this religion, that fpirit of enthufiafm, which at once animated and empowered its profeffors in the infancy of it to fpread their conquefts is greatly declined, and their zeal for making profelytes almoft grown obfolete. The Arabs feem to have given over all thought of extending their dominion either on a fpiritual or temporal account, as if their ftrength and their fanatical frenzy had left them all at once.

As to Mahomet himfelf, there is a faint reverence kept up for his name; which is, however, more more matter of habit than of devotion: neither was their fuperftitious regard for him ever pufhed that length which is commonly imagined. That furious zeal of which the firft Saracen conquerors made fuch a parade, and fo fuccefsfully availed themfelves, had not fo much a veneration for Mahomet for its objeƈt, as the unity of the Supreme Being; in the invocation of which, if they joined the commemoration of his name, it was purely out of gratitude for his being the miffionary of that unity, and for his deftroying that idol-worfhip, to which Arabia had continued fo long under bondage. For the reft they looked on him as a mere man, fubjeƈt to all the failings and paffions of one, and fo far from addreffing him as a faint, that in their mofchs and orifons, they do not pray to him but for him, recommending him to the divine mercy: nor is there any fuch thing, as what has been vulgarly believed, of pilgrimages to his tomb: thefe being, in a religious fenfe, folely direƈted to what is called the Cahabah, or holy-
houfe

house at Mecca; which, having long been an idol-temple, was by Mahomet dedicated to the unity of God, and wherein he retained, in complaisance to the idolaters, the famous black-stone, which had been worshipped by them as representing Akbar their *greatest* god. The prophet's tomb is at Medina, visited by the Mahometans, purely out of curiosity and reverence to his memory; but the Indian Moors frequently return without ever seeing it at all, though it is so near Mecca.

If some of their bigots were weak enough to consider the Koran as an inspired book, by much the greater number of the Mahometans, giving it all the praise they think due to it for its containing their favorite doctrine of the unity, at the same time insist, that in other respects it is no more than a common performance of which many other Arabians might have been capable, either in point of matter or language. The famous Motazales was the first that more openly broached this opinion, and was followed in it not only by great numbers of the Mahometans, but by several of the Khaliphs themselves of the race of Mahomet, who even persecuted to death many who declared for the divine and uncreated essence of that book. A book than which surely never any thing appeared with more evident marks of imposture, full as it is of inconsistencies, incoherencies, and pitifully absurd fictions; so manifestly written from day to day, according to occurences, that some of the chapters came out expresly and adaptedly to the various circumstances of Mahomet's interest or passions. Sometimes, in order to regulate the distribution of the plunder; at others to quiet the scandal he gave, either by taking another man's wife away from him, and that man, even his adopted son, or by his commerce with his Egyptian slave Mary: not but that there are here and there

scattered

scattered through it some excellent passages and sentences of morality, set off with the pomp of figure and metaphors, and with the usual Asiatic swell. Yet most of them are mere common-place, and such as may be supposed to have been penned for him, as he could neither read or write himself, by his co-adjutors a Jewish Rabbi, and Sergius the Nestorian monk, known among the Arabs by the name of Baheerah. Upon the least reflection on them then every thing that is worth notice in that extraordinary book shrinks to little more than nothing. Even the greatest zealots for it esteem the 112th chapter equal in value to a third part of the whole Koran, though containing no more than the following few words, " * *Say God is one God : the* " *eternal God : he begetteth not ; neither is he be-* " *gotten, and there is not any one like unto him.*"

HAVING in the preceding chapter mentioned certain apparent points of imitation of the Orientalists, in the innovators, or rather defacers of the christian system, in favor of that stupendous fabric of church-power they have raised on its ruins; there appeared to me another point of designed conformity, or at least of accidental co-incidence, doubtless too obvious to have escaped others; though their having taken notice of it may easily escape me.

IT is well known that after Mahomet's death, the succession to his power in spirituals and temporals devolved to the Khaliphs; and though the popes were of a more ancient institution, they had not risen to that summit of power and dominion, which they afterwards did, until some centuries after the establishment in form of the Mahometan religion, with the princes of which some of them

---

* Sale's Koran.

kept a correspondence; whilst all of them seem to have copied, and improved on the model of the government of the Khaliphs, at least if the following striking points of resembling may be allowed to warrant such a conjecture.

THE title taken by the successors to that pretended prophet was that of Khaliph, or vice-gerent of Mahomet: the popes assumed the modest one of vice-gerent of Jesus Christ. Nor were the Mahometans ever fonder of their tenet of the unity of the god-head in heaven, than the papists of asserting the unity of the pope's vice-god-head on earth.

THE Khaliphs, who were originally stiled *commanders of the faithful* in a temporal sense, as being generalissimos of the mussulmen, even on their decline from that power, still retained it in a spiritual one, asserting a supreme jurisdiction and the right of disposing of, and of conferring the investiture of kingdoms and dominions that did not belong to them, on princes of their belief. Have not the popes, in that identical quality of spiritual *commanders of the faithful*, arrogated to themselves the same prerogative?

THE Khaliphs had a peculiar ecclesiastical state or district, subjected at once to their spiritual and temporal authority, and of which the town where they kept their court was considered as the metropolis and see of their religion: so had and still have the popes.

THIS parallel, if needful, might yet be pushed further, to shew that the Romish church, amidst all its insolence and presumption, was mean enough to copy the very originals it affected to despise and condemn; and for want of the talent of invention, was forced to submit even to the heathens and Mahometans for all its principal points of ambition and avarice. Nor were the papists entirely to blame for this recourse of theirs to the enemy,

enemy, sure as they were to find nothing of that sort to favor their purposes in the scriptures; which it was yet more sacrilegious in them, supplementally to force into their services, by torturing texts, into saying whatever they pleased. Thus, however, they at length succeeded in composing that strange phantom, or rag-doll of their church-authority, which they set up as the queen of nations, and which they never could have compassed, but through the profound ignorance, and its concomitant superstition in which the laity was then immersed, and liable to all the frauds and encroachments of the popes. Yet it seems to be some mitigation of the guilt of those Roman Khaliphs, to suppose, that they could not have conceived so transcendently impudent a scheme as what they carried into execution, if they had not been encouraged to it by some example. That this conformity might be only matter of purely chance, there is no being positive in the negative: but so much is certain, that the Khaliphs were greatly too haughty to borrow any institutions from the popes, on whose side the imitation, if at all, must have been.

ALL that fanaticism of the Mahometans however, being now pretty well subsided into a more sober common sense; and that not only in India, but even on the spot whence it originally sprung; they grow much less troublesome and tyrannical to the christians, and indeed to all sects who live peaceably under their government; though they are still as rigid as ever, in their not suffering any converts to be made out of their religion into another. Nor can I find, that the Roman missionaries are ever fond of aspiring to the crown of martyrdom in attempting it. Their chief quarry is the Gentoos, and even towards them their apostolical zeal is greatly slackened; probably from the jest of it being grown more stale, from being more seen through by their own laity; besides that, their conversions generally cost them money, which they could not lately so well afford.

The Mahometans seem also to grow the more purely Unitarians, in proportion as their zeal for the mere ceremonial part of their discipline relaxes; nor will they so much as hear with patience any argument against that fundamental point of their religion. At the article of death they invoke no name but that of Allah, God, and generally die with it in their mouths, especially the Tartars; whose distance of country from the local spring-head of that religion, and whose original principles of pure Deism, render them more indifferent to any mention of Mahomet. In fact, most of his sectaries push their veneration for the Supreme Being so far, as not only never to mention God with the least irreverence; but they think it even blasphemous to praise or define a Being, whom they look on as so infinitely above all praise, definition or comprehension. They do not approve even of terming him Good, Righteous, Merciful, or the like; not only for their thinking such epithets just as superfluous, or even impertinent, as if one was emphatically to say of a man that he had a head, legs, arms, or any other members implied by the very name of man, and of whose having them no one could doubt; but as they conceive it is profaning the sacred Majesty of the name of God, to associate it with human attributes or conceptions, and that nothing fills the idea due to that Being so well as the name itself, a substantive singularly and for ever above the company of an adjective.

As to their gross notions of a sensual paradise, the stress they lay upon their ablutions, and their other rites and ceremonies; it can hardly be thought, that so great a genius as Mahomet must have been, was not himself sensible of the absurdity

THE EAST-INDIES.

dity of his impoſture in thoſe points: but knowing, as he did, the reach and temper of his countrymen, he moſt probably adapted his religion to their ſwallow, and might never have paſſed it at all, if he had not ſo let it down to the level of their apprehenſion, and the coarſeneſs of their palate. But as the particulars of it have been ſo fully deſcribed by numbers of authors, it became ſuperfluous for me to enter into a further diſcuſſion of it, than might juſt ſerve to ſhew more expreſly the ſtate of it in India, ſo far as it fell under my obſervation there, or in my way to get the beſt accounts of it.

CHAP. IV.

Of the GENTOO *religion. Paradox of their zeal and tolerancy, and how to be accounted for. Their veneration for* COWS: *ſtory on that occaſion of* ECBAR-SHAH, *great* MOGUL, *and a* BRAMIN. *Metempſychoſis. Tenacious of their points of religion: ſtory of* LOLDASS VITULDASS, *a* BANYAN, *on that occaſion. Nicety of civil diſtinctions: ſtory thereon of a* NAYR *and* THYVEE. *Impracticability of recovering the caſt when loſt. Story of a* Gentoo *and his wife: fidelity of the* Gentoo *wives, to what owing. Suicide not ſo common now among the* Gentoos *as formerly: ſtory of one who drowned himſelf. Account of the* GYMNOSOPHISTS *or* GIOGHYS: *ſtory of one. Trials by ordeal on the* MALABAR *coaſt: ſtory of an* ENGLISH *lady on that occaſion. Diſtinction of the* Gentoos *into tribes or caſts. Account of the* Bramins: *antiquity of their religion: conjectures on the* PAPHIAN VENUS: *a prayer of the* Bramins: *devotions to* JAGGERNAUT. *Conjecture on the pyramidal form of certain idols. An*

objection

objection to HERODOTUS *attempted to be solved; as also another to* PLUTARCH *and* JUSTIN. INDIANS *probably initiated by the* EGYPTIANS. *Quotations in favor of the wisdom of the* Indians : *their polytheism resolveable into the unity of God.*

BALDÆUS, and many others, have already given to the public such full accounts of the Gentoo mythology, that they have left me little or nothing to add to them. It is however true, that though the bottom of that religion is every where nearly the same, yet in various parts of that extensive country called Indostan, there are such various modes of opinions and practice built upon it, as would require many volumes to specify the differences. I shall only mention those particulars of it that struck me the most, in which some will perhaps appear either not to have been touched upon, or but transiently by others, as all objects do not affect alike.

NOTHING appeared more paradoxical to me, than the violent tenaciousness of the Gentoos in their religion and customs ; and yet at the same time their perfect acquiescence, humanity, and toleration of others who differ from them in those points that are so sacred to them.

THEIR obstinacy, however, may be accounted for physically, from that weak flimzy texture of their bodies chiefly, and especially of the Bramins and Banyans, raised upon rice, vegetables, and water; which, joined to the relaxation from the heat of the climate, softens and effeminates them so, that they are not capable of a strong and manly exertion of their reason, to shake off the yoke of a prejudice once thoroughly imbibed. This constitutional indolence, or *vis inertiæ,* running equally through the temporal and spiritual notions of the Asiatics in general, may also be one of the causes

of

THE EAST-INDIES.

of their abject paffive refignation to flavery, and fubmiffion to that defpotifm which reigns over all the Eaft.

As to that fpirit of toleration in religion, for which the Gentoos are fo fingularly diftinguifhed, it is doubtlefs owing to their fundamental tenet of it, of which the purport is ; " that the diverfity of modes of worfhip is apparently agreeable to the God of the univerfe : that all prayers put up to him from man, are all equally acceptable and fanctified to him, by the fincerity of the intention : that the true univerfal religion is no other than the religion of the heart ; that the various outward forms of it are only acceffaries indifferent in themfelves, and merely accidents of time, place, education or birth ; and that therefore all change of religion is at beft but a dangerous and needlefs experiment, fince, according to them, every honeft man is fure to be faved in his own." Upon this principle, inftead of perfecuting and burning others for not being of it, or " of compelling them to enter," they will abfolutely admit of no profelytes to theirs ; and though whole nations have adopted their principal tenets, as the vulgar of the Chinefe for example, thofe of the tranfmigration of fouls, and their idol-worfhip imported into that country by Fohi, who was in all probability no other than a roving Gioghi ; they neither admit of a community, or hold any correfpondence with them, and would as foon fit down to eat, or intermarry with chriftians and Moors, as with their fellow-religionifts in China. When any of their religion renounce it, even in the countries where they are mafters, they charitably fuppofe it was through a confcientious perfuafion, and never perfecute them in any manner, unlefs by cutting off all communion with them, and expelling them irrecoverably out of the caft or tribe in which they were born. This they think abundant punishment, and for any thing else content themselves with only pitying them: many of such were, in truth, literally speaking, objects of pity, being of the poorer sort, won over in times of famine, by the Romish priests, who for that purpose watched and relieved their necessities on condition of their conversion. Nor was it always in those times, but often wherever they could discover objects with whose indigence they could work, that they succeeded by these mercenary means: and this is so true, as for those proselytes to be proverbially known in India, by the appellation of *Christianos de Arroz,* or rice-christians; which is a further confirmation of what has been before said, on the head of those so much celebrated conversions.

But nothing more strongly exemplifies the tolerating spirit of the Gentoos, than their conduct with respect to those who differ from them in their treatment of cows, or of that species in general. Their superstitious veneration for these animals is too well known to insist on here; but by all the discourse I have had with Bramins on that head, it appeared very clearly to me, that the spirit of that law of theirs, which forbids the slaughter of them, is chiefly gratitude; from their arguing against the cruelty of such a retribution, as killing a creature so serviceable to mankind, both in agriculture, and in furnishing so innocent, and by them esteemed a good diet, as milk, butter and cheese, relatively to which last articles they always mention that species in the feminine gender. The lawgiver, probably for a greater enforcement, added the fabulous fiction of the Cow Camdoga; which, however has had such an effect, that the Gentoos in general annex a sanctity to every thing that comes from that animal. They purify themselves

with

with its urine; they burn its excrements into a greyifh powder, with which they fprinkle their fore-heads, breafts and bellies; they alfo, when the dung is recent, make a compoft of it, with which they fmear their houfes, pavements, and fides of them in the ftyle of a luftration. In fhort, fo exceffive is their veneration for this animal, that there could hardly a Gentoo be found, that if under a forced option to kill father, mother, or children, or a cow, would not, with fcarce a hefitation, but prefer facrificing any or all of the former: and yet with all this religious horror for the flaying thefe creatures, they have no fort of averfion or ill-will to thofe who do. They fcruple neither converfation, nor even friendfhip with thofe who ufe them for their food; and this purely from their enlarged notions and allowance for the difference of religions. In fome countries indeed, efpecially on the Malabar coaft, immediately under the domination of Gentoos, they do not fuffer the openly killing of cows, though they will wink hard not to fee it; and even this moderate reftriction is not warranted by the tenor of their religion, at leaft to judge of it by the following ftory.

ECBAR-SHAH, one of the great Moguls, who was great-grandfather to Aurengzeb, and remarkable for that indifference to all religions, for which I have before accounted on the principles of Deifm, had, it feems, a favorite Bramin, to whom he hardly refufed any thing he could afk. This Bramin, imagining he could not make a more meritorious ufe of his influence with the Mogul, than to follicit a royal edict, forbidding the flaughter of cows in the province wherein he was born, requefted and obtained it. A few days after, the Mogul was furprifed at the Bramin appearing before him with a forrowful petitioning face, and entreating him to revoke the edict which had
been

been so graciously granted to his sollicitations. Ecbar-shah gratified him in this second request; but was curious in course to know the cause of this change of mind. The Bramin satisfied him by imputing it to a dream, in matter of which the superstition of the Orientialists is too well known to need a commentary here. The dream he alledged was, that in his sleep, he had been beset by a number of those animals, furiously goring and butting at him; when on his expostulating with them on such an ungrateful return for his care of the preservation of their species, one of the herd, speaking for the rest, said as follows; " It is for " that very reason of thy mistaken zeal, that we " thus persecute and shall for ever persecute thee: " thou knowest, that at our dissolution we migrate " into more noble forms, and though thy religion " forbids the forwarding of that end, it does not " forbid thy suffering others to procure us that " advantage which is now by thy means re-" tarded."

It is not however to this horned species alone that this principle of tenderness is confined. Their belief of the Metempsychosis makes them extend it to every animated creature, none being so minute, or of so low a class, but that they think it may be the receptacle of a human soul, consequently of that of their parents, relations or friends. Thence it is, that the difference or size which mechanically, one may say, affects the eye with contempt or regard, and lessens or augments compassion towards an animal in the act of destroying it, has no such effect on them. They cannot without horror think of dispossessing by violence any being of that precious gift of God life, and do not less respect it in the flea that bites them than in the elephant. But this is only to be understood of the Bramins, Banyans, and some other of their

stricter

stricter tribes, in whom this aversion to bloodshed does not suppose a great stomach to fighting; nor indeed do they value themselves upon courage; yet, like the Quakers, they know perfectly well how to esteem it in those who have it. That a country too so tempting to the conquest of it from its natural treasures and deliciousness, might not want for military defenders, which could not be expected from out of those peaceable tribes, the province of war was, according to the Gentoo system of religion, left to other divisions of casts, especially the Ketterees, out of which their Rajahs, kings, chiefs, and generals are taken, whose hereditary profession is that of arms. The Rashpoots and others are in the like manner warriors born. Such being the men of action and rule among the Gentoos by the constitution of their religion, it is the less wonder that they run into those injustices and violences which generally accompany the sword. This also solves that seeming paradox, of a religion breathing nothing but humanity, mildness and universal charity, having produced no better a government; and is one more proof, that no consideration, human or divine, is sufficient to soften the ferocity, or moderate the oppressions of any power that is purely a military one.

There is also another point in their religion, which appears as unaccountable as it is singular. Tenacious as they are of it, they are yet liable to lose irrecoverably their right of communion, not only for voluntary breaches or derogations from it, but for even involuntary ones, or for such as one would imagine extream force or necessity might justify. Certain it is, however, that numbers of them, though in other respects cowardly and afraid of death, would sooner incur it than violate any of those fundamental points, on which depends their right of communion; such, as for example, kill-

ing

ing a cow, or tasting of beef, drinking or eating but out of the same vessel with those of another religion, which is a defilement never to be repaired, and many others too tedious to enumerate. They will even, on such occasions, impose on themselves martyrdom, under no circumstance of violence, but of an accidental necessity, rather than forfeit what they call their cast. Thus, when Loldafs Vituldafs, a considerable Banyan merchant beforementioned *, was on his passage from Bombay to Surat in an English ship, he having made a provision of water, in vessels of his own under his own seal, such as might serve for that short run, being usually of no more than two or three days, it happened that, through retardment by calms and contrary winds, the same was expended, and he reduced to a condition of perishing with thirst, though there was plenty of water on board, But that being profane as to him, no entreaties could prevail on him to break his law, though his life was in such imminent danger: he felt all the torments so well known to be in thirst, and he would actually have sunk under it, if a favorable breeze springing up, had not brought him to Gundavee, just near Surat, but so faint as to have his soul, as they say, between his lips.

THIS delicacy of religion does not only subsist among the Gentoos, in respect to those of other religions, but between the different degrees and denominations of tribes of their own religion, who never eat, or intermarry, with one another under the same penalty. In some parts this nicety extends even to civil distinctions; as on the coast of Malabar, where it is made capital for a Nayr, or noble of that country, to approach so near an in-

---

* See p. 161.

ferior

THE EAST-INDIES. 189
ferior caſt, as to receive a wound that ſhould draw blood from him. It is not many years ſince, that near Penany, the reſidence of the Samorine of Calicut, an extraordinary accident of this nature happened. A Nayr happened to have a ſort of ſtruggle with a Thyvee, or land-tiller, when, as in half jeſt, half earneſt, they grappled each other, the Thyvee's ſickle by chance wounded the Nayr, who no ſooner ſaw his own blood, than he looſed his hold, and entreated the Thyvee to make off as ſoon as poſſible, and to keep the accident a ſecret for both their ſakes. It happening however to take air, the Nayrs aſſembled upon it, and one of the elders getting up and expoſing the caſe, they inſtantly fell on the poor Nayr, and hacking him to death with their ſabres, ſerved him as it is ſaid of the porpoiſes, when one of their ſpecies is wounded, whom the reſt, whilſt he is bleeding, inſtantly tear to pieces: after which, and groaning over him, they proceeded, by way of revenge for this ſacrifice, to which they had been thus compelled by their law, to the exterminating the whole tribe of the Thyvees, in the village of which the author of the miſchief was inhabitant. Yet even in this they ſhewed, that in the midſt of their wild ſuperſtition they could remember equity; as they were well informed how the thing had paſſed, care had been taken to pre-adviſe the Thyvees of what was intended, that they might timely ſave themſelves, till the day particularly ſet for the maſſacre was over, after which it is not lawful for them to revive the procedure; ſo that when the ſtorm was over, they might without danger return to their habitations. However, if a woman in that country lies with one of an inferior caſt, they do not indeed put her to death, but as being *ipſo facto* degraded, ſhe is ſeized and ſold for a ſlave.

As

As to the impracticability of a re-admission into the Gentoo-cast, when once, whether wilfully or involuntarily forfeited, I never heard of an exception being allowed; unless the following story may pass for one, which strongly but justly characterises the rigorousness of the Gentoos on that head.

One of them, a man of substance, residing on the banks of the Ganges, had a wife of great beauty, with whom he lived happy in the utmost reciprocal affection. One morning early, as she went, in the simplicity of their manner of life, to fill a water-vessel at the river, a Mogul nobleman chancing to pass by, was so struck with her at the first sight, that, yielding to the impetuosity of his passion, he spurred up his horse to her, seized her, and laying her a-cross his saddle-bow, rode off with her, regardless of her cries, and over-powering her struggles. Whether she was alone or accompanied, no one it seems could inform her unfortunate spouse, who was the ravisher, that he might have implored justice against a violence, certainly not tolerated under the Mogul government; or of what road he had taken, that by his perquisitions he might find her out and reclaim her. In this dilemma, life being grown odious to the inconsoleable husband, he quitted his habitation, and turned wandering Gioghi, with a double intention of humoring his melancholic turn to solitude, and of searching the whole country for her. But whilst he was thus employed, the Mogul nobleman had accomplished his brutal purpose, and though at first very cautious of allowing her the least liberty, for fear of a discovery, on having two children by her, grew relaxed in that point, even more than the Mahometans commonly are, thinking perhaps to gain her heart by that indulgence, customary among the Gentoos. After two years, her husband, now a Gioghi, came by chance to a garden-den-door, at which she was standing, and begged alms of her. It is not said whether he knew her or not, but at the first sight, and sound of his voice, she knew him, though in a plight so fit to disguise him. Then it was, that in a rapture of joy she welcomed him, and related to him all her adventures, and the innocence of her heart in all she had suffered, concluding with her detestation of her present condition, and an offer of immediately making her escape, and returning to his bosom. To this the Gentoo made no other answer or objection, but to represent to her the inviolable rule of their religion in such a case, which did not admit of his receiving her again as his wife, or having any communication with her. However, after joining in the bewailment of the cruelty of their separation, and of the law that prohibited that reunion, for which they both ardently sighed, and after abundance of consultation, about what measures could be taken, it was agreed between them, that the husband should instantly repair to the great temple of Jaggernaut, near the sea-side, in the kingdom of Orixa, near the mouth of the Ganges, there to consult the high priest and his chief assistants, whether any thing could be done to restore her at least to her religion. Accordingly he went, and returned to her with such a countenance as prepared her for the worst. He then told her, that he came to bid her an eternal adieu, for that the taking off the excommunication she had innocently incurred, could not be effectuated but on such conditions, as he could neither expect, or advise her to comply with. They were these; that she should destroy the children she had by her ravisher, so as to leave no living monuments of her pollution by his profane embraces, then fly with her husband to the temple of Jaggernaut, and there have melted lead poured down her throat,

by

by which means only she might be admitted to die in her cast if she could not live in it. The wife on hearing these terms accepted them, hard as they were, notwithstanding all the tenderest dissuasions on the man's part. Urged by the manifold incentives of zeal for her religion, love for her husband, and a hatred for her ravisher, that made her see in those children of hers nothing but his part in them, all conspiring to steel her heart against the motions of nature, she perpetrated the first part of the injunction, and found means to escape undiscovered with her husband, who durst not even renew with her the privilege of one, as her person still remained polluted, and unapproachable by him under the penalty of a mortal sin, and of falling into the same predicament in which she stood. Arrived at the temple, she presented herself with the utmost constancy and intrepidity to the priests, of whom she demanded the fulfilment of the rest of her sentence. After a sequestration of a few days and other preparatory ceremonies, she was led to the appointed place of execution in the area before the temple, where, in the presence of an innumerable concourse of people, she appeared without the least symptom of fear at the dreadful solemnity and apparatus of the fire, and instruments of her suffering. After a short prayer she was blind-folded, and extended on the ground, with her mouth open ready to receive her death in the melted lead. Instead of which, some cold water prepared for that purpose was poured into it, and she was bid to get up, and then assured, that the sincerity of her intention having been thus proved, was accepted by the Deity, and that she was thenceforward at liberty to live with her husband as before, being now re-instated in all her rights divine and social.

WHETHER

WHETHER this story be true or false, it is certain, that it contains nothing but what the law of the Gentoos renders probable; and as certain, that the article of it annexing an expulsion from their communion to any violation of the conjugal faith, more especially with those of another religion, or with any of an inferior tribe (for it seems the sin, though still a mortal one, is not so great if committed with those of their own cast) keeps an effectual check on the wives, and makes it so hard for the Europeans to avail themselves of that liberty they see the Gentoo women enjoy. I know that some indeed have boasted of their successes in gallantry among them; but I have strong reasons to think they are much rarer than has been said, or at least were chiefly among the very lowest tribes, who are not so scrupulous, and with whom money might prevail. In short, the wives of the principal Gentoos, with all their apparent freedom of shewing themselves, are, by their never going abroad unless accompanied, and by their superstition, as effectually defended from the approaches of strangers, as those of the Moors are by their walls, bars, lettice-windows, and impenetrable veils.

ANOTHER reason for their prodigious affection and veneration for their husbands, is their early marriage. A father is reckoned inhuman and careless of his childrens happiness, if he does not make the earliest provision for having them suitably matched: therefore they marry them at the age of three, four, or five years, sometimes younger, and often run into ruinous expences in the celebration of that ceremony: after which the parties, in the tenderness of that ductile age, are brought up until that of consummation, in the constant

constant inculcation to them of mutual dearness, as a sacred point of religion. The women especially retain such strong impressions of this doctrine, that notwithstanding the influence of a climate far from favorable to chastity, instances of infidelity are at least as rare among them, as in any people of the world besides. Thence too the readiness of numbers of them to embrace that cruel practice of burning themselves with their husbands, or in due season after his death. Some of them living under governments where that superstition was not suffered, have voluntarily gone to Gentoo countries barely to enjoy the liberty of that act. Others, after bringing up their children to a state of maturity, which seems an allowable reason of dispensation with them, and many years after the death of their husbands, have, as if they had endured life only till that duty to their children was fulfilled, paid that one to their deceased husbands, of seeking to rejoin them, by burning themselves with the usual ceremony. Some indeed, who had not the courage either to undergo that fate, or the patience to brook the indignities and slights that fall upon those who decline it, and which form a kind of compulsion to it, though they call it matter of choice, such as cutting off their hair, which to them is the most intolerable of all pains, servile offices, and wearing a particular colored garment, of a dingy red, will, especially if they meet with encouragement, turn Christians, or Moors. It must not however be understood, that this practice of voluntary burning is very general. Many of the tribes, especially of the lower ones, are totally exempted from it, and it is only with respect to the more considerable personages that it is ever used, and even among them,

THE EAST-INDIES. 195

them, the inftances begin to be much rarer, and that point to be lefs infifted on *.

THE examples of that cool philofophical fuicide, for which the Indians are by the ancients fo much celebrated, as being matter even of common cuftom among them, are grown extremely rare. I could not, whilft I was in India, hear of one that had reforted to that extremity, except a merchant of Surat, who, many years before my time, had ordered himfelf to be carried, faftened on a bed, the bottom of whofe corner pofts were provided with a weight to fink it, into the river Tappy, on men's fhoulders, who had their cue to let him gently down into the ftream, as foon as he had finifhed his own funeral harangue to a croud of people, among whom were his fons and relations, of which he acquitted himfelf with great compofure and even eloquence. He had however no motive for this fpontaneous departure out of life, but that fort of philofophy once fo prevalent in thofe parts, and for which the Gymnofophift Calanus made him-

---

* Mr. Eyre, brother to that truly worthy and amiable gentleman who perifhed among the other unfortunate perfons in the black-hole at Calcutta, as will be hereafter particularly mentioned, was chief at Patna fome few years ago, when a Gentoo woman underwent this ceremony of facrificing herfelf to the memory of her hufband, who had been a man of fome confideration, and the woman was perfonally known to Mr. Eyre. The place appointed for the ceremony was clofe to the walls of the Englifh factory, and when the woman approached, Mr. Eyre advanced up to her, advifed her to defift from her fatal purpofe, and offered her protection in the factory; which fhe refufed, and perfifted in her defign, alledging, that fhe had already undergone that ceremony four times, that this was the laft, and then fhe fhould attain a ftate of eternal happinefs. The ceremony was awfully performed, and fhe perifhed in the flames with the conftancy of a chriftian martyr.

O 2 felf

self be so much admired by Alexander and his whole army.

THESE Gymnosophists were undoubtedly not Bramins, as has been erroneously advanced by many authors; but of that sect of men now called Gioghys; which, like other human institutions, have been at length vitiated by abuses, hypocrisy, and the admission of corrupt members. Their original regulation turns upon a renunciation of the world, a hermitical or itinerant life, violent ascetics, and that stark-nakedness from whence they derived their Greek name. At present, indeed, when they occasionally travel into Christian or Moorish jurisdictions, they dispense with this last precept, and wear, out of deference to their customs, a scant rag that scarce covers their parts, to which their own opinions annex no idea of shame or turpitude. As to the self-martyrizing postures, and other cruelties they impose on themselves, they do not mean by these to insinuate, that any torments of the creature can be acceptable to its Creator, but purely for the sake of the merit they apprehend in the intenseness and constancy of their spiritual contemplation of the Deity; being such as enables them to master their attention so far, as to call it off from the feelings that pain their bodies, and to fix it unremoveably on the only idea they think can worthily fill their minds. It is also in the sense and character of contemplatists, absorbed in this single object, that they prove what is perhaps harder to attain to, their insensibility to pleasure. Thus some of them will sit on a pedestal, by the side of the tanks or ponds where the Gentoo women perform their ablutions, whom they suffer to salute with the utmost reverence and simplicity, the living Priapus they exhibit for that purpose, whilst their eyes roll frightfully in their heads, and no symptom or gesture of theirs betrays the least indication

indication of human feeling, senfual emotion, or attention to the fight or touch of thefe females, who imagine there is great prolific virtue in this ftrange act of adoration. Thefe Gioghys alfo generally have that part bored, with a fmooth foldered ring paffed through it, as an atteftation of the impracticability for them of incontinence. But though I am well perfuaded, that vanity and fpiritual pride enter for a great deal into all thefe their felf-tortures, aufterities and felf-denials, yet it is hard to think that all of them are equally fufpectable. There is alfo reafon to believe, that fome of this fect have made very valuable difcoveries, efpecially in Botany, from the opportunities of their roving life, through wilds, forefts, and among the mountains where they ofteneft fhelter, being abfolutely forbid to lie in houfes, or under any built cover, unlefs occafionally the open porches of their pagodas. The Gentoos however, to whom the abufes of this profeffion are perfectly known, and to whom their impoftures are grown ftale enough to put them on their guard, retain the higheft veneration and awe towards fuch of them as they have reafon to think are fincere in the exercife of it: they pretend even to produce, in their excufe for this branch of their bigotry, fome miracles recent within the memory of man. To this purpofe, they relate an event, of which they will have it there are now living witneffes, and which may ferve at leaft to expofe their credulity, though one cannot help at the fame time doing juftice to their talent of invention. One of thefe Ginghys, as the ftory goes, came to a large inland town, in Afhmeer, and going directly to the governor of it, a Gentoo, prefented to him a bill of exchange, drawn payable to the bearer by the god Ram, for 2000 rupees, or about 250 l. fterling; at which the governor protefted

tefted with a laugh at him as an impoftor. The Gioghy then went round the town, and was every where received with the fame kind of fcoff, except by a rich oilman, who very devoutly accepted it, and paid the amount: upon which, returning him a bleffing in behalf of the God, whofe draught he had thus honored, the Gioghy left him and the town, but not without fulminating as he paffed the gates, a curfe of leprofy to continue twelve years upon all the inhabitants except the oilman and his family, which inftantly took effect. And fo popularly was this ftory propagated, that it was brought to Bombay fome years ago by a Banyan, who declared, that he had himfelf feen a fon of the deputy, or affiftant governor of the town, who was a leper from that malediction, but the fymptoms of whofe diftemper were greatly mitigated by his being then in the twelfth or expiring year of the term affigned. The Gentoos are not content with occafional fiction or forgery of miracles from time to time, but infift on the exiftence of a conftant and ftanding one in their trials by ordeals, of melted lead or boiling oil, fuch as they are now actually in ufe on the Malabar-coaft. So much however is certain, that thefe ordeals are not in the leaft managed by any prieftcraft, unlefs it could be fuppofed combined with the whole governing laity, againft the intereft of juftice, and their own, having been for ages practifed as the criterions of innocence, through the various provinces on that coaft. I never faw one of thefe trials myfelf, but believe that numbers of eye-witneffes to them are now in England, who can better afcertain the nature and manner of them than I dare pretend to do. It has however been affured to me, that feveral of the Englifh chiefs of fettlements on that coaft, have ufed their utmoft care and precaution to detect whatever fraud might be in this method of

trial;

trial; that they have caused the party that was to undergo it, not only to be locked up in their own guard-room, or prison, but seen the hand that was to be plunged into the boiling lead or oil, bound up with a handkerchief closely tied round the wrist, and sealed with their own seals, which remained unbroke till the instant of the public ceremony of it. Notwithstanding all which precaution, and every other that the most determined incredulity and suspicion of fraud could devise, they could never discover that there was any trick or juggle in it; to say nothing of the improbability of so many princes of different and discordant dominions, for so many ages, joining in a cheat of no sort of use but to skreen obnoxious criminals, and to baffle that justice, by which alone any government can subsist. Some unable to deny the fact itself, have endeavored to account naturally for it, by averring, that neither water, oil, or lead, when boiling, can effect a hand dipped into it, so as to burn it. If this were true, the whole of this pretended miracle of the Gentoos would fall at once to the ground, and the miracle would be that it could ever pass for one. An English lady however could have contradicted this from her own experience: for at Tellicherry, where she then resided, and where scandal had not entirely respected her, happening to be present at one of these ordeal-trials, where an Indian culprit drew his hand unharmed out of a cauldron of melted lead, she said, she was sure it was all a jest, and that it could not burn; but on putting her finger in to prove it, skreamed out with the pain. "That trial (said the then go-
"vernor Adams humorously) I suppose, madam,
"was for your virtue."

THE ceremony is however performed with great solemnity. The party to be tried, on appeal to it for his innocence, whether on suspicion of murder, theft,

theft, conjugal infidelity in the women, in short of any crime, or even in civil cases, on denying a debt, is brought in public, to the side of the fire, on which is set a cauldron or ladle full of boiling water or oil, but most commonly lead ; the prince or magistrates of the country assisting. His hand is previously clean washed, and an ola, or leaf of the wild brab-tree, with the matter of the accusation written on it, and girt round his waist, when, on a solemn invocation of the Deity by a Bramin, the culprit plunges his hand in, scoops up the boiling fluid, and if he draws it out unhurt, is absolved ; otherwise he receives the punishment prescribed by the laws for the crime on which the accusation lay. And so sacred and firmly believed in general on that coast is this method of purgation, that I have been assured, that even some of the Indian Christians and Moors have voluntarily submitted their cause to its decision on their own personal experiment.

As the princes of those countries, where this custom stands at this day in full force, use no sort of reserve, or refuse any examination that might be required, certain it is, that on the least intimation from any person of authority here, to any of the English gentlemen on that coast, such an enquiry would be very readily set on foot, as would satisfactorily liquidate what truth or falsehood there is in this practice ; and surely even the Royal Society has vouchsafed to take cognizance of points of not superior importance or curiosity to this. The issue must be, since the fact is incontestably true, either to discover a natural method of resisting fire, far more subtle than what is known to our European jugglers ; or to prove, that Divine Providence, when solemnly appealed to, does not disdain its immediate interposition in favor of innocence, an act which, though surely not unworthy

THE EAST-INDIES.

thy of the goodnefs of God, the Romifh priefts in thofe parts, not denying the fupernaturalnefs of the effect produced, attribute to the power and craft of the devil; with what propriety let any one judge.

THE diftinction of the Gentoos into their tribes or cafts, forms another confiderable object of their religion, which has its conveniencies and inconveniencies. Priefts, warriors, merchants, hufbandmen, and in fhort all the divifions of mechanics and artificers known among them, are each claffed in their refpective tribes; and though all under the bond of the fame religion, neither eat, drink, or intermarry with one another, fo that a goldfmith for example, cannot marry his child to a druggift's. All muft be born in the profeffion they exercife: no tranfition or mixture is allowed: by which contractednefs of difpofition great injuftice is often done to talents and genius, to which no refpect is had, or allowance made for their infinite diverfity. Thus fome are confined to make an indifferent figure in one fphere or way of life, who would have fhined in another: yet fuch juftly fuppofeable inftances excepted, this diftribution has in general the advantage of order on its fide, and the power of the prejudice of education in favor of cuftom, diminifhes and even annihilates the fenfe of the injury thereby done to a few. Moft of the tribes too have each, under every government, a particular perfon who is reckoned the chief of it, and is in fome meafure accountable for the conduct of the individuals of it; which alfo makes it the eafier to eftimate, number, or affemble them refpectively on any neceffary occafion. But though one would imagine that moft profeffions, and manual arts efpecially, thus for ages hereditarily tranfmitted, would proceed from father to fon, to the utmoft perfection, it does not appear that this confequence

quence follows in effect: for, by all tradition and accounts, they stick pretty near at the same point they were at many ages ago; whether emulation has been rather deadened than excited by this confinement to the vocation of birth; or whether, what is the most likely, the people of those soft climates want that solidity, application and curiosity, necessary to carry them beyond a certain pitch, to say nothing of the discouragement for ever existing under despotic government, from the precariousness of property.

The Bramins or Butths, as they are often called from the idols which all have that name; if these did not take it from them, vindicate pre-eminence of rank and esteem from their appropriate functions in divine worship. There are some of them, however, often employed in purely civil matters without derogation to their character. They have a learned language peculiar to themselves called the Hanscrit, in which the Vedham, Shaster, and other of the books of their law are written. As to those who stick purely to the duties of their office, the simplicity of their lives answers to that of their diet, into which they admit of no animal food, and which one would think had its influence on their minds as well as bodies, being generally free from the violenter passions and vices, in which the cold one of avarice is certainly not included; for in this, those of them, at least, who enter into temporal affairs, vye with any other condition of men. With respect to their constitution they are generally healthy, though not strong bodied. Their senses of smell and taste are exquisite, which they doubtless owe to their abstinence from flesh. Thus flowers produce to them a much stronger odor than the same sort would to Europeans; and they are as nice in the taste of different waters, as we are in that of wines, and make as great a point of luxury in the choice of them. It is also observed, that the wounds of those used to a vegetable diet, are much sooner and easier cured than those of such as eat flesh, from the greater grossness of humors bred in these last by that food. The Bramins are likewise said to possess many valuable secrets in natural philosophy, acquired by their studious and contemplative turn, and which if not brought to Europe, is not so much owing to any uncommunicativeness of theirs, as to the want of curiosity and inquisitiveness in the Europeans, who seldom travel to those parts in search of knowledge, and are too much engrossed by their pursuits of fortune, to give sufficient attention, or employ sufficient means to come at such discoveries.

UPON the whole, whoever will combine all the absurdities of their mythology, their incarnations of Vistnow, the exploits of the ape Singa, the wars of their god Ram, the virtues of their cow Camdoga, and the rest of their ridiculous fables, with that exquisite morality, practical and speculative, that may be collected from what they collaterally teach, must own, that the human mind is capable of uniting in it the greatest seeming incompatibilities.

YET it must be owned that their religion, all gross as it is, does not exclude the idea among them of the God of the Universe, as it evidently turns upon deities merely local, and proper to India, which even their own doctrines subordinates to a certain superior and more extensive power. For as to Brama, he is never understood by them, but as the supreme God, the Jupiter Indiges of specifically their country.

THAT their religion is one of the ancientest in the world there are many reasons to think. Nothing

thing of so remote an original being to be less suspected of borrowing from others, especially in a people who have ever made it a sacred point to follow their own peculiar institutions, without deigning to admit of any foreign admixture. It is then highly probable, that the doctrine of the Metempsychosis, which so particularly distinguished Pythagoras, was derived from them, with many other articles and modes of worship, and opinion, which from certain resemblances might be evestigated from the same spring-head. Thus, among many other conjectural instances, may be quoted the image of the Paphian Venus, for the form of which Tacitus could not account *, not being in any thing resembling the human one, but orbicularly rising from a broad basis, and in the nature of a race-goal, tapering to a narrow convex a-top; which is exactly the figure of the idol in India, consecrated to such an office as that heathen deity was supposed to preside over, and to which, on the borders especially of the Ganges, the Gentoo virgins are brought to undergo a kind of superficial defloration, before they are delivered up to their husbands. At the first view indeed one would imagine that this Indian effigy was, especially from this application of it, meant for a kind of representation of a Phallus, or Ithyphallus; but besides that, the form is too imperfect and remote an imitation; besides that, the Indians make no scruple of expressing clearly the parts of generation in both sexes, joined together, in an image of them, they call Quivelinga, which they

---

* Simulacrum Deæ non effigie humana, continuus orbis latiore initio tenuem in ambitum, metæ modo, exsurgens, et ratio in obscuro.　　　　Tacit. Hist. Lib. II.
Albæ Pyramidi haud dissimilem dixeris.
　　　　　　　　　　　Tyrius Maximus.

wear

THE EAST-INDIES.

wear about their perfons, or hang about their necks, as an amulet; befides alfo, that they have pagodas appropriately dedicated to Priapus, under the name of Gopalfami; this pyramidal ftone may be plainly traced to its original; that idol, which in the fame but a larger form is worfhipped by the Gentoos under the name of Jaggernaut, which, according to all accounts, and to captain Hamilton's efpecially, is no other than a pyramidal black ftone, fabled to have fallen from heaven, or at leaft to have miraculoufly prefented itfelf on that place, where ftands his temple before-mentioned. Now, according to the beft information I could obtain from the Gentoos, this ftone, of which all the images in that form in India are efteemed but copies, is meant for the power prefiding over univerfal generation, which they attribute to the genial heat and influence of the fun acting under fubordination to it; and to whom the following formulary or prayer is addreffed, and often repeated in a day by the Bramins efpecially, with their eyes towards the fun. " *Thou Power!* " *which illuminates that refplendent Orb, deign alfo* " *to illuminate my mind, fo as that I may thereby be* " *directed to walk in the way the moft pleafing to* " *thee.*" Now confidering the dignity attached in the idea of the Gentoos to the generative power, it is no derogation to the fupremacy attributed to Jaggernaut, manifefted by their making his temple and image the head place of their worfhip, to infer that he is their god Bramin under that title, juft as Jupiter had feveral names, according to his various functions, and equivalent to the Mythras or Venus Urania of the Perfians, or fimply the Venus of the heathens. That the Deity, however reprefented by fpecifically that image and under that name, was held to prefide over the genial fire, is plainly proved, by the ceremonies with which

which at a certain time of the year they perform their worship to it, especially on the banks of the Ganges. For the Gentoo inhabitants there form domestic idols after that of Jaggernaut, to which they give its name, and which are niched in a conveyance that is to serve them for a triumphal car, all together decorated with gilding and tinsel. Formerly it used to be so with jewels and expensive finery, according to the circumstances of the owner, but of late they have much abated on that point. This machine is kept for some days in the best apartment of their house, during which time it is matter of devotion with them to exhibit all the obsceneſt postures, and to act all manner of lasciviousness in sight, as it were, of the idol, and as the most acceptable mode of worship to that deity it represents. After which they carry it in its gilded car processionally to the Ganges, and throw all in together, as an acknowledgment to that river of its congenial fertilization with that of the sun. Their reason too for relaxing in their expence on this head was, their finding that the Christians and Moors, watching the places where they were committed to the stream, made a practice of diving for the jewels or valuables with which they used to be adorned, and by this means gained what to the Gentoos seemed a sacrilegious booty at their expence.

As to the cause of the Gentoos predilection of this pyramidal form, it seems lost in the remoteſt antiquity. But if I might be allowed to hazard a conjecture, it should be, that it was originally suggested to them by that pyramidal aspiration of flame, which is one of the most conspicuous properties of fire.

If the above is not sufficient to establish the conjecture of the Paphian effigy of Venus, being originally derivable from the form of this Indian deity,

THE EAST-INDIES.

deity, perhaps the following account may ferve at leaft to corroborate it, and into which I enter purely, as I think it may throw fome illuftration on a dark point of antiquity, which has perplexed fo many authors, and relatively to which fome of the antients will probably appear to have been unjuftly condemned.

The learned and laborious Dr. Hyde has particularly taken Herodotus to taſk for ſaying, that * Venus was the Perfian Mythras, Myhir, or in plainer Englifh the fun: but in this point not a little may be faid to juftify and reconcile him to hiftorical truth.

As to the objection of the nominal difference of fexes, in Mithras and Venus, that is folved by the plain matter of fact of the Parfees not admitting any fuch diftinction of genders, in thofe fpiritual beings, which they efteemed as provincial fuper-intendants, or agents, and which the heathens dignified by the title of Gods.

That the Sun and Venus were by the Perfians, confidered as one and the fame divinity appointed to prefide over univerfal generation, may be inferred without much violence from many points of fact.

Mythras the Sun, or Myhir, in the primitive Perfian language, fignified Love; and the Sun being deemed the genial infpirer of it, has that quality evidently in common with the Venus of the Heathens.

Venus was imaged in that conic form, mentioned both by Tacitus, in his relation of the firft

---

* Cur autem Herodotus addit eam (ſc. Veneram Uranam) Perfis Mythram plane nefcio: nam cum eo nomine femper fignificatur Sol, quamnam erroris anfam arripuerit nefcio. Hyde. De. Rel. Vet. Perf. Page 99.

Vefpafian's

Vespasian's visit to her temple in Paphos, and by Tyrius Maximus.

Mythras, or the Sun, was also precisely imaged in the same form, that is to say, of a conic stone, in Cœlo-Syria, and among the * Emissenians, and from its shape took the name of the Round-God, or Agli-Baal, whence the emperor Heliogabalus, who had been a priest in the temple of it, derived his appellation, and in the sense of this Mythras being the same as Venus, he was doubtless no improper minister of that dissolute deity.

From this conformity of offices, attributes and form, it is no wonder that Mythras and Venus, called by the Assyrians Mylitta, or Mauledta, the parent of all things, might be deemed one and the same presiding Power, and as such reported by Herodotus. It is also in respect to the above conformity, that his cotemporary Artaxerxes Mnemon, did not make quite so violent or strange an innovation, as Dr. Hyde seems to imagine it, in introducing the statue of Venus in an human form, being then nothing more than another mode of representing Mythras, or Myhir, of whom the adoration, never however more than reverential, and such as was used towards their great men, was before so thoroughly established. This construction too if received, though offered only as a conjecture for want of a better, would absolve Justin, and reconcile the difference between him and Plutarch; the former placing Aspasia, the concubine of Artaxerxes, at the head of the priestesses of the Sun; the latter of those of Venus. Both then, in this case, might be right.

---

* Solem sub forma saxi ab imo rotundi et conici apud Emissenos cultum fuisse quod et a cœlo delapsum fuisse Jactabant Testatur Herodiannus.   Hyde, p. 115.

The

THE EAST-INDIES.

The refemblance, however, above fet forth of the image of the Paphian Venus, and of the Perfian Mythras, to that of Jaggernaut in India, is entirely fubmitted to the reader, for his judging of the degree of probability of their being imitations of the latter: but I cannot omit another corroborative circumftance of the progreffion from the Eaft to the Weft, of that Indian fymbol, pervading fo great an extent of continent.

This pyramidal ftone or image of Jaggernaut was faid to have come miraculoufly from heaven. The fame was pretended of the effigy of the fun, in the fame form, among the Emyffenians. Nay even the Greeks, with their ufual fondnefs for the marvellous, a quality which is fpecifically the loadftone of lies, adopted a fiction of much the fame, though rather of even a groffer nature. Anaxagoras, one of their not leaft confiderable philofophers, imagined that the Sun itfelf was a large roundifh red-hot ftone, and according to Pliny the elder (book I. chap. 58.) foretold the very day on which a fragment of it would fall in that part of Thracia near the river Ægos, " which (fays that author " very gravely) came to pafs accordingly, and the " ftone, of the bignefs of a common cart, and of " an adult color, is *now* extant, and to this day to " be feen there." So credulous, and at the fame time fo imitative a creature is man, that even his fictions are feldom purely original.

That thefe pyramidal and conic forms were, from the antienteft times, the felect ones of the Gentoos, for the moft facred of their images is certain: but whether they were imitated by other nations; whether the pyramids and obelifks of Egypt, the form of which is at this time actually among the ornaments of our gardens and viftos, were brought thither and improved on by the Egyptian Ofyris, together with many other articles;

Vol. I. P fuch

such as the tranfmigration of fouls, the divifion of the week into feven days, under the influence of the feven planets, the names of fome of which are retained to this day in the Englifh ftyle or kalender, or the diftribution of the Zodiac into figns, the ufe of incenfe, all which points are ftrongly claimed by the Bramins of India; it is hard, at this fo remote diftance of time, to decide on merely certain points of conformity, and as hard to think thofe points were all purely accidental.

But to avoid any fufpicion of my leaning to that common weak fide of travellers, finding a kind of fatisfaction to their vanity in over-rating the countries where they have been, as if themfelves were to come in for a fhare of their diftinction, I beg leave to remind the reader, that I have not exaggerated the wifdom and learning of the Bramins beyond what their general reputation will ftrictly bear me out, and efpecially that in which they ftood with the Perfians, who, as their neighbors, may be fuppofed to have known them beft. Towards which I need but felect two quotations, and both furnifhed by Dr. Hyde; for which I fhall perhaps be thought the more excufeable, as that even their being in fome meafure foreign to his fubject did not hinder him from introducing them.

The firft from Ammianus Marcellinus.———
" That moft wife prince Hyftafpes, the father of
" Darius, who ventured to penetrate into the in-
" terior of India, in a private character, came at
" length to a fhady recefs embofomed in woods,
" where the Bramins exercifed their fublime facul-
" ties in the tranquil cultivation of the fciences.
" There he learnt from them the abftrufeft rea-
" fons of things. They accounted to him for the
" motions of this fublunary world, the planets,
" and the whole ftarry hoft. They taught him
" the

"the pureſt forms of worſhip: and when he had
"collected as much knowledge as he could for
"the time, at his return he communicated as
"much of it to the magi, or prieſts of Perſia, as
"he thought proper. Hence it plainly appears,
"that he drew the rudiments of his erudition from
"the Indian ſages *."

THE ſecond is from an oriental author. "Per-
"ſuya, head-phyſician to the king Naſhirwan
"(who was cotemporary to the emperor Juſtinian)
"brought for him a book, entitled, The wiſdom
"of the Indians, or a dialogue between Kalil and
"Dumnee †, or the crowned head and the en-
"quirer. This he tranſlated into Perſian, and
"deſerved by his work eternal reputation among
"that people. The king too looked on it as ſo
"great a merit, that he ordered Boorzumgheer,
"his firſt counſellor, to write the life of Perſuya
"from his infancy, to the age of which he then
"was. And this was done."

EVEN the Mahometans themſelves pay a profound reſpect to the learning of the Bramins, and
would not be ſo averſe to the Gentoos as they ſeem
but for that Polytheiſm of theirs, which makes
them admit of ſuch innumerable gods; eſpecially

---

* Hyſtaſpes reigned A. Mundi 3484, or 519 years before our Savior's time.

† This book is in the catalogue (page 19) appendixed by Mr. Frazer, to his hiſtory of Shah Nadir, under the various titles of Ayar Daniſh, the criterion of wiſdom; and a moderner edition under that of Anhar Soheili, the flowers of Soheili, and of Kalil Dumnee. He obſerves, that the king Naſhirwan the Juſt made it his guide, not only in affairs relating to government, but alſo in private life. Sultan Mahmud Ghazi put it into verſe. (Frazer, app. page 19.) I never heard that this book was tranſlated into Latin or into any European language. Every one knows that the Indian Lockman was generally believed to be the original of the Grecian Eſop.

in some parts of India; as for example, on the Malabar-coast, as far as three hundred and thirty three millions; though they consider this only as a consequence, in course of their departure from the unity of the deity, after which there appears to them no end, or knowing where to stop. Yet after all, if these gods of the Gentoos were to be candidly scanned and liquidated, it might fairly come out that they were considered even by them as no more than a kind of secondary beings, or local superintendants and ministers, subordinate to one supreme God, and thus would the whole legions of them ultimately center in unity. At least I can safely aver, that so it appeared to me from the answers of the Bramins, being far from contradictory to that interpretation, when I pressed them on that point.

CHAP. V.

Of the religion of the PARSEES. *Division of the religion of the* Parsees *into two states, ancient and modern. Introductory mention of* ZOROASTER, *or* ZARATOOSHT: *he reforms the religion of the* PERSIANS. *Their horror of ditheism: their accounting for the appearances of evil: their notions of fire; and of the human soul: their belief of the immortality of the soul: doctrine of rewards and punishments. Zoroaster's books being lost, his religion undergoes an innovation. The Parsees scandalized as fire-worshippers in a literal sense: their innocence of manners. Account of the* SOUFFEES.

IF I presume to add any thing, on a subject which seems already exhausted by the learned and judicious disquisitions of Dr. Hyde, on the religion

ligion of the antient Perfians, or of the modern Parfees, it is moſt certainly not from any preſumption in me of improving on that excellent author. On the contrary, perhaps the remarks which occured to me, and were the reſult of my own perſonal converſation with ſome of thoſe deſcendants of the ancient Magi in Perſia, now refugees in India, may ſerve to corroborate ſome of thoſe points advanced by him, that ſeemed to me ſuſceptible of a further illuſtration.

EVEN in ſome reſpects where I may appear to differ from him, the prejudice moſt certainly ought to be in his favor, who ſtudied the matter ſo much more methodically and deeply, as to deſerve a preference to all the information I could obtain though on the ſpot: but then it was only by ſnatches from perſons, whoſe broken Engliſh I could not always be ſo ſure of underſtanding, as to depend upon my not having miſtaken their ſenſe, and leſs yet when interpreted by them at ſecond hand, from ſome that could not ſpeak our language at all. Beſides, that ſuch as fell in my way, in this purſuit of inſtruction, were none of them profoundly verſed in their religion, being either purely commercial characters, or ſuch as knew little more of it than the vulgar tradition, or the preſent practice and ritual part of it. Yet even their imperfect accounts, as they turned on a point of ſuch high curioſity, which religion is generally admitted to be, and open into ſuch a wide field of reflection, appeared to be conſiderable enough for me, not to ſuppreſs in them any thing that might perhaps throw a further light on this ſubject.

FROM all the enquiries I could make, it appeared to me, if not clearly, very probable, that there are two diſtinctions neceſſary to be made in this religion of the Parſees. The firſt, the pure one of Zoroaſter, for ſo I ſhall call him, that name being more generally familiar than his true one of Zaratoosht, from which the other was corruptly formed by the Greeks. The second and more modern one, such as it is at present in practice among the Parsees of Persia and India, disfigured by various adulterations.

It was under the reign of Hystaspes, about five hundred years before the nativity of our Savior, that Zoroaster florished. The limits of my plan do not here allow me to enter into the particulars of his birth, education, or introduction of his doctrine; besides that other authors have rendered such a task superfluous. I shall only mention their concurrent attestation of his having been profoundly versed in the mathematics and natural philosophy; whence he probably drew those sublime notions about fire, on which he founded the basis of his religion, and which are to this day retained by his sectaries.

It is very plain, however, that he found the homage to, and perhaps the adoration of that element, already established in that country, since there were Pyræums, or conservatories of perennial fire, known to be there long before his time. But that worship of it, whether religious or only gratefully reverential, or whatever else, was accompanied with so much idolatry or Sabaïsm, that enlightened by a sounder philosophy, he set himself to purge it of its gross errors, and reduce it to the two great cardinal points on which his religion entirely turns: the belief of one supreme God; and of the sun or element of fire being his first minister throughout all his works, as well as the symbol and eternal monitor of purity. The rest of his tenets were only subordinate to, or emanations from them.

As to God, the followers of Zoroaster, agreeably to his doctrine, are so penetrated with his immensity, menfity, and confequently omniprefence of power, that they efteem it a kind of impiety, or at leaft a fign of narrownefs of conception to erect temples to him, as conveying an idea of locality or confinement of the deity between four walls that fhocks and indignates them. Thence that celebrated faying of theirs, " that there can be no " temple, worthy of the Majefty of God, except " the whole univerfe, and the heart of an honeft " man." But of all their opinions, that which they hold the moft facred, is, That God is the fole neceffary felf-exiftent Being from all eternity, fupreme and author of all good. Thence their thorough deteftation of the fchifm of the Perfian dualifts, admitting the co-eternity and co-ordination of the two principles of good and evil, and of the blafphemous abfurdities of manicheifm, founded on that hypothefis of a ditheifm.

THEIR manner of accounting for the appearances, and but the appearances of evil, is as follows,

THEY fay, that God the arbiter and author of all Being, and all modes of Being, created a firft matter or fluid, in which were effentially comprehended all the conftitutives of thofe forms, into which it became under his pleafure infinitely modifiable; fuch as the globe itfelf, men, animals, vegetables, minerals, &c. whofe effence they thus pretend is at bottom all the fame matter, fire *. That every thing is generated out of it, and ultimately refolveable into it; its particles being what they imagine the minims of *all* exiftence. An opinion, which by the way was alfo that of fome of

---

* The Latin word *purus* is evidently derived from the Greek one πυρ fire: as *uro* to burn, probably comes from the Syriac one *ur* fire.

the Grecian philosophers. In this infinitely subtile celestial fluid the parent-substance, or crude matter of all future forms, they say, there existed no distinction of any, till the separation ordained by God took place, by a regulated diversified coagulation of the grosser parts contained in it. In this consisted that division of essentially the same matter at bottom into spirit, and matter or that which is commonly understood by matter in contra-distinction to spirit; or into light, and into the interceptor of light, opaqueness. Between these, through the principle of activity imprinted on that first matter, or elemental fluid of fire by the immediate hand of God, there results a perpetual struggle and conflict. On the side of fire, to rarefy and reduce all things into their original minuteness and fluidity; on the side of hardened matter or opaqueness, a resistance to the returning into it; to which principle they attribute the cohesion of bodies, and their mechanically passive aversion to dissolution. That but for this impression of activity on light, or what they understand by light, the elementary fire, though light is but a part of it, no motion absolutely could be in the universe, nor any thing be kept in order, but by its qualities of expansion and impulsion. That the coagulations formed out of it would be condensed into one hard impenetrable substance, collapsing for want of fire to expand it, or to bring it back to its original state, and compacted with cold, and involved in utter darkness. Neither of which circumstances, as some authors have mistaken the opinion of the Parsees, are positive qualities in matter, but negative ones consequential to the privation of heat and light. That but for the resistent *vis inertiæ*, or inert principle in opaque matter, the *vis vitæ*, or vital power in fire, would want whereon to exercise itself in those its omnimodal operations, which, under its

primary

THE EAST-INDIES. 217

primary original laws, ferve to give motion, and animation to all forms of being. That this conflict was inftituted for the wifeft and beft ends, fince inftituted by a power incapable of any other. That it is precifely from this conflict, that all the evil that appears to exift in the world, as well as all the good refults; but that the evil is entirely fubfervient, and even inftrumental to the infinitely greater good intended by it. That the ftubbornnefs of the grofs opaque modes of being refifting the operations of fire, and producing all thofe appearances of evil, both in the moral and material world, fuch as the rebellion of the flefh againft the fpiritual light, and the diftemperatures of the elements, is an incomparably fubaltern confideration to the good, which is both apparently and prefumably the confequence of the conflict occafioned by it. They make a *toto cœlo* difference between God's being the author of pofitive evil, and his being the permitter of fuch a comparative evil, as they hold it the utmoft prefumption in the narrownefs of the human underftanding to object to it, without knowing or comprehending all the depth and wifdom of the divine purpofes and meaning in it. Efpecially as nothing can be more clear, than that many of thofe feeming diforders or imperfections, of which nature (which is but another name for the great *fiat* of God throughout all his works) is fo unjuftly accufed, appear on examination to be conducive to the harmony of the whole, and often in quality of falutary admonitions to mankind. The conclufion then deducible from this doctrine is, that fince many effects in nature, which appear at the firft view to be evils, are juftified, as to the wifdom of their caufes, by their ultimately iffuing in a known fuperior good, it is but fair to refignedly believe, that all the reft are not one jot the lefs prefumably fo, for
their

their ends being, moſt probably for very good reaſons, concealed from, or impenetrable to us. That
it is therefore the utmoſt raſhneſs and impiety to
infer abſolute evil from ſome parts, or individuals,
occaſionally appearing to ſuffer in the courſe of
things, from thoſe primordial laws, to which God
has ſubjected all his works in general, without excepting that part of them, man, whoſe good has
been, doubtleſs, though without indeed conſulting
him, as much conſulted as was fitting it ſhould be,
of which God ought ſurely to be held a competent
judge. Perfection too being the appropriate attribute of God, they think it no injuſtice to man,
nor that there was any obligation on that ſupreme
Being to create him as perfect as himſelf. Thence
they abſolve omnipotence of the abſurdity and in-
conſiſtency of evil being introduced into nature by
the very author of all good, or which is nearly the
ſame thing, by any ſubordinate creature under his
permiſſion; allowing no evil actually to exiſt in
nature, any other than an imaginary, partial, temporary one, bearing no ſort of proportion to real,
infinite and eternal goodneſs, and therefore not in-
compatible with it. This fantom of evil then,
ſuch as it appears in the actual ſtate of nature, they
figuratively imperſonate in the eaſtern manner, and
give to it the name of Harryman, whence the
Greek word of Arimanius; as the good principle
or that of light, they term Oroozm, or Oroſma-
des, by which they alſo often underſtand God, for
its immediately proceeding from or repreſenting
him, for whom they have the reſerved appellation
of Yeſd, or Yeſdan. The above-mentioned conflict they alſo believe will laſt until the conſumma-
tion of all things, when at God's appointed time
the powers of light or pure ſpirit, will ultimately
prevail over thoſe of darkneſs or opakeneſs, and

when

when even the shadow of evil will be driven from the face of things.

ACCORDING to this doctrine, the Parsees are, in a double sense, so far from being materialists, that the name of spiritualists is more adaptable to them, since they rather resolve all matter into spirit; and for that they make a perfect distinction between that spirit and God, whom they assert to be the Creator of it, and whose essence, or mode of existence, they do not however pretend to comprehend or define, content with believing him the supreme Author and Governor of every thing, and different from every thing, but himself.

As to fire, they place the spring-head of it in that globe of fire the sun, by them called Mythras, or Mihir, to which they pay the highest reverence, in gratitude for the manifold benefits flowing from its ministerial omnificence. However, they are so far from confounding the subordination of the servant with the majesty of its Creator and Master, that they not only attribute no sort of sense or reasoning to the sun, or fire, in any of its operations; but consider it as a purely passive blind instrument, directed and governed by the immediate impressions on it of the will of God: nor do they even give that luminary, all glorious as it is, more than the second rank among his works, reserving the first for that stupendous production of divine power, the mind of man.

As to fire itself, exclusive of the supposed denser coagulations out of it, that go by the name of matter, the Parsees opinion of it, such as I had it from one of themselves, is, as nearly as I could understand him, as follows. They very clearly distinguish its existence as fire, into two states; the one that violenter one of ignition, such as in the sun, and common burning fire, quick, and with different degrees of fierceness, never without heat,

though

though sometimes without light; the other, and necessary to feed the first, by which it is constantly attracted, like a stream rushing to an opening, is that of its primitive elementary simplicity, universally diffused as in the atmosphere, or co-existent with all substance in various proportions, as in salt, spirits, water, in short where not? capable of even giving a sensation of cold, in the too long absence or too great distance from it of the same element ignition; elastic, but losing its elasticity in becoming fewel to that other, whether in purely that its kindled state, or that of its supplying life to the whole animal and vegetable creation, tempered by the fluids with which it mixes, and which damping it, return it effete and unserviceable, till it recovers its spring; every where diffused, in us, round us, and above us, though always impalpable and often insensible, freely permeating, saturating, and impregnating the whole terraqueous globe, to its innermost depths, operating every thing in both its states, by its presence or retreat, and in both its states essentially in incessant motion, though in different degrees, so as that nothing in the universe can be said to be in perfect rest, from its constant work of generation, preservation, or destruction; for the rest of such infinite subtility, as to mock all grasp, all comprehension, all exactness of definition. Such too is precisely the notion Zoroaster established of its omnipresence, that one would be tempted to think he had from his known skill in natural philosophy, and the curious mathematical machines for which he was so celebrated, the specific proof of it from electricity, that so modern discovery with us.

As to the soul of man, they pronounce it, without hesitation, to be generated and constituted out of this elementary fire, according to the peculiar organization of his body, of which they imagine the heart to be the principal laboratory, sending up the

the spirits, as the lightest secretions to the brain, where they are stopped by that soft substance, and receiving a further coction, become thought, reflection, memory, reason, &c. through the exquisite workmanship of that part, which, as before remarked, they as far exalt above the element of fire itself, as we more esteem a watch for the value it receives from the artificers hands, than for the crude materials out of which it is formed *.

From the persuasion also that God would not make any thing so unmeaning, so much in vain, as so valuable a work as the soul, to have no longer a duration than this transient temporal life, and from the unperishableness of the element out of which it is made, and in which, to use our terms, they comprehend equally the material and spiritual part of the body, only distinguished by different degrees of density and rarefaction, they deduce and firmly believe the immortality of the soul. But for how its individuality is to be preserved they do not pretend to account, nor think their ignorance lessens in the least the probability of that point, since they are sensible they cannot even account for the mode of their existence here in this world.

Their doctrine of rewards and punishments in the other life, they found upon the clear self-evident flambeau of reason lighted up in the human soul, which at the same time that it gives them the

---

* This opinion of the essence of the human soul, Boerhaave seems, in his treatise on fire, to have gone round and round, without daring to strike into it, or to express more than his suspicion that it consisted of fire, "animam ex igne constare," the discovery of electricity, had he then known it, would perhaps have emboldened him to a more peremptory decision. And even Sir Isaac Newton's ethereal fluid may, on examination, be found something analogous to this doctrine of Zoroaster's of fire, according to which this globe, and indeed the whole universe is, strictly speaking, an empyreum.

per-

perception of right and wrong, of the conflict in short, to speak in their figurative stile, between Oroozm the good principle, and Harryman the evil one; or, as in ours, between the gross flesh, and the purer spirit, inclines them naturally enough to the side of virtue, to constitute them guilty if they prefer that of vice, the temptation of which was given to them for an occasion of merit in combating and conquering it, and never great enough to excuse their yielding to it, if they did but justice to their gift of reason, or gave it fair play, as they ought to do, if only out of gratitude and respect to the Divine Power, and to follow where he leads.

As to their punishments, they do not admit material burning to be any part of them. They think the element of fire to be too pure, too noble, to be employed in the vile office of executioner. Nay, they pretend that the business of Mihir, fire, or rather divine love, is to be that of moderating the inflictions of justice on the guilty souls in the place of their suffering, which the modern Parsees paint as a dark, dreary, disconsolate region, where every thing is big with horror, pain and disgust; caverns abounding with serpents, water as thick as melted pitch, and as cold as ice. Yet just as those torments are held, and even tempered with mercy, they do not believe them to be eternal; but that after a certain time, the objects of them will be delivered and assumed into a state of bliss, though of an inferior one, to that of the good, from whom also they will be distinguished with a brand in the forehead. They think, in short, that punishments will be, both in point of degree and duration, proportioned to the human frailty and finiteness: but that rewards will be infinite and unmeasurable, like the divine goodness.

Such was the bottom of the doctrine of Zoroaster, as it may even to this day be collected out
of

THE EAST-INDIES.

of the traditional remains of it, among the adulterations it has undergone fince his time, and of which I now proceed to give the beft account of their origin that I could obtain.

THIS religion of that great man was it feems too fimple, too uncompounded to fatisfy the grofs conceptions of the vulgar, or to anfwer the lucrative purpofes of the chief Moghs, or Magi, now known, in India at leaft, by the name of Duftoors, or directors of their ritual, not improbably derived from the Perfian word *Duftoor*, fignifying form or cuftom.

A NUMBER of years being elapfed fince the death of Zoroafter, his religion was no longer fuffered to continue in its original purity. His books had been deftroyed; but whether by accident, or purpofely to make way for innovations that could not fo well take place whilft they were exifting in judgment againft them, I could not learn from any Parfee that I confulted. However, loft they all were, and the prefent capital law-book, called the Zendavaftaw, in the fame Pehlavi language, or old Perfian, was pretended to be compiled by memory from it, by Erda-viraph, one of the chief Magi. But to judge of it by the abftract or tranflation of it into the modern Perfian, by the fon of Melikfhadi, a Duftoor, who lived about two hundred and fifty years ago, and entitled Saad-dir, or the hundred gates, that fame Erda-viraph muft have greatly fophifticated and new-fangled the original doctrine by interpolations, additions, and foifting in fuperftitions that much disfigured the groundwork of it. Thence probably fo many of thofe abfurd rites and ceremonies now in practice among the prefent Parfees, too tedious to particularize here, and fo unworthy the fenfe of fo great a law-giver; fuch as, for example, their laying fo much ftrefs on their cufhee or girdle, as not to dare to be an

inftant

inftant without it; their over-acted reverence to that fire, which Zoroafter appointed to be kept in only as a conftant monitor to them to preferve their purity, of which that element is fo expreffive a fymbol; and which they carry fuch a length, as not venturing to pray before it, without their mouth is covered with a fmall fquare flap of linen, like a fhort apron, left they fhould pollute the fire by breathing on it. Nor did thefe innovations take place with impunity: for without attributing their utter fubfequent ruin and defolation to any judgment on them, it is enough to obferve, that thofe very acts of fuperftition expofed them to that conftructive fcandal, which rendered them fo odious to the Mahometans efpecially, and fo ridiculous to other nations, of their paying a religious adoration to fire, which they never did or intended: but the appearances were by their own fault againft them. Neither were thefe additions of Erda-viraph without a view to the temporal advantages of the Magi, to whom a neceffity of applying for occafional purifications, not without a fee or gratuity, was made a part of them in the new Zendavaftaw. As to this book in the Pehlavi character, whatever difficulty there might be of obtaining a copy of it in Dr. Hyde's time, there has been none lately, it being eafy enough to get one, at fcarce any more expence than paying for the work of tranfcribing. I am alfo affured, there are feveral copies of it in England. If there are any other works, as I am not affured but what there are, that go in Zoroafter's name, they are certainly none of his, there being no genuine remains of his original writing, or tranflations from them, but are all compiled and probably adulterated, in the fame manner as the Zenda-vaftaw, and very likely by the fame perfon.

YET

YET notwithstanding this spurious ingraftment, such was still the force of the sap of the original stock, as to hinder the fruit from being intirely spoilt; for by what even to this day appears, it is certain that no morals are purer and more innocent, either in public or private life, than those in general of the Parsees in India at least. For as to those in Persia, chiefly known there by the name of Ghebers, Gaurs, or Attash-perests, Fire-worshippers, I have little or no knowledge of them. There are, it is true, reports not so favorable of them, but which there are many reasons for rejecting; besides this strong one, that calumny is often added to oppression, if only for the sake of justifying it.

THERE is also great reason to think that the Souffees of Persia, so named either from their *white* garments, or that the term imports the same as the Grecian one Sophos, wise, are but a continuation of the antient Magi, although they outwardly conform to the Mahometan religion for peace-sake, as numbers do of the modern Sabaïtes, or the Drusians and Kalbains, about mount Libanus, and in the confines of Bagdat. These Souffees save appearances in respect to the Persian government under which they live: but the bottom of their doctrine is the purest mysticism, which contradicting no religion, can put on the forms of all, and assimilate with all. This may be evidently proved by a comparison of the works of those Asiatic mystics, or contemplatists, with those of our Christian ones, where the same spirit of refinement reigns congenially in both; boasting an intimate union with the deity, and a sublime detachment from all worldly matters; and even the fire-philosophy is in a great measure adopted by Jacob Behmen, the most celebrated of our modern mystics, and a protestant, who almost wholly builds

builds his visionary system of theology upon it. The principal aim, however, of the Souffees, is to frame within themselves a mental Elyzium, by an extinction of all the passions, in sacrifice to God: in which state of quietism they say they feel a certain pleasure, like that of the body, when after being over-heated it is cooled by a refreshing breeze. They also, especially in the conduct of social life, recommend three points to observance; 1st, That of a grateful return to friendship and benefits; 2dly, To win all hearts by generosity; 3dly, Never to depart from sweetness of temper, truth and candor.

AND here, on taking leave of this subject, I entreat the candid allowance of the reader for any obscurity bred by the abstruseness of some parts of it; especially, for the difficulty naturally cleaving to it, of finding terms to express ideas originally unfamiliar and new to me; and that difficulty greatly enhanced, as before observed, by the imperfectness of communication in a broken language.

CHAP. VI.

Of the GENTOO *funerals. Ceremony of interment: of cremation: and similarity of customs therein with the antient western world.*

IT was at Bombay that I had occasion to see the different ways in use among the Gentoos, for disposing of their dead, that of burying, and that of burning them, which last is much the most common.

As to the first, it was on the downs, that succeed to the sandy beach of Back-bay, that I happened to be present at the funeral ceremony of a

Ketteree,

Ketteree, or rather one of a particular caſt of the Ketterees, burying his wife, a young woman that ſeemed to be about twenty years of age. Thoſe who accompanied the huſband dug a pit exactly in the ſhape of a well, in one ſide of which there was a nich hollowed out for the corpſe to be depoſited in a ſitting poſture, with room enough for a plate of raw rice, and a jar of water by her ſide. As ſoon as the pit was ready, they put her into it, with all her cloaths and jewels, exactly as ſhe wore them when alive. But as ſoon as ſhe was placed, her huſband, who had until then ſtood ſtill, as a ſpectator, jumped into the grave, and very compoſedly took off all her jewels, and brought them up with him, after which the pit was filled up. It is to be obſerved, that though thoſe of the caſt of the Ketterees are commonly to be buried, the Rajahs, and the great men of it, have the privilege of being burnt after their death. The wives of thoſe who are not burnt, and have a mind to bear their huſbands company, have their necks twiſted round by a Bramin, on the brink of their graves, and are then interred with them.

As to the ceremony of burning, I ſaw it performed on the corpſe of a youth of about eighteen, the ſon of a Banyan. The funeral pile was prepared on the beach, the father aſſiſting at it bareheaded, with what little cloaths he had on him, coarſe and torn, which is their general manner of mourning. As ſoon as the corpſe was placed on the pile, and ſome prayers muttered by the attendant Bramin, fire was ſet to it at one of the corners; and the wood being dry, and in great quantity, it ſoon blazed up and conſumed the body to aſhes, without any noiſome ſmell; ſuch as however does not unfrequently happen if there is a ſcant of wood, or rain intervenes to damp it. The aſhes are gathered and thrown with ceremony into the sea by a Bramin, who for that purpose wades into it as far as he safely can. Those who are the most bigotted and can afford the expence of it, leave orders for their ashes to be collected in an urn, sealed up, and carried to be thrown into the Ganges, to whose waters they attribute a peculiar sanctity. But what drew my attention most in the course of the above ceremony, was the behavior of the father, who, according to the Gentoo custom of its being always the next and dearest male relation, to set fire to the pile, walked thrice round it with a sort of desperate haste, and then with his face averted, thrust his hand behind him, and gave fire to it, after which he, with the appearance of the utmost agonies, rolled himself in the sand, beating his breast, and tearing his flesh.

This also presents another striking conformity with the Indians, of the Romans and western Heathens, as may be seen in more than one description of their burning their dead *. This, however, and numberless other instances that might be produced of similarity of customs, religious and civil, seem to countenance the opinion before-mentioned, that the practice of the Indians had progressively penetrated so far west as Italy, in the very earliest ages, and even before Rome itself was founded. Nor will the channel of pervasion of the continent appear doubtful or obscure, to those who consider the connections of Egypt with Greece, and of Greece with Italy, and how naturally the importations of the Indian customs may be traced to the expeditions of Osyris and Bacchus (whom some authors have confounded with Osyris) and others into that coun-

---

* ———Subjectam, more parentum,
Aversi tenuere facem.——— VIRG. En. Lib. VI. Verf. 223.
  The circumstance of going thrice round the pile, may be met with in other authors.

try.

try. As to the latter ages, there is no doubt, but that the knowledge of India was as familiar in Rome, as it may now be in England; embaffies having even come from the princes of it to Auguftus Cæfar, after the Roman wars under his aufpices had been pufhed to the borders of it. Befides, that there was undoubtedly a confiderable trade carried on between India and the Roman dominions, through Egypt by the Red-fea, by the Euphrates in the Perfian Gulph, and over land through Perfia itfelf; which kingdom gave alfo paffage to the firft filk brought from China, then called the nation of the Seres, whence the Latin word of Sericum for filk. India, however, ceafed for a long time to be fo well known, from the interruption of all commerce with it, by the troubles that followed and defolated both the Roman empire, and the intermediary countries, till at length it was refumed by the Salernitans and Venetians, opening indirectly a trade with it by the way of Grand Cairo, and Aleppo, by means of the Arabs, and the Perfian Caravans which florifhed confiderably, till the Portuguefe Vafco Gama, in 1497, difcovered the navigation to the Indian ocean; fince when India itfelf is once more become familiar to the weftern world, and the trade to it more commodioufly extended.

BOOK V.

MISCELLANEOUS OBSERVATIONS.

CHAP. I.

Variety of the GENTOO *customs, and of the weather in the peninsula of* INDOSTAN. *Account of a species of* PIGMIES *in the* CARNATIC *country. Remarks on the* Gentoos *to the north of proper* MALABAR. *Story of a female warrior challenging a* MORATTOE *general.* Gentoos *expensive in their marriages; affect corpulence; fond of high-seasoning, pepper, myrabolans, creeatt, and sagoe: practice of chewing betel; cachoondah, cachoo, confectionary. Some Casts drink strong liquors, and eat fish and other animal food. Effects of a fish diet. Reservedness of the* Gentoo-women. BRAMINS *and* BANYANS *revengeful. Poisoning in* INDIA *has been exaggerated. Account of a particular poison.* Bramins *in secular employs; confess the unity of God. Great difference of the proper* Malabars *from the more northern* INDIANS. *Plurality of husbands: nudity of breasts. Story thereon of a queen of* ATTINGA: *the sovereigns of* Attinga *always females. Manners of the* Malabars: *articles of their dress. Missionaries scheme of passing for* European Bramins: *story of the hypocrisy of one.* Malabar *feasts. Rajah of* SARIMPATAM's *forces trained up to nose-cutting.* — *Of* EUROPEAN
settlements

THE EAST-INDIES.

settlements on the Malabar *coast.*——*Plagues and earthquakes not common in* India. Bramins *treatment of bloody fluxes: mordechin, barbees: sunrise, its unwholsome effect. Chronical distempers rare in* India.

HOWEVER the Gentoos are comprehended and known to the Europeans under that common appellation, which is derived from the corrupt Portuguese Lingua Franca, generalized over the maritime coasts of India, signifying Gentiles or Heathens; and though their religion is every where at bottom the same; it is inconceivable how much the various nations of them in that vast peninsula of Indostan differ in their civil customs and manners, not extensively on the same coast, but where they are only separated by the Ball-a-gat mountains, which are extremely high, and so called from *Bal* mountain, and *gatt* flat, because one part of them affords large and delicious plains on their summit, little known to Europeans. They divide that tract of land, of which one side is called the coast of Coromandel, the other that of proper Malabar, beginning as before noted, at Mount-Dilly; the whole peninsula narrowing to the point, like a tongue, to Cape Comorin, which terminates that part of the continent of India to the southward. Nor is the variety less in the weather itself, which nothing more than the partition made by those hills renders so different at the same time of the year, that the winter monsoon reigns along the Coromandel side, whilst the summer one prevails on that of Malabar, and yet they lie all under one latitude, and in some places there are scarce a hundred leagues from the coast to the other side.

But as the land northerns, the continent grows broader and broader, and the inland-parts in some places

places towards the hills are covered with immenfe impenetrable forrefts, that afford a fhelter for wild beafts of all forts. But in that which forms the inland-boundary of the Carnatic Rajah's dominions, there is one fingular fpecies of creatures, of which I had heard much in India, and of the truth of which the following fact, that happened fome time before my arrival there, may ferve for an atteftation.

VENCAJEE, a merchant of that country, and an inhabitant on the fea-coaft, fent up to Bombay to the then governor of it, Mr. Horne, a couple of thofe creatures before mentioned as a prefent, by a coafting veffel, of which one captain Boag was the mafter, and the make of which, according to his defcription, and that of others, was as follows.

THEY were fcarcely two feet high, walked erect, and had perfectly an human form. They were of a fallow white, without any hair, except in thofe parts that it is cuftomary for mankind to have it. By their melancholy, they feemed to have a rational fenfe of their captivity, and had many of the human actions. They made their bed very orderly in the cage in which they were fent up, and on being viewed, would endeavor to conceal with their hands thofe parts that modefty forbids manifefting. The joints of their knees were not re-entring like thofe of monkies, but faliant like thofe of men; a circumftance they have (if I miftake not) in common with the Oranoutangs in the eaftern parts of India, in Sumatra, Java, and the Spice-iflands, of which thefe feem to be the diminutives, though with nearer approaches of refemblance to the human fpecies. But though the navigation from the Carnatic coaft to Bombay is of a very fhort run, of not above fix or feven degrees, whether the fea-air did not agree with them, or that they could not brook their confinement, or that captain Boag had

not

THE EAST-INDIES. 233

not properly confulted their provifion, the female fickening firft died, and the male giving all the demonftrations of grief, feemed to take it to heart fo, that he refufed to eat, and in two days after followed her. The captain, on his return to Bombay, reporting this to the governor, was by him afked, What he had done with the bodies? He faid, he had flung them over-board. Being further afked, Why he did not keep them in fpirits? He replied bluntly, that he did not think of it. Upon this the governor wrote afrefh to Vencajee, and defired him to procure another couple, at any rate, as he fhould grudge no expence to be mafter of fuch a curiofity. Vencajee's anfwer was, He would very willingly oblige him, but that he was afraid it would not be in his power: that thefe creatures came from a foreft about feventy leagues up the country, where the inhabitants would fometimes catch them on the fkirts of it, but that they were fo exquifitely cunning and fhy, that this fcarcely happened once in a century.

If the above relation fhould be true, as there is no reafon to doubt it, we have here a proof, that the exiftence of pygmies is not entirely fabulous, as nothing can nearer approach the defcription of them.

As to the differences between the various nations of the Indians of thefe countries, they are fo many, and fo great, as to treat of them fully and in order would be impoffible to me, both for the extenfivenefs of the matter, and my not being thoroughly acquainted with them. I fhall only mention a few particulars.

The Gentoos to the northward of Mount-Dilly, as the Canarines for example, and the Sundahrajah's fubjects, all follow pretty nearly the fame cuftoms as the Morattoes before defcribed, except that trade is more encouraged in their dominions.

As

As for the Angrias and Kempſaunt, a petty Rajah on the coaſt, they chiefly dealt in piracy; as alſo the Malwans, whoſe capital reſidence was a ſmall iſland on that coaſt, fortified quite round, where they kept their cruizers; but theſe, as well as Kempſaunt, were rather friendly towards the Engliſh, whoſe paſſes they reſpected, on account of their jealouſy of Angria. Next to Kempſaunt's country lies a ſmall independent government, conſtitutionally ſubject to a woman, or petty Rannee, which is the feminine gender of Rajah. It is but lately that one of theſe female ſovereigns, by name Debooree, who could raiſe about five thouſand horſe, which is their way of computing their ſtrength, had ſo much the amazon in her, that on a ſon of her's being killed in battle by the famous Badgerou, the head general of the Mar-rajah's, the ſame who lately conquered Baſſaïm, and the iſland of Salſet from the Portugueſe, ſhe ſent him a challenge in form, which Badgerou very ſenſibly declined, giving for anſwer, that the ſtake was not equal, for that ſhe might gain immortal reputation by conquering Badgerou, but that he could not poſſibly acquire any by conquering a woman.

The Gentoos are in their marriage ceremonies extremely expenſive, though frugal in every other article of life. Some of them will even go near to ruin themſelves in the celebration of their childrens nuptials, and laviſh away upon them what would be a handſome proviſion for the married couple when grown up. For, as I before obſerved, they make a point of entering them very young into the ſtate of wedlock. Then it is they ſpare no coſt for feaſting, ornaments of their houſes, proceſſions, muſic, dancing-girls, fireworks, and the like, in the pomp of which they out-vye one another; it being a matter of ambition with them to have it ſaid, how much was expended at a ſon's wedding.

wedding. The Bramins too come in for their share of the entertainment and presents, their function being necessary to perform the ceremony. Some of the great merchants, especially at Bengal, have been known to spend a lack of rupees, about twelve thousand pounds; and, besides making considerable presents, have invited the English gentlemen to an entertainment furnished at their charge exactly in the English manner, under the direction of an English steward, for which they have allowed as far as five hundred pounds. In short, there are few of them who do not in this point stretch their abilities.

THE Gentoos too, as well as many of the Orientalists in general, affect corpulence, which they imagine adds to the dignity of their port, as they strut behind a prominent belly, like the pidgeon called the Dutch cropper. To compass this, some of them will drink every day large quantities of Ghee, a kind of liquid butter, preserved by being melted, and is kept in that fluid state by the heat of the climate. This they imagine breeds fat, though it is hard to conceive, that it should not rather destroy their stomach by the rankness it must produce in it. They pretend however that experience authorizes this practice. It might so, as to their intention, for any thing I saw to contradict this opinion, in the size of some of those who made use of it; but I have reason to think it unwholesome even for them, if but for that gross habit of body it is supposed to produce.

THE Banyans, especially at Surat and Bombay, as they eat no flesh or drink any spirituous liquors, aim at something supplemental to that heartening diet, not only in the heat of the spices, and of the long-pepper, red or green, which they eat raw, or pickled with their rice, or mix with their currees, but are fond of the drug
Assa-

Assa fœtida, which they call Hing, and of a finer and more transparent sort of it called Hingurah, both brought from Persia. The consequence however of which fetid part of their cookery is, that they smell exceeding strong of it, not only at the mouth, but from its perspiration through every pore. They say in their defence that it is very wholesome, cordial, and a great corrector of all crudity, or indigestion.

PEPPER too they insist on being cooling; but with what truth, I know not, only that it is certain, that on the Malabar coast where it grows, and where one would think whole ages should have instructed them in its qualities, it is their constant practice to give it in great quantities, in the vehicle of congee, which is a kind of rice-gruel, and that in the most burning fevers.

MYRABOLANS they generally use in purging, and have the highest opinion of their effects, either as a preventive, or a medicine. Their are various sorts of them: some they pretend are so strong, that they will operate by barely holding one in the hand clutched. But perhaps this may be only an Asiatic exaggeration.

THEY have also a dry reed, which I have been told has some affinity to the Centaury major. They call it Creeatt, and on infusion in warm water it yields a bitter potion, which they say is a sovereign stomachic, and promoter of digestion.

OF the Sagoe, from the eastern parts of India they have no sort of opinion, insisting, that the appearance it has of a jelly, or mucilage, when boiled, is a false promise of nourishment, being essentially waterish and unsubstantial.

ALL these I have only mentioned for the sake of suggesting reflections to better judges, and without taking on me in the least to determine how far the Indians are right or wrong in their notions.

THE

THE EAST-INDIES. 237

THE practice of chewing Betel is univerfal over India, as well as on the coaft of China. It is produced at all vifits and entertainments among one another, and even to the Europeans, fome of whom, efpecially the Portuguefe, and very rarely indeed fome of the Englifh, have adopted the habit. It is fometimes offered only in the way of civility, as a glafs of wine among us; but in large companies, it is brought in ready made up on Japan chargers, which they call from the Portuguefe name Bandejahs, fomething like our tea boards, and diftributed round.

THE dofe, if I may fo call it, muft neceffarily confift of the three ingredients, the Betel-leaf, the Arek or Betel-nut, and Chunam; for wanting any of thefe, that deep red color, which refults from their mixture in maftication, would alfo fail.

THE Betel-leaf is fomething like that of a laurel, and grows upon poles like the hop. The leaf is full of large fibres, which with that of the middle they generally ftrip off with the nail. It has a hot, biting tafte, not unpleafing when one is ufed to it.

THE Arek-nut is exactly in form and bignefs like a nutmeg, only harder; marbled in the infide with white and reddifh ftreaks; infipid to the tafte, and muft be fhredded with a kind of fciffors, they are never without for that purpofe, fo as to wrap it up with the leaf. They ufe it both raw and boiled, which laft they fay preferves and adds ftreng'h to it. But I would not advife any one to tafte it green, fince it affects the animal fpirits fo powerfully, that inftantaneoufly as it were, thofe who are not ufed to it, fall down as in a trance; it is true they recover prefently, and without any ill confequences.

THE Chunam is only a lime burnt and made of the fineft fhells. For ufe it muft be wetted, exactly

a 6

as if to ferve for mortar, and is held in gold, filver, or metal round boxes.

To thefe three articles is often added for luxury what they call Cachoonda, a Japan-earth, which, from perfumes and other mixtures, chiefly manufactured at Goa, receives fuch improvement, as to be fold to advantage when re-imported to Japan. It is made up in little round cakes of fcarce the breadth of half a crown, but fomewhat thicker. The furface is a dark dingy brown, the mafs of a brittle gritty texture, and breaks white. The tafte is at firft little better than that of common chalk, but foon turns to a favor that dwells agreeably upon the palate.

ANOTHER addition too they ufe of what they call Catchoo, being a blackifh granulated perfumed compofition, of the fize of fmall fhot, which they carry in little boxes on purpofe. They are pleafingly tafted, and are reckoned provocatives, when taken alone, which is not a fmall confideration with the Afiatics in general.

THEY pretend that this ufe of Betel fweetens the breath, fortifies the ftomach, though the juice is rarely fwallowed, and preferves the teeth, though it reddens them; but, I am apt to believe, that there is more of a vitious habit than any medicinal virtue in it, and that it is like tobacco, chiefly matter of pleafure.

THE Gentoos in general are fond of fweetmeats and confectionary, and have an infinite variety of forts of them; many of them unknown to us in Europe, and fome of them may doubtlefs be very good, though I never tafted any I could call fo.

THE Rajahs and great officers among the Gentoos, though prohibited by their law to drink fpirituous liquors; yet being of the Ketteree caft, which is far lefs ftrict than that of the Bramins and Banyans,

Banyans, assume to themselves a dispensing power in this point, and will indulge themselves especially in cordial drams. They may also eat fish, and some particular sorts of animal food; but as to beef, they are to the full as rigorous in their abstinence from it, as any of the strictest casts of the Gentoos whatever. They allow themselves a greater latitude in the plurality of wives and concubines; most of the Bramins and Banyans contenting themselves with one, unless she is, on competent experience, found to be barren, which is among them reckoned a great misfortune and reproach, but which is however very rarely the case.

THE women begin to bear children at twelve years of age, and even much younger; for I have seen them pregnant in their tenth, but then their teeming time is soon over. It is not common for them to have any after thirty, about which time, and often before that, they go entirely out of bloom, and lose all that plumpness and delicacy for which they are so justly remarkable. This is, however, not to be understood of the celebrated beauties of Cashmeer, who being born in a more northern climate, and in a purer air among the mountains of that country, bordering on north-east Tartary, retain their charms and prolific faculty, as long at least as any European women. But these generally fall to the share of the principal Moors or Moguls.

I COULD not help observing the efficacy of a fish-diet, wherever there were fishermens villages by the sea-side, which were constantly swarming with children, beyond what could be any where else seen. Surely then the president Montesquieu was not out in his remark, that such a diet must diametrically counter-act the intention of the ecclesiastical legislators of the Romish church, who so judicious-

ly

ly prescribed it by way of mortification of the flesh, or in aid of continency. Such is their infallibility!

I HAVE before mentioned the liberty of the Gentoo women, and their rarely abusing it. When they appear abroad, or stand at their doors, they seem, by their looks at least, and their muttering, to resent it as an high affront, if any one stops to view or consider them. Some of them will with a disdainful air speak out aloud, and often use these words, "Deckh na mur," look and die, and certainly they are in general shy of any men speaking to them unless their husbands. Was a woman seen to suffer any of the other sex, except some very near relations to talk to her, though it were ever so innocently, she forfeits her reputation, if not her cast, as much as if things had been carried to extremities. The Bramins and Banyans too, with all the seeming liberty they allow their own wives, reproach the Europeans for suffering theirs to converse familiarly with other men; and when they are told, that we entirely depend on their virtue, they shake their heads, and answer with a proverb, that will sound but coarsely in our language, " That if butter is trusted too near the " fire, it will hardly keep from melting "

THE Gentoos in general are not only tenacious of their religion, but of all their traditional customs; their manner of life having probably admitted of little or no variation from what it was in the first ages. They live almost entirely by rule, and the whole tenor of life in one, according to his respective cast, is exactly the same in every point, as that of his ancestors and cotemporaries; which makes that the description of them by former travellers, is precisely conformable to what may be seen at this day.

IT is also observed, that the Bramins and Banyans do not want for that vice of cowards, vindictiveness.

THE EAST-INDIES.

dictiveness. Averse as they are to blood, they stick at nothing to compass their revenge by the ruin of their adversaries : and if incapable of effectuating it personally themselves, like women, and those of a non-fighting profession, so true it is, that the human heart is every where the same at bottom, they are but the more obstinate in pursuing their point, by all the arts their inventiveness can suggest to them. They know perfectly well how to insinuate themselves with governors, and men of power, by the suppleness of their character, and the use they make themselves of to them, so as to induce them to be the instruments of their revenge. This is especially the practice of the Banyans, where they have conceived an envy or jealousy of trade, when they spare for no cunning to hurt or supplant one another, and yet have so much the art of preserving appearances, as not to be suspected of the mischief they cause under-hand, and employ such refinements of policy, as the most thorough European courtier would not disown.

MUCH has been said of the prevailingness of the art of poisoning in the East-Indies : but by the best information I could procure, there is neither more of that infernal practice, nor greater skill in it than in any other part of the world. I have heard it indeed said, that on the banks of the Ganges, there is produced a seed, that if once swallowed will adhere closely to the coats of the stomach, where it vegetates, and spreads its ramifications so as to destroy a man, without its being in the power of medicines to extirpate, or obstruct its growth. But before reasoning on the naturally seeming impossibility of such an effect, it would be first necessary to verify the fact; which was never in my power, and I have only mentioned it for the singularity of the invention, if, as most probable, it is one.

The Bramins, as being the hereditary depofitaries of all the literature, as well as of the religion of the country, are generally in the higheft confideration, and employed by the Gentoo Rajahs as their minifters and fecretaries. Thefe laft, under the title of Nagur-Bramins, or Scribes, have, in fome parts, a fingular way of prefixing the cypher of the number one, at the head of their letters, as fome Romanifts do the fign of the crofs. By this they mean to reprefent the unity of God, which, though rather out of its place, I could not omit, in confirmation of what has been before advanced, of their fimplification at bottom of all the divinities of their mythology, into the fervants of one fupreme God. But as if all thefe politically minifterial Bramins had renounced the virtues of their condition, with its practical and fpeculative duties, they moft commonly take the bent of the court, and adopt its principles of rapine and oppreffion, of which they will even fubmit to be the inftruments, and occafionally give as little quarter to their own brethren, as to any others; which fpirit of theirs makes a total difference between the worldly Bramins, and the religious contemplative ones, who remain within their fphere, and preferve all the fimplicity and purity of their fequeftered life.

Yet even this corruption, reproached to the others, has not hitherto entirely penetrated to the Malabar countries, properly fo called: where, though the Bramins are in the fame or rather greater efteem, and have more the lead of affairs, they retain more of the humanity and difintereftednefs of their primitive inftitution.

But indeed nothing can hardly be imagined more different in general, than the cuftoms and manners of the Malabars from the more northern parts,

parts, though undivided from them but by an imaginary line, beginning at Mount-Dilly, in the latitude of 12 north. Here the whole government and people wear a new face and form. The country, known by that name, comprehends a tract of land extended to Cape Comorin, and is bounded in-land by that vast chain of mountains which separates that coast from the Coromandel, and runs up through the whole Indostan, till it loses itself in the extremities of northern Tartary, or even extends farther to the very Pole itself.

This mass of country called Proper Malabar, is divided into a multitude of petty kingdoms, or chief-ships; through which are diffused nearly the same modes of religion, manners, and policy.

The highest dignitaries among the Bramins are called, by a Malabar name, Namboorees: next to these are the common Bramins, or Nambyars; after whom come the Nayrs, a sort of military nobility that runs hereditary, as all professions do in the other tribes of India. It is among them that principally prevails the strange custom of one wife being common to a number: in which point the great power of custom is seen, from its rarely or never producing any jealousies or quarrels among the co-tenants of the same woman. Their number is not so much limited by any specific law, as by a kind of tacit convention, it scarce ever happening that it exceeds six or seven. The woman however is under no obligation to admit above a single attachment, though not less respected for using her privilege to its utmost extent. If one of the husbands happens to come to the house when she is employed with another, he knows that circumstance by certain signals left at the door, that his turn is not come, and departs very resignedly. It is owing however to the doubtful paternity, which such a practice must necessarily create, that inheritances descend by the females, and that the nepotism by the sister's side constantly takes place, in quality of the surest proximity of blood.

THE women of those countries are not allowed to cover any part of their breasts, to the naked display of which they annex no idea of immodesty, which in fact ceases by the familiarity of it to the eye. Most Europeans at their first arrival experience the force of temptation from such a nudity on the foot of the ideas, to which their education and customs have habituated them: but it is not long before those impressions by their frequency entirely wear off, and they view it with as little emotion as the natives themselves, or as any of the most obvious parts of the body, the face, or hands.

IN some parts of the Malabar, this custom is however more rigorously observed than in others. A Queen of Attinga, on a woman of her country coming into her presence, who having been some time in an European settlement, where she had conformed to the fashion there, had continued the concealment of her breasts, ordered them to be cut off, for daring to appear before her with such a mark of disrespect to the established manners of the country.

THIS Queen of Attinga is the hereditary sovereign of a dominion, in which the English have their settlement of Anjengo, towards the Cape Comorin. By the constitution of its laws, it must be always a female that governs. It is against the law for her to marry; but that heiresses of her blood may not be wanting she may choose whom, and as many as she pleases to admit to the honor of her bed. The handsomest young men about the court, generally compose her seraglio. The sons fall into the rank of the nobility; and the daughters only can pretend to the succession.

FROM

The North East View of Anjengo Fort on the Coast of Malabar.

FROM such strange customs one would naturally enough conclude, that nothing but such a barbarism reigns in the Malabar as among the savages of America: yet this is far from being the case. The Malabars have in general even a certain politeness, and especially a shrewdness of discernment of their interests, which those who deal or treat with them are sure to experience. Like most of the Orientalists, they are grave, know perfectly well how to keep dignity, and are great observers of silence, especially in their public functions. They despise and distrust all verboseness in the management of state affairs. Their harangues are succinct and pathetic. A king of Travancore, for example, on two ambassadors being sent to him by the Naïck of Madura, a neighboring prince, and one of them having made a prolix speech, and the other preparing to take it up and proceed in the same manner, where the other had left off, austerely admonished him in these few words, " Do not be long, life is short."

MOST of the Malabars, male and female, are particularly fond of having their ears hang almost as low as their shoulders, which is effected while they are young, by boring the lobes of them, and introducing a slip of a brab-tree leaf spirally folded, and renewed in proportion as the hole grows wider and wider, from the constant elasticity of its endeavor to recover its streightness, and when arrived at its utmost, they adorn them with ear-pendants, heavy enough one would imagine to burst the gristle; in the upper-part of which they also stick jewels of value according to their circumstances.

IT is on the southernmost part of this coast that, taking the benefit of the usual indulgence of the Gentoos in matters of religion, some Romish missionaries penetrated into the country; and the better

ter to infinuate themfelves put on the Bramins drefs, and even adopted the ftring, which is chiefly their badge of diftinction, worn acrofs their fhoulders exactly like the ribbons of orders in Europe. It is compofed of brown cotton threads, knotted at diftances, and is what the Bramins efpecially are never feen without. With a view to palm themfelves upon thefe people for European Bramins, the miffionaries alfo decorated themfelves therewith; but not without a previous application to the court of Rome, where they reprefented it as a purely civil, not a religious matter; which was undoubtedly falfe, fince thofe tribes who wear it boaft of it as a facred inftitution of the God Brama himfelf. But if they had not been profoundly ignorant of the hiftory of their own church, they might have fpared themfelves the expence of fuch an untruth: for it is well known, that in the three firft and beft ages of chriftianity, the clergy, fuch as it then was, could hardly be diftinguifhed from the laity, unlefs by its greater innocence, and fanctity of manners. The fucceeding priefts foon departed from that primitive fimplicity, and made no fcruple of adopting the garb of the Gentiles; as for example, the particular cloak of the philofophers, now their efpifcopal pallium; nor of borrowing from the priefts of the heathen gods their taudry fafhions of drefs, which to this day furnifh the chief articles of their confecrated toilet.

ONE of thefe miffionaries, on an Englifh gentleman afking him, how he durft venture himfelf among fo many naked-breafted beauties, defended by no armor but that of a frail chaftity, anfwered, that he had not been infenfible to the temptation, but that his method of fubduing it was, by dropping melted wax on the peccant flefh, thus to correct one burning by another: on which the Englifh
gentleman

gentleman put him into a confusion, equivalent to a confession of his impudent hypocrisy, by telling him, with a very philosophical coolness, that he supposed, by his answer, he took him for a Portuguese.

The princes and chiefs of the Malabar dominions, and especially the Samorin of Calicut, often, on particular occasions, and festival-days, make entertainments to which the whole country round is invited; and where the quantity, rather than the quality of the victuals provided, inflames the charge of them, being chiefly rice, the pea-like grain of Dholl, with the sauce of turmeric, coconut, and other vegetables, all which articles are in those parts extremely cheap, and the beverage is never but pure water: they are however, literally speaking, cramming-matches; for it is not uncommon for some of the guests, tempted by the free-cost of them, to overcharge their stomachs, so as to die under it. This is treated by the rest as matter of pleasantry; and when they mean to celebrate the magnificence of any such feast, they do it by telling the numbers that burst at it.

On the back of the Samorin's dominions, and contiguous to them, lies the country of the Rajah of Sarimpatam; not that I could hear of yet subdued. It has been a constantly received law with them, never to make any but a defensive war, and even then not to kill a man though it were in battle; instead of which, they practice a singular method of fighting that has not, it seems, been without its success. Their military was trained up to a particular dexterity, at cutting off the noses of their enemies in an engagement; and the dread of incurring this deformity, a dread equal in many to that of death, proved sufficient to keep neighbors, not much more martial than themselves, from effectually attacking them. This reminds one of the famous stratagem of Julius Cæsar, at the battle of Pharsalia, riding round the ranks of his hardy rugged veterans, and directing them to aim specially at the faces of the young delicate effeminate Patricians opposed to them. " *Miles faciem* " *feri.*"

The Europeans, English, French, and Dutch have lined as it were the coast of Malabar with their fortified settlements and factories. Some were obtained by force, others by insinuation: but in general the powers in those parts are not displeased with having them in their countries, to which they are undoubtedly a benefit by the protection they occasionally afford them against their enemies, as well as for the trade they bring to it, and for the vent they procure of the natural and artificial produce of them, by which their revenue is encreased: and to do them justice, it is seldom their faults if any quarrels with them happen. It is oftener that of the European governors and chiefs, whom private passions, prejudices, and interests mislead into engaging their employers into expensive and detrimental feuds or wars, which they represent as honorable and necessary; or under such plausible, though false colors, as to obtain their approbation and sanction, whilst at such a distance, it is hard for the mis-information to be discovered. Those princes who are not a match for the European artillery and discipline, on conceiving any disgust or resentment, have fallen on a way distressing of such settlements, not only by harrassing them with alarms, and a war of ambushes to the very gates of their fortifications; but by laying a general interdict on the trade and dealings of their subjects with them. It is true, that themselves

are

are in the mean time not a little fufferers by the ceffation of their emoluments, and even of the fub-fiftence of their people; but this they can ofteneft difpenfe with for a time long enough not to be the firft tired. Not unfrequently too, they turn the channel of commerce into other European governments, always alert to fupplant one another, and avail themfelves towards it of thefe mif-underftandings, of which they have perhaps under-hand fown the feeds, or fomented the growth.

As to the climate in general of India, it is far from unwholfome, unlefs where particular accidents of fituation difaffect the air; as the neighborhood of fwamps, the dry burning fands on the fea-coaft, or the freedom of ventilation intercepted by woods. The heats are rarely fuch as to be intolerable, efpecially on abftaining from any excefs in fpirituous liquors, ftrong indigeft foods, or violent exercife.

It is alfo remarkable, that thofe countries are feldom if ever afflicted with thofe two fcourges in nature, earthquakes and plagues.

As to the firft, the ftate of the cave at Elephanta is a proof, that for at leaft thefe two thoufand years, thofe parts have been exempt from it; though their mountainous fituation near the feafide, like that of Naples, Sicily, and Lifbon, might make fuch a vifitation naturally expected.

And as to plagues, I never could learn that there was any tradition, or hiftory of any remarkable ones known there beyond certain epidemical diftempers, fuch as the bloody fluxes chiefly incident to Europeans, and the fmall pox more peculiar to the natives; and which fometimes rages fomewhat in the nature of a plague, making

great

great havock among them, especially on the Malabar coast.

For bloody fluxes, the Bramins suggest a very simple, and as they pretend a most infallible remedy, consisting in a strict abstinence from every thing but rice stewed dry; to which they allow no sauce of any kind whatever, and attribute to it an absorbent quality, that is excellent against that acrimony which preys on the entrails, and breeds the disorder. For drink they give nothing but water, corrected by a very moderate quantity of cinnamon or Cassia-lignum. As to the Tellicherry-bark, long boasted as a specific in this distemper, it seems to have lately greatly declined in practice, probably from experience having shewn, that it was not so much to be trusted to as was imagined.

There is likewise known on the Malabar-coast chiefly, a most violent disorder they call the Mordechin; which seizes the patient with such fury of purging, vomiting, and tormina of the intestines, that it will often carry him off in thirty hours. For this the physicians among the natives know no more effectual remedy, than the actual cautery applied to the soles of the feet, the powerful rerevulsion of which rarely fails of a salutary efficacy.

The Barbeers is another dreadful illness of the paralytic kind, that attacks mostly the Europeans, and deprives them of the use of their limbs. The natives, with what reason I know not, say, that it is most commonly brought on by venereal excesses, having irrecoverably exhausted the radical moisture and spirits of life. The Portuguese apply to such as are in this condition, from that circumstance, the term of *Esfalfados*: but I am far from clear, that by it they mean all who are afflicted with the Barbeers; which, not denying, but it

may

may sometimes be the effect of that cause, is not always so; being sometime produced by colds caught by lying out exposed to the dew, or night-air, and by the consequences of fevers, especially by being over-physicked for venereal complaints.

THE Malabar physicians particularly are of opinion, that it is unwholesome to be out in the air at sun-rise; for that at that time it gives a certain life and activity to the noxious damp vapors of the atmosphere, risen during its absence; but which its power encreasing with its ascent, conquers and dispels.

CHRONICAL disorders, such as the gout, rheumatism, stone, consumption, &c. are rarely known in those parts; and indeed none of the distempers, more particular to them, are so frequent or general, as to form a just objection to the venturing into that climate. Those who live any thing regular, or who listen to the preventive advice of such as are acquainted with the nature of it, rarely incurring more danger from it, than what they might find in their native spot.

CHAP.

CHAP. II.

Summary reflections on the trade of INDIA. *That trade advantageous to the nation. Certain objections to it discussed.*

THE trade to, from, and in India, has so long been carried on in an established known rote of practice, that the public could certainly learn nothing new from any particular accounts of it into which I might descend. I shall only then hazard here such reflections, as occured to me on the view of it, in its totality.

It has been said, speciously indeed, but falsely, that the returns from India, consisted chiefly either in articles of pure luxury, or such as tended to discourage the industry of our native manufacturers, by interfering with the produce of it, from their being to be afforded cheaper ; and that these articles, ruinous in either sense, were yet further so by their not being to be had but in exchange for bullion, of which they consequently impoverished the nation, and for so few of our home-manufactures, as did not form an object considerable enough to counter-balance the exportation of the other.

To this heavy accusation has been opposed a very solid defence, consisting of proofs, that admitting of no falsification, admit of no doubt ; proofs from accounts easily verifiable, of the balance of national advantages being greatly in favor of that trade.

NOTHING is plainer, than that manufactures or employment being wanting to the industrious or useful subjects is so far from being the case, that of these there is rather wanting a sufficient number
of

THE EAST-INDIES. 253

of them to the work that might be found for them at reasonable rates, and to the demands of the government for the service and defence of their country.

Whoever will enter more than superficially into this disquisition, will find, that pretended superabundance of subjects, having reasons to complain of the labor of the Indians defrauding them of the livelihood to be got by theirs, might be more profitably, to the public and to themselves, employed in branches that would encrease the national wealth and power; such as the more thorough cultivation of our old colonies, foundation of new and useful ones, improving of agriculture, and especially strengthening that great national bulwark our marine, to which the complement of hands is felt, as its greatest need, so sensibly wanting; points rather preferable to many of the arts and trades, purely dependent on luxury, and which at once soften and unman those who exercised them, and those for whose sake they are exercised.

What first gave rise to the idea in me, was the observation of the wretchedness and insignificance to the defence of a country, of those so much envied artists, the whole tribes of weavers, callicostainers, and in short all the retainers to the looms of India, whose incessant and ingenious industry never scarce extricates them out of the depths of poverty; whilst it at the same time disqualifies them for any other effectual service, being scarcely more of men than the machinery of their fabrics. Whatever advantage is made of their industry is entirely engrossed by the Banyans, Chittys, or head-merchants; men as effeminate as themselves; and in whose coffers, generally speaking, all that money stagnates that is not invested in the usurious advances which are so hard upon labor, by un-
conscionably

confcionably fcrewing down its price; which being their great point in trade, leffens the commendation due to their fpirit of it, lucre being their fole object, and the public good quite out of the queftion.

STILL it will be faid, that fuch manufactures not only hinder the exportation of money, but actually bring it into their country. This is too evidently true to be denied, and fo far they are a commendable advantage, even though fufceptible of being abufed: but furely it is not ultimately a lefs one for the nation that deals with them, or that even furnifhes them with bullion, if fuch a trade is carried on with a moral certainty of an outlet or market for the returns, that will reimburfe it with profit; at the fame time that thefe of its fubjects, who might otherwife be employed in producing the like manufactures at a much dearer rate, fhould, by a found and comprehenfive policy, be diftributed into the many branches in which they are actually wanted, to anfwer much more valuable ends, in the increafe of the protective force of the nation, and of its power to extend its trade, navigation and influence. Such a refervation of fubjects, would be only preferring a greater good to a leffer one, to which it would be far from giving the exclufion; as it is far from implying fo grofs an abfurdity as that of difcouraging home-manufactures, or from meaning any thing more than a juft modification, and choice of them. For in the choice of which to encourage moft lies the great ftrefs of policy, and thefe inconteftibly are thofe claffes of mechanics who give to the crude materials produced by this country, fuch as wool, iron, tin, lead, &c. that additional value of their manual labor, which is fo much net profit to the nation. Imports that interfere with fuch, doubtlefs deferve to be difcouraged, and we

fee

fee that they actually are fo. But as to thofe articles appropriate to India, grown into a kind of neceffaries by cuftom, and to which the reproach of luxury can only lie in declamation, the revenue might probably find its account as much in even the quantity of their imports being increafed, as in the exorbitance of the duties on them. If more enlarged and comprehenfive notions were to take place, under the fanction of proper regulations, the Weft Indies, and our American colonies, might receive a greater benefit than they do from the Eaft India trade, ftill preferving to England its right and advantage of being the centrical point of union of both. Thus if, by any means or device, the commerce with India could afford an augmentation of its number of fhipping, the marine of the kingdom would receive a proportionable increafe, and employ the greater number of hands, inured to the change of climates, and the experter for thofe voyages of a long run; which would be a far preferable confideration, to that of their being funk in fuch of the lower and more flavifh branches of the mechanics, as only procuring them a bare livelihood, rob fpheres of occupation, fitter for freemen and Englifhmen, of their requifite number of hands, who in them would be more effentially ferviceable to the ftate, in the advancement of the live-force, navigation, and truly profitable trade of the kingdom. I fay truly profitable, becaufe even trade itfelf may be ruinoufly diverfified and extended, if the other principal objects of government are neglected, or even not preferred, and a nation languifh with faintnefs, amidft thofe riches, which ought to procure its ftrength and happinefs. But this can never be the cafe, if the increafe of the protective power, which has fo juft a right to be fupported by the revenue from trade, is at the fame time duly confulted, and fo ordered

as

as to keep pace with it. No folly being greater than that of exalting the mercantile above the military spirit, both being of such mutual benefit, that they ought never to be considered in distinct views. However, if it was necessary to sacrifice the object of one of them, it undoubtedly ought to be that of trade, which must decrease in its value in proportion to its decrease of security, and because the safety and honor of a nation are points preferable to a momentary profit. But the truth is, that there is no necessity of neglecting either, and that it must be a wretched policy that does not sufficiently take care of both, and make both serviceable to each other.

THE expedience of which management stands no where more fully illustrated than in the East-Indies, where it is scarce possible to carry on a commerce on other than a precarious, dishonorable, disadvantageous footing, unless a state of force procures a respect to, or confidence in our arms; the country-governments of India being constitutionally such, as scarce ever to neglect occasions of oppression or plunder, where they have no opposition, or vengeance to fear. Nor do they ever solidly bestow their countenance or friendship, but where they can depend on a protection in the revolutions, to which it is in the very nature of their despotism so often to expose them. The merchants especially prefer dealing with that nation, which they see the most powerful and able to shelter them from the tyranny of their own country-men. Thence their predilection of our government to live under, and to which they are of such notable benefit. As mere traders, the English would never have got the footing they had, if they had not added to that character the profession of arms both at land and sea. This is so

true,

THE EAST-INDIES.

true, that the special privileges, fortified settlements, and favorable grants obtained from the several Princes of India, will, conformable to their original dates, appear to have been owing to the figure our nation formerly made there in war, when its victories over the Portuguese, who sunk as fast as we rose, gave it such a reputation, as that hardly any thing was denied to it; and, to say the truth, it is principally on that old foundation, that the extraction of our commerce has since subsisted: I say principally only, because no doubt our frank, unaffectedly and generous national character, amidst all the faults of some of its subjects in power there, I can safely aver, without any partiality, also once bore in the eyes of the Indians a very favorable comparison with the silly, senseless, sanguinary bigotry of the Portuguese; with the unsocial dryness, imperious conduct, and keenness after gain of the Dutch; and the super-refined designing politeness of the French. And yet the advantages of these last over us in the affair of Madrass, did not a little shake our estimation in those parts, no people being more apt to be dazzled and influenced by success than the Orientalists, and those of India above all.

THE Dutch especially insult us, in their insinuations to the country-governments, of our inferiority, in that we are not possessed of a head place of arms, such as Batavia is to them, from whence our operations might be more timely, and more effectually applied to any exigence, than as there now exists a necessity for waiting for orders and aids from Europe. They do not consider, or at least do not add a candid confession of the treacherous and cruel supplantment of us, in a time of full peace, in the Spice-islands, which are the mines, from whence they draw the means of supporting

porting the extraordinary charges of that their boasted capital place in India, a competition with which our trade, circumstanced as it has been since that fatal epoch, could never well afford; though it is impossible but it might have gained a much more considerable extension, if either the settlements we actually have, had been better cultivated, useful new ones had been formed, or other channels of commerce explored; or if, in short, more attention had not been given to the temptation of momentary profits and present dividends, than to the founding of permanent establishments upon greater views, but of which the immediate requisite expence appeared to be as so much lost in the distant futurity of the returns. This narrow consideration it is, which combined with a certain generally prevailing indolence, and the facility of humoring that indolence, since the opening of those fatal gulphs, the public funds, which, swallowing up the very aliment and support of trade, have set up a class of men called the moneyed interest, to the destruction of the commercial one, upon the produce of whose stock, which itself has depauperated, it projects lazily to live; all these, I say, have more contributed to extinguish the antient English spirit of discovery and extension, than any certainty that could with reason be pleaded, of there being nothing further to be found or hoped for from it.

CHAP.

CHAP. III.
Of the PROTESTANT MISSION *in* MALABAR.

IN this country is the city of Tranquebar, or Taragu Wadhi, a Danish colony, with a fortified castle, which Ofre Giedde, a gentleman of that nation, purchased of the princes of Tanjaour in 1621; since which time it has belonged to the kings of Denmark. The place contains about 5000 souls; the greatest part Pagans, or Papists.

THAT good king Frederic IV. of Denmark was touched with concern, that so many of his subjects should live under heathen darkness, and was ashamed that Protestants should be wholly intent on commerce, without the least thought, though obliged in meer gratitude, of the salvation of those people, with whom they carried on so gainful a traffic. Not that the name Jesus Christ was unknown in Malabar. There were many years ago, on the western coast, a very considerable number of christians, disciples of St. Thomas, and of the Syrian communion. We presume not to fix the time of their conversion; and the Danish missionaries have proved the famous crofs, pretended to be found near St. Thome, and of which a description was published in Lisbon, in 1722, an absolute deception: they have demonstrated, that the names of the kings Pandijen and Choren, which appear in the inscription, are more antient than Jesus Christ. These Syrian christians are divided into two communions; and a great part of them were brought over to the Romish communion, when the Portuguese were masters of Cochin. Near seventy churches were united to that of Rome, and their head in those times was called

S 2 Mar-

Mar-Gabriel: but Mar-Thomas, coming from Antioch, formed a party againſt him, to the peril of his own life; Mar-Gabriel having ſent aſſaſſins to murder him in his own houſe. He was ſucceeded by another Mar-Thomas; and this antient church recovered ſome part of its liberty. They have no veneration for images, and they reject tranſubſtantiation: but have embraced the doctrine of Eutychius.

The metropolitan church of theſe chriſtians was very near Madraſs, on the famous mountain of St. Thomas; whither the chriſtians of the weſtern coaſt travelled to perform their devotions; though it was a dangerous journey of ſixty days. This holy place was lately ſubject to the Portugueſe; and notwithſtanding they were diſpoſſeſſed of their ſettlements on the coaſts of Coromandel, it was the reſidence of a Romiſh biſhop: but the diviſions among his people hindered him from making it his conſtant abode.

Nearer Tranquebar, and in the city of that name, are other chriſtians vaſtly more numerous. It is about one hundred and fifty years ago, that the Romiſh miſſionaries ſettled themſelves in the kingdom of Tanjaour; and Pondicherry was always well ſupplied with French Jeſuits, who applied themſelves to the converſion of the Pagans, under the dominion of France. There are other miſſions in Madura and the Carnatic.

The Portugueſe is the common language of the ſlaves and ſoldiers of the company, who are compoſed of ſuch tawny Portugueſe, deſcended from thoſe firſt conquerors of the Indies, who choſe to ſtay in the country after they were deprived of their fortreſſes by other nations.

The Malabarian language is very difficult for an European. Baldæus and Gedaes have pronounced it impoffible to be learnt by one not born in the country. The Romifh miffionaries feldom enjoin themfelves fo hard a tafk; and indeed what means are there of learning it? M. Ziegenbalg found but one European, who knew enough of Malabarian to make a tranflation of it: and there was no book to ferve him for a guide. There was but one way for him to be inftructed in it, and that very mortifying for a perfon who had no other views than the fervice of the gofpel. He made a bargain with a Malabarian fchoolmafter, and went and feated himfelf among the naked children of the country, who learned to read and write: there he learned to draw in the characters of founds, the fenfe of which was wholly unknown to him; and fubmitted to the fame tafks as the fchool-boys. Such was the ardent zeal of M. Ziegenbalg, that in lefs than a year he attained a perfect knowledge of the Malabarian tongue; and the learned of that country admired the elegance of his diction. After that, in 1708, he applied himfelf to the tranflation of the Bible, which he finifhed in 1711, and had it printed at Tranquebar in 1714. He compofed alfo a Malabarian dictionary of 20,000 words, taken from the poets. As foon as he could fpeak the language, he employed this new talent in the propagation of the chriftian faith. He reforted to the Pagan feafts, to the pagodas, to the confecrated fifh-ponds, and wherever thefe Gentiles had their affemblies: there he confulted the Bramins; reprefenting to them the ridiculoufnefs of their religion, and raifed the admiration of the people, who never heard any man talk like that German prieft. The principal perfons among the learned, both Pagans and Mahometans, held frequent affemblies for regular conferences, and entered into formal difputations with him; in which the purity of the chriftian morals difplayed itfelf in fuch a manner, as to affect the moft barbarous hearts. The Pandarams, the Mahometan priefts, and the Bramins themfelves, yielded to the force of truth. Mr. Ziegenbalg and Mr. Plutfchau foon found, it was an eafy matter to get the better of them at difputing; but that their adverfaries had not the leaft concern in fuch a victory. Mr. Bourguet, in a remarkable latter addreffed to Mr. Ziegenbalg, advifes him to begin with a phyfical demonftration of the Being of a God. The Pagans are fufficiently convinced of this point, and befides, they want not to be confuted, but reformed. Here lies the main difficulty of converfions, and the difference between the labours of the miffionaries of Rome and of Tranquebar; the Romans aim at nothing but perfuafion; the Proteftants endeavour to inftruct and to render their converts wifer as well as better.

M. ZIEGENBALG, to try another method unknown to the Romifh miffionaries, and to which their pride would never condefcend, propofed to himfelf the inftruction of children, whofe tender hearts were free from prepoffeffion, and not to leave them till he had thoroughly feafoned them with the principles of the true religion; for this end, he and his collegue gave public notice, that they would open a free fchool, where all forts of children fhould be taught reading, writing, and accompts, with other things proper for their age, gratis. The concourfe to thefe fchools was furprifing: in 1714, there were 21 fchools in the city and fuburbs, and the number of children 575, who there received inftructions. At firft, while the miffionaries had none but Pagan affiftants and overfeers, they could teach the children nothing but morality, and choice fentences taken out of the Bible; which, for their elegance, were acceptable

THE EAST-INDIES. 263

able to the Heathens themselves; but at laſt they found means, by degrees, to convince governors of the ſchools, and to convert the children; and to this the eſtabliſhment of the goſpel is principally to be aſcribed. The Malabarians themſelves admired that ſpirit of charity which animated thoſe ſchoolmaſters, and regarded thoſe ſchools as one of their beſt public works.

ALL nations have their prejudices, and the Malabarians in particular; though not ſo ſtrong as thoſe of the ſouthern people of Europe. They have the ſame reſpect for the antiquity of their religion, the ſame fondneſs for frivolous ceremonies, and the ſame confidence in good works and penances. They have beſides, an extreme repugnance to what they eſteem impurity. The more intelligent perſons among them had nothing to object to the miſſionaries, but the wine which the Europeans drank, the beef which they eat, the confuſion of ſects, and the omiſſion of ceremonial ablutions. Theſe prejudices operate with more force in proportion to the natural indolence of the nation, which hears and anſwers with docility, but ſuffers little or no impreſſion from the force of reaſon.

TRAVELLING in this country is attended with great difficulties. The king of Tanjaour is extremely jealous of every white man who paſſes through his territories. At every village, the toll-gatherers are intolerable in their exactions upon Europeans, and detain them until they obtain their liberty from the court by preſents. Beſides this, the burning ſands, and the heat of the ſun, and the want of food dreſſed after the European manner, are great obſtacles, if not unſurmountable at ſome times: but theſe difficulties could not retard the zeal of the Daniſh miſſionaries, who, in 1707, applied one half of their penſions in erecting a mean church, which was called Jeruſalem; and which has ſince

S 4 been

been rebuilt in a better manner. The other half was dedicated to the service of the schools; reserving only a bare subsistance for themselves.

IN 1712, there were 117 Malabarian Gentiles added to the christian church, and the number of converts amounted to 221. The labours of Meff. Ziegenbalg and Plutschau were soon become famous in Asia and Europe; and the veneration which these apostolical persons attracted from all ranks, procured them assistances, as powerful as they were unexpected. The king of Denmark settled on them 2000 crowns a year, payable from the post office, to defray the necessary charges of the mission; and this sum was often doubled by extraordinary presents. The piety of the king disposed him to augment this fund, which was so well employed to the advancement of true christianity.

GERMANY, excited by the accounts published at Hall, since 1709, sent large sums towards the support of the mission. But the greatest contributions came from England, which exerted itself on the occasion. Since 1709, the society established there for the propagation of the gospel in foreign parts very liberally assisted Mr. Ziegenbalg; and, in 1713, the sum sent from England amounted to 1194 l. sterling, which much exceeded the entire annual revenue for some years past.

IT was indeed very affecting to see the protestants at last awake out of their lethargy. Mr. Plutschau, who was returned into Europe, had many marks of esteem conferred upon him, and favours were accumulated upon the Danish missionaries; who, from that time, almost constantly took their voyage to the Indies by way of England, and in English vessels. Since that time, there has been erected a Portuguese printing press, which was taken by the French forces, commanded

by

THE EAST-INDIES. 265

by M. du Gue Trouin, when he plundered Rio de Janeiro in 1711, and afterwards purchafed and fent to Tranquebar; on which occafion 250 copies of the New Teftament in Portuguefe, printed at London, were difperfed among the Portuguefe in Brafil, who were the firft of their nation in thofe parts, that ever had an opportunity of reading the gofpel.

ENGLAND, from that time, continued powerfully to affift the miffionof Tranquebar, and alone fuftained the miffion of Madrafs, and that of St. David. Of late years, thofe miffions have been in a more particular manner the object of their charity. Two archbifhops of Canterbury, Tennifon and Wake, fet on foot a collection for this purpofe: the Univerfity of Cambridge followed the pious example of thofe prelates, and king George I. honoured the miffionaries with a letter written with his own hand.

IN 1715, was eftablifhed at Copenhagen, a fociety for propagation of faith, which has fince that time had the particular infpection of the miffion. Loaded with honours and the charities of all nations through which he paffed, Mr. Ziegenbalg, in 1716, returned to Tranquebar, the country defigned for the laft fcene of his devoted life and labours.

AT his return things affumed a new face: there were two printing preffes already in the country; for Germany had furnifhed them with one for the ufe of Malabar. The preffes were employed on an edition of the Bible, and other books defigned for the converfion of the Gentiles, which were three fhort treatifes; one entitled, Letters to the Malabarians; another, The way of falvation; and the third, Paganifm, a ftate of damnation. The publication of thefe books, and efpecially the New

Teftament,

Teftament, had a furprifing effect. The very Romans themfelves then acted in difobedience to their priefts, which they had never done before, and came and afked for the gofpel, which they had received for the foundation of their faith, without knowing what it was.

M. Ziegenbalg began tranflating the whole Bible into the Malabarian language, which was not finifhed before 1725, by Mr. Schulze, who catechifed the children publicly, to oblige in a manner the Gentiles to hear the gofpel. He eftablifhed an excellent order in the exercife of piety; and Mr. Stevenfon, an Englifh minifter, who paid a vifit to Mr. Ziegenbalg at Tranquebar, fpeaks with admiration of the decency of divine fervice, and of the good order which he obferved in all his minifterial labours.

The king of Denmark had honoured M. Ziegenbalg with the title of fuperintendant, which he had hitherto borne among the miffionaries. Three new affiftants were come to him from Europe, when death carried him off, on the 25th of February 1719, in the 36th year of his age. Mr. Grandler, his faithful affiftant, who had particularly devoted himfelf to the care of the fchools, furvived him but a year, and had only time to leave his orders to Schulze, the oldeft and moft active of the three minifters of the gofpel. The death of thofe two perfons reduced the miffion to a very low ftate, and the new miffionaries found themfelves in the fame circumftances with Meffrs. Ziegenbalg and Plutfchau, when they firft entered on their work, being obliged to learn the language, without any other affiftance than what they found in the books of their predeceffors. The fchools were diffolved, becaufe the contract ceafed between the fchoolmafters and the furviving miffionaries,

THE EAST-INDIES. 267

fionaries, who could not be comprehended under it. This doctrine of the miffion lafted feveral years, and the number of converts in 1724 amounted but to 28. The number of converts has confiderably increafed fince 1736. There were in all 6252, in the 35 years of the miffion, ending October 5, 1742, a number of which, without being fabulous or miraculous, muft however be accounted a confiderable acquifition made by the gofpel, and a recompence proportionable to the number and labours of the miffionaries. Thefe converts live partly at Tranquebar, and the reft are difperfed over the kingdom of Tanjaour, where the miffionaries have formed five diocefes, or particular diftricts of the Gentiles.

The miffion of Tranquebar in 1742, was under the direction of eight miffionaries, two national priefts, three catechifts of the firft order, befides thofe of an inferior rank, with a proportional number of affiftants. The fchools in the city are in very good order, and confift of near 200 children, maintained at the expence of the miffion: and new fchools have been eftablifhed in the country of Tanjaour. The Dutch Eaft India company has done many good things for the propagation of the gofpel: but it is in its power to do fomething more, without hardly touching thofe immenfe funds which it poffeffes.

CHAP.

CHAP. IV.

Of some particular ANIMALS *of* INDIA. *The* ELEPHANT *and* RHINOCEROS. *The* CAMEL, DROMEDARY, *and* CAMELOPARD. *The* LION *and* LIONESS. LEOPARD *and* PANTHER. *The* TYGER. *The* APE.

IT is not in men alone, that the difference of talents and dispositions is remarkable: all nature is full of similar examples. Every climate is not proper for every fruit; happy is that which produces the best. It is true, that India is deficient in some of the conveniencies of life; but this loss is amply made up by the great abundance of all that is necessary, and of several things that are peculiar to it, which draw thither all other nations of the world, either to admire its curiosities, or to make a profit of its riches and fertility. For there is none of them, but whom either necessity or luxury lead to the Indies: but the Indians themselves are not obliged to go any where else to give proofs of their indigence: they can even boast with justice, that they have more rarities than all other nations together; of which every one may be convinced, when acquainted with the nature of some animals familiar to them, and of the fruits which they gather in the fields.

No other countries in the world but the Indies, and some southern provinces in Africa, produce Elephants: but the Indian are much better than the African in quality. This animal, the largest, and the most extraordinary in its nature, which the earth produces, deserves to be considered in the first place. As savage of itself as the lion or the

tyger,

tyger, it muft be hunted like other wild beafts; and there formerly were none among the Indians, but the fhepherds who had that permiffion. They inclofed, by a large and deep ditch, a plain about a quarter of a league in circumference; where they built a bridge of wood, and hovels into which they might retire; into this inclofure they carried fome tame female elephants, who drew the wild ones thither in the night-time. As foon as they entered, the hunters retired out of their inclofure, drew off the bridge, and went into the neighbouring villages to feek for aid. Several days after, when they faw the elephants weakened with hunger and thirft, they returned upon tame elephants, with which they purfued and harraffed them, until they had exhaufted their force. Then they bridled them, and made incifions about their mouth, and round their neck, to render them more fenfible, and ftop them when they made too violent a motion: afterwards they mounted, and drove them into ftables by the force of blows.

NOTWITHSTANDING the enormous bulk of this animal, being twenty feet in circumference, he is of a docility and ingenuity approaching to the human intelligence. He is fufceptible of love, affection and gratitude to fuch a degree, as to pine away with grief when he has loft his keeper: he is obferved to be tranfported with grief, and ready to kill himfelf, when, in a furious moment, he has killed or treated him ill.

To this inftinct of humanity, the elephant joins an extraordinary force, proportioned to his ftature, which renders him the ftrongeft of all animals. The Indians have always trained them to war, and made them the terror of the enemy, by the flaughter which they occafioned when they gave them the fignal to advance. This happened by the

found

sound of drums and trumpets, by the sight of blood already spilt, at which they have a horror, or by a view of certain liquors which resemble it, as the juice of mulberries or grapes. In an instant they make a furious assault, throw themselves across the battalions, and carry every where terror, disorder and death. The smell and dreadful bellowing of these animals occasion still more disorder among the horses than the men. At the first attack, they are struck with terror, they cannot be made to advance; they fall back upon one another, and even throw their riders. Cæsar had but one elephant, when he gave battle to Cassibelan, king of the Britons, and he alone put the whole army to flight. This was the principal use which the Persians, Syrians, and Romans made of them.

SOMETIMES they built upon the back of those monstrous creatures great wooden towers of several stories, upon which the archers mounted, and shot in safety, having almost their whole body under covert. In the battle which Antiochus Eupator gave to Judas Maccabeus, that king of Syria had more than thirty elephants of this kind, on each whereof were thirty-two archers, who shot arrows from all sides; and an Indian who guided them. In the Indies they were ranged in the front of the army, at a hundred paces distance the one from the other, where they served as a rampart against the enemy, until the moment when they were to be roused and united. Porus placed two hundred in the same line, when Alexander came to attack him.

THIS animal is sixteen or eighteen months in the belly of its mother, after which he comes forth about the bigness of a calf. He does not arrive at his full strength, until the age of fifty or sixty years;

THE EAST-INDIES. 271

years; it is only then that they can build a tower upon his back. From his nose there hangs a mass of long and hollow flesh, which they call his trunk, and sometimes his hand, because it is of infinite service to him whether for feats of advantage, or of strength: he makes use of it to carry things to his mouth; from that arise two teeth, or prodigious tusks, which grow to six feet in length, from whence we have our ivory. As if this animal was acquainted with their value, or apprehended being killed on their account, he hides them in the earth whenever they fall from him through age, or any other accident. The skin upon his back is like a thick buckram, or rather a suit of armour, which can scarce be cut through; but under his belly it is much thinner.

Their ordinary food is grass or corn; but they are very fond of sweets, such as barley-sugar, and this is given to tame them. They make those whom they design for war drink the wine of the country, that is a kind of beer: but others who are weaker, and used for labour, drink only water, which they love best when it is muddy. They are subject to different distempers, of which the Indians know the remedies; and this makes that animal live two or three hundred years. Apollonius Tyaneus, or Damis, related that they had seen in the city of Taxila, the elephant of the famous Porus, with two circles of gold round his tusks, in which it was written, in Greek characters, that Alexander, in esteem of him, had consecrated him to the Sun. At the same time he must have been above four hundred years old. But their too great love for the marvellous renders this suspected.

The Rhinoceros, called by the modern Indians Abadu, comes very near the elephant in bulk and

figure.

figure. This creature is chiefly found in the island of Java; but is common enough in the kingdoms of Bengal and Patna. The ancients have frequently mentioned this animal, but without giving an exact description of it.

We must then have recourse to the moderns for a knowledge of this extraordinary animal. Bontius and Father le Compte, who had examined it several times, speak of it pretty much in the same manner. Here follow the words of the missionary. The Rhinoceros is one of the most extraordinary animals in the world. He is somewhat like the wild boar, if it was not that he is much larger, that his feet are thicker, and his body more unwieldy. His skin is all over covered with large and thick scales of a blackish colour, and an uncommon hardness. They are divided into small squares or buttons, raised a little above the skin, and nearly like those of the crocodile. His legs appear to be set in boots, and his head wrapt up behind in a smooth capuchin, which has given occasion to the Portuguese, to call him an Indian monk. His head is large; his mouth little; and his snout down to a great length, and armed with a long thick horn, which makes him terrible to the tygers, buffaloes, and elephants. But what appears most wonderful in this animal is his tongue, which Nature has covered with so rough a membrane, that it is not at all different from a file, and flays every thing which he licks. As we have animals in Europe that make a grateful repast on thistles, whose small points agreeably stimulate the fibres or the nerves in their tongue; so the rhinoceros eats with pleasure the branches of trees bristled all over with the largest thorns. We are told by some travellers, that they have frequently given him of these, whose points were very rough and

and long, and it was wonderful to fee with what greedinefs and dexterity he immediately licked them up, and chewed them in his mouth without the leaft inconvenience. It is true, it was fometimes a little bloody, but that even rendered the tafte more agreeable, and thefe little wounds to appearance made no other impreffion on his tongue than falt and pepper make on ours." The author might have added, that this animal has two kinds of wings of a fkin extremely ugly, which cover his belly like a houfing, and in fhape refembling the wings of a bat.

THOUGH the reft of his body is in a manner wrapt up in armour, and thofe who attack him are expofed to great danger; yet the Indians hunt him as they do other animals, becaufe he is of great ufe to them after his death. The Moors eat his flefh, however hard it may be. His horn is not lefs curious than ufeful: when it is cut through the middle, on each fide is feen the figure of a man, whofe outlines are marked by little white ftrokes, with thofe of different birds and other things, as in the Egyptian flints. The greateft part of the Indian princes drink out of cups made of this horn, becaufe they fay, it fweats at the approach of any poifon whatfoever. The people of Java likewife fet a great value on this animal, becaufe there is no part but is found in fome degree ufeful in medicine. They make ufe of its flefh, horn, blood, teeth, fkin, and even its excrements. They are perfuaded there cannot be a better antidote againft all kinds of poifon, and they attribute to it the qualities which the ancients did to the Unicorn. Frequently they make bucklers of its fkin with its fcales.

THE camel and the dromedary perform to the Indians, and the greateft part of the eaftern nations, the same services which we receive from beasts of burden, with this difference, that they will carry a thousand weight and above, and go fifty leagues in a day without being fatigued; but they are not fit to draw carriages.

The camel is naturally fearful, insupportable to the horse on account of his bad smell, and suffers himself to be devoured by the lion and the tyger without the least resistance. We are assured he lives a century, if no accident happens to him. He has no teeth, except in his lower jaw; and he differs from the dromedary in this, that he has only one bunch on his back, and the dromedary two, disposed lengthways.

The Camelopard is not so well known. It does not resemble the camel, whose name the ancients had given it, but in the head and the manner of carrying it, bearing it in a bolder and more upright manner. His skin is reddish spotted with white, or white with spots of red; and his size bigger or less, pretty near that of a fine horse; but he is very slender about the loins, somewhat like the ape.

The Indians, according to the ancients, had even the art of taming the lion, and making him hunt like a dog, or to draw like a horse. His strength, his courage, and majesty have occasioned him to be called the king of beasts: and indeed he uses them as a demesne appertaining to him, having no other food. All of them respect him; all tremble before him; " but I know not by what instinct, says Ælian, he himself trembles before the cock and the elephant." He never attacks a man, says Pliny, but when old age prevents his overtaking other prey. It is then he draws near to cities, devouring those he finds in the fields. Sometimes the sense of his weakness incites him to join with
others,

others, to afford each mutual aid; and this union becomes so much the more dangerous, that one cannot be attacked without engaging the rest which are in full strength. At other times he is not daunted at the most formidable hunter, whom he views with confidence and fierceness. He receives his first attack; he beats the ground with his tail, lashing his sides, and thus by degrees kindles that fury which has no example, and to which the most violent transports of passion may be compared. As there are always many engaged against him, he examines with attention from what hand those arrows are sent which wound him, whom he distinguishes from those who only flourish their weapons, or miss him. He fixes chiefly on those who have struck him; and if he can lay hold of them, tears them in pieces; but his vengeance is satisfied with overturning the others, and tossing them about. The lioness is not so distinguishing in her fury: as sensible to the loss of her young as to her own wounds, she, with her head to the ground, her eyes fixed upon those who would ravish them from her, never fails to save them, or to perish in their defence. That which Ælian and other naturalists relate of the fertility of this animal is peculiar to itself. They say she brings forth but five times; the first time she has five young ones; the second four; the third time three; the fourth no more than two; and the last time only one. Sometimes she couples with the leopard, and they distinguish the lions that proceed from thence, by their not having so fine a mane as those of the genuine species. Both the one and the other are much afraid of fire: some of them are white and some tawny.

THE leopard and panther, according to Pliny, Ælian, and others, are the male and female of the same species. Although this creature is not so large as the lion, he is not less cruel and dangerous when attacked; but seldom invades man first; yet the Indians despise his fury, and know how to profit by it. They hunt him among other wild beasts; they eat his flesh, and preserve his young ones. When they have tamed and familiarised them, they present them to the king, or keep them to make use of them in hunting. The leopard is naturally adapted to it, and carries that about him which attracts his prey. So sweet an odor exhales from his body, that the roe-bucks and does are charmed with it, and approach him without knowing their danger: but as the sight of his head terrifies them, and as they betake themselves to flight the instant they perceive it, he has the cunning to conceal it under the leaves of trees, and makes not the least motion till they are so near, that he can unexpectedly spring upon them. This kind of hunting is still in use among the Indians; though permitted to none but the king.

It is pretended, that while the panther has young, the leopard dares not defend himself against her, although much the stronger, and that she makes him suffer every kind of abuse. Because this animal loves wine, says Appian, the ancients have looked upon it as a symbol and attendant of Bacchus.

All these animals are as frequent in Arabia and Lybia as in the Indies: but it is here chiefly that the tyger is found, whose very name recals the idea of fierceness. In order to take them, the shepherds or hunters watch the moment when the mother is gone to seek food for her young, and carry them off. But when she returns, and finds them not, she becomes furious; she traces them by the smell, and runs with incredible swiftness till she has

has overtaken the Indians, who fly before her on the fleeteſt horſes. When ſhe comes near, they drop one of her young, which ſhe takes between her teeth and carries back to her den : the hope of recovering the reſt in the ſame manner, inſpires her with ardor, and cauſes her to return with greater alacrity. But the hunters have boats prepared on the banks of a river, and thus eſcape her fury. They tame the young ones, and make the ſame uſe of them as thoſe of the panther.

It were almoſt needleſs to ſpeak of the ape, unleſs it were to take notice, that he has his origin chiefly from the Indies. They are ſeen in that country of all colours and of all kinds; grey, red, white and black; and ſome have been brought into Europe larger than an ordinary dog, whoſe faces were of a perfect azure color.

Their attachment to one another is perhaps without example, among other animals; and we may judge of it by a ſingular inſtance which Tavernier relates. " Returning from Agra with the Engliſh preſident, who was going to Surat, about four or five leagues from Amenabad, we paſſed thro' a little foreſt of the trees called Mangoes. We ſaw a good number of large apes, male and female, many of the laſt holding their young ones between their arms. We were each of us in our chariot, and the Engliſh preſident ſtopt to tell me, that he had a fine fowling-piece; and knowing that I was a good markſman, begged of me to try it on one of thoſe animals. One of my ſervants, who was of the country, having made me a ſign not to hazard it, I endeavored to diſſuade the preſident from his deſign. But in ſpite of all I could ſay, he ſhot and killed a female ape, which hung among the branches, letting her young ones fall to the ground. What my ſervant had foreſeen came to paſs immediately,

mediately, all the apes who were on the trees, to the number of more than sixty, descended immediately in a fury, and fell upon the president's coach, whom they would have strangled, had it not been for the ready assistance afforded him by shutting the doors, and setting all our domestics to drive them away; although they came not near me yet I was afraid of the fury of these animals, who were strong and large: they pursued the president's coach near a league, so much were they enraged."

Mr. Eyre, who was chief of Patna in 1750, met with a similar accident, as he was going through a wood near the Ganges, with a guard, and many others in company. They saw a great number of large apes among the trees, chattering and making a loud and menacing noise: one of the soldiers fired and killed a large ape; upon which some apes ran and lamented over it, while others advanced, as if they would attack the destroyers; but another fire made them disperse.

CHAP.

CHAP. V.

A description of the country of TRANQUEBAR. *Of the coins, money of accompt, weights, and measures of* INDIA. *With a list of our* EAST-INDIA *company's present forts and factories.*

NOTWITHSTANDING the simplicity and rudeness of their tools, the Malabarians are very good mechanics, as may be seen by their fine painted chints. Here a joiner is likewise a carpenter and turner, and in all these trades he only uses a kind of a very imperfect hatchet, a wimble, hammer and plane. As there are no European mechanics in the colonies, the natives do all the work, and much cheaper than the Europeans could do it.

THEY have their sciences, as well as we; and will not be persuaded they were ever known to the Europeans. They are great admirers of physic, so that the Romish catechists have a general passport, by applying themselves to this science; and such has been their success, that the late Mr. Grundler has given us an entire system of it; and in a great measure we owe to their labours the magnificent garden of Malabar, a description of which is published by M. de Rheeden; a work no less remarkable for the exactness of the figures drawn by the natives, than for the number of the plates.

THEIR physic consists in the knowledge of their plants, and how to use them in prescriptions, which their physicians learn by observation, or have transmitted to them by their ancestors. Yet they do not neglect cultivating chymistry; for they use several calcined stones, or powders; and they even give into alchymy. And their fondness for it it is furprifing, confidering that fuel is very fcarce, and that cow-dung cannot produce that degree of heat neceffary for the fufion of metals. Their phyficians are not in fo great efteem as thofe of the miffion. The great people in the Indies never fail, when they can have an European phyfician, to prefer him to their own; even the Mogul employed a furgeon, who came to Dehli in the retinue of an envoy, from the Englifh Eaft-India company.

These people compofe verfes; at leaft the miffionaries call fuch as make them poets; but the Danifh miffionary could not find a rhyme or meafure in the fpecimens publifhed in the Tranquebar relations; for their language does not feem adapted to poetry: they themfelves affirm that it is copious, clear, regular, and formed upon confiftent, and even upon eafy rules. They are fond of the repetitions of Patta, and Kappa, which feem difagreeable to Europeans; and their words, efpecially thofe called poetical, are of a length unknown in other languages.

The ftudy of the fciences is not fo common among the Malabarians. Scarcely one in ten thoufand can read and write his own language with accuracy; this being a hard ftudy, requiring fix years application, and the pronounciation very difficult. M. Ziegenbalg, whom the moft learned Pandarams admired for the purity with which he fpoke their language, has left to his fucceffors a great number of faults to be corrected. He wrote d for t, and tch where it ought to be ch, or f. There are two letters in particular, that can hardly be decyphered to foreigners; the one which M. Ziegenbalg wrote rh, is pronounced almoft as rch or even ch: but Europeans pronounce it as an l. For inftance, Piliacatta, inftead of Parhejakadhu;

kadhu; the other is expreſſed by dh, and is rather an r: the ſame river being written Collarum, by M. la Croze, and Collodham by Mr. Ziegenbalg.

Their knowledge of phyſics is very groſs, as appears from their anatomy laid down in the Wedam, which is altogether in manner of the Egyptians. Bruhma reſides in the brain; Pulejar in the arteries of the hip; Wirchtnou about the navel, and Ruttiren about the heart. They reckon a great number of metals; but they have not learned the art to ſeparate heterogeneous ſubſtances, which are not malleable. They have two very ſingular metals; one the genuine Tambac, a kind of copper preferred even to gold; the other a founding metal, confiſting of two parts of tin, and eight parts of copper, of which they make their kitchen utenſils. Their hiſtory goes back an incredible number of years. In fabulous hiſtory they are well verſed; but their knowledge is very deficient as to modern and true hiſtory; it hardly reaches to the beginning of the ſeventeenth century, as no author among them has taken the pains to leave to poſterity a true account of his own times. They tell us of Darma, Choren, Pandijen, and other kings, who were before the æra of the world; but they know not the names of thoſe princes who reigned three centuries ago.

The Malabarians pretend they have profeſſors who teach ethics, logic, rhetoric, geography, politics, mathematics, muſic and geometry; at leaſt they have names for all theſe ſciences: however, their profeſſors make but a poor figure, if we may judge by the wretched ſpecimens in their Wedam, or ſacred books. They do not ſucceed but in ſuch ſciences as depend ſolely on the laws of nature, implanted in the minds of all nations.

Of the coins, monies of accompt, weights, and measures of India.

1. COINS. The principal, and those most generally current on the continent of India, and its islands, are the pagoda, rupee, and fanam, both of gold and silver. They have also several little pieces of copper money, among which is the peca or pice.

AT Surat, 16 pices make the ana of $7\frac{1}{2}$ d. sterling; and 4 anas make a rupee of 2s. 6d. sterling.

AT Bombay, 72 pices make the rupee of 2s. 6d. sterling.

AT Goa, the xeraphim is worth 240 Portugal reas, or about 16 d. sterling; 2 reas make a basaraco, 15 basaracos a vintin, 42 vintins a tangus, 4 tangus a paru, $2\frac{1}{2}$ parues a pagoda of gold, or between 3 and 4 l. sterling.

AT Carwar, 6 pices make the juttal, and 48 juttals a pagoda.

AT Tellicherry and Calicut, 16 visims make a fanam, $4\frac{1}{2}$ fanams of Calicut, and 5 of Tellicherry, make a rupee of 2s. 6d. sterling.

AT Anjengo, and other parts of the Malabar coast, 16 visims make a fanam, and $5\frac{3}{4}$ fanams make a rupee of 2s. 6d. sterling.

AT Madrafs, and other parts of the coast of Coromandel, 80 casches make a fanam, or 3d. sterling; and 36 fanams a silver pagoda, or 7s. 8d. sterling.

IN Bengal, 12 pices make the ana, or $1\frac{7}{8}$ d. sterling; and 16 anas the rupee of 2s. 6d. sterling.

AT Bencoolen, in the island of Sumatra, a settalee is worth $7\frac{1}{2}$d. sterling; 2 settalees make 1 socoo, or 1s. 3d. sterling; and 4 socoos make 1 real, or 5s. sterling.

THE EAST-INDIES. 283

But there are three kinds of silver rupees current in India: the rupees siccas worth 2s. 11d. sterling at Bengal; the rupees of Surat, worth 2s. 3d. sterling; and the rupees of Madrafs, worth 2s. 6d. sterling: which is to be understood of the new rupees, as the old ones of each kind are less in value; those of Madrafs being but 1s. 11d. sterling, those of Surat 2s. and the siccas 2s. 4d.

2. Monies of accompt. At Surat, Agra, and some other cities of the Great Mogul, they use lacks or lacres; implying a hundred thousand: thus a lack of rupees is one hundred thousand rupees.

Throughout Malabar, and at Goa, they use tangas, vintins, and pardos xeraphin. The tanga is of two kinds, good and bad alloy: hence their custom is to count by good or bad money; the tanga of good alloy being 1-5th better than the bad; so that 4 tangas good being allowed the pardos xeraphin, there will be required 5 of the bad; 4 vintins good make a tanga likewise good; 15 baruccos a vintin; the good barucco equal to a Portuguese ree, or 1-13th of a penny sterling.

3. Weights. At Agra, their weights for gold, silver, musks, civets, and other valuable articles, are called the troll, which is 12 masses; and the mass contains 40lb. For other commodities their common weight is the seer, which varies in several parts of Indostan: in Agra it is of two kinds, the one 26 pices, which is $26\frac{1}{3}$ ounces; and the other is 30 pices. They have also hundred weights called maunds, 14 seers to a maund, being 33lb. English: the maund weighs 69lb. avoirdupois; but the maund they weigh their indicos with is only 53lb.

At Goa, their weight for spices is the Bahar; it weighs $3\frac{1}{2}$ quintals Portugal weight. Their
other

other weights for sugar, honey, &c. is the maund of 14 lb.

At Bombay, 15 pice is one seer; 40 seers is 1 maund, or 28 lb. 20 maunds is 1 candy, and 1 pucca maund is $74\frac{2}{3}$ lb.

At Surat, 40 seer is 1 maund, or $37\frac{1}{3}$ lb. and 20 maund, is 1 candy, or $6\frac{2}{3}$ C.

At Anjengo, 80 pullums is 1 telong, or 16 lb; and 35 telongs is 1 candy, or 560 lb.

At Callicut and Tellicherry, 20 maunds of $29\frac{3}{4}$ lb. is 1 candy.

At Carwar, 25 pice is 1 seer, 40 seers is 1 maund, or $25\frac{3}{4}$ lb. and 20 maunds is 1 candy, or 515 lb.

Along the coast of Coromandel, 20 maunds is 1 candy, or 500 lb. English, and a maund is 40 seers of 22 maces, or 25 lb. English. But at Madrass, 25 lb. is 1 maund, and 20 maunds is 1 candy, or 500 lb.

In Bengal, 20 pice is 1 seer, 40 seers is 1 maund of 75 lb. 20 maunds of 25 lb. each, 1 candy, 80 couries 1 pun, and 16 pun 1 cahaun.

At Bencoolen, a bahar is 560 lb.

4. Measures. At Surat, the covid for silk and linen is 1 yard English.

At Bombay, 5 pecks is a parah, and 25 parahs a morah of uncertain measure.

At Madrass, 3 pints make a measure, 8 measures a mereal, 5 mereals a parac, and 80 paracs a grise of uncertain measure; but 1 gorge is 20 pices, and a covid $\frac{1}{2}$ a yard.

At Bengal, the covid is the same as at Surat and Madrass.

At Bencoolen, 1 bamboo is an English gallon.

The list of the English company's forts and factories.

In the viceroyalty of Bengal, to which are, or ought to be subject, the provinces of Bengal, Bahar, and Orixa: Fort

THE EAST-INDIES.   285

FORT WILLIAM, in the city of Calcutta. Is the prefidency, or chief fettlement of the company, in the viceroyalty, and ftands upon the eaft fide of the right branch of the river Ganges.

MOORSHEDABAD, or Muxadabad, is the ufual refidence of the viceroy, or Subah, fituated between the two branches of the Ganges, about 60 miles below, where the river divides itfelf into two branches.

PATNA. The chief market for faltpetre, ftands upon the fame river, about 150 miles above where it divides itfelf.

DACCA, or Daka. Stands upon the eaft fide of the left branch of the faid river, about 60 miles above its mouth, or influx into the bay of Bengal.

LUCKIPORE, or Juckidore. An inland factory in Bengal.

BULRAMGURRY, or Balafor. In Orixa, near the mouth of the river Ganga, a famous road, where fhips bound up the Ganges ufually take in their pilots.

NEGRAIS. A little ifland, near Negrais Point, on the coaft of the kingdom of Pegu, and eaft fide of the bay of Bengal, under the faid prefidency at Fort William.

IN the viceroyalty of the Deckan, to which are, or ought to be fubject, the provinces of Golconda, the Carnatic, Malabar, and, in fhort, the greateft part of the large peninfula, lying between the two famous rivers, Ganges and Indus.

AND, Firft, upon the eaft fide of the faid peninfula, commonly called the coaft of Coromandel, all under the direction of the prefidency at Madrafs:

VISAGAPATNAM. Upon the faid coaft, and on the frontier between Golconda and Orixa.

MASULIPATNAM. A city upon the fame coaft, farther fouth.

FORT

FORT ST. GEORGE, in the city of Madrafs. Is the prefidency upon the fame coaft.

ARCOT. An inland city, weft of Madrafs.

WANDIVASH. An inland place, fouth of Arcot.

CARANGOLY. A coaft town.

ALAMPARVA. A coaft town, about 60 miles fouth of Madrafs.

PERMACOIL, or Perumal. An inland city, well fortified in the Indian manner, weft of the former.

FORT St. David's, demolifhed by the French.

DAVECOTAH. A coaft town, fouth of St. David's.

CARICAL. A French fettlement reduced by us.

SECONDLY, Upon the weft fide of the faid peninfula, commonly called the Malabar coaft, all under the direction of the prefidency of Bombay:

ANJENGO. About 35 miles north of Cape Comorin, at the fouth end of the faid peninfula.

TELLICHERRY. Near 200 miles north of the former, and a little to the north of Calicut.

ONOR. About the fame diftance north of Calicut.

CARWAR. About 40 miles fouth of Goa, the Portuguefe chief fettlement.

BOMBAY. An ifland upon the northern part of this coaft, ftrongly fortified, and wholly poffeffed by us.

SCINDY, or Tatta. Near the mouth of the Indus, called Sindi, by the natives.

IN the large ifland of Sumatra. Fort Marlborough, upon the fouth-weft coaft, and near the fouth-eaft end of the ifland; a prefidency under whofe direction are all the factories on this ifland, but the fort was lately demolifhed, and the factory plundered, by the French.

MOCCOMOGO. Upon the fame coaft, about 100 miles to the north-weft of the former.

THE EAST-INDIES. 287

NATTAL, Tapanooly. Both upon the fame coaft, but further to the north-weft.

UPON the fouth coaft of China. Canton. Is, at prefent, the only port of China frequented by European fhips.

GOMBROON. At the mouth of the gulph of Baffora, in Perfia.

MOCHO. On the Red Sea, in Arabia, near the Strait of Babelmandel.

ST. HELENA. An ifland, in the middle of the Ethiopian fea, and many leagues from any land, ftrongly fortified, and wholly poffeffed by us.

CHAP. VI.

Of the principal COMPANIES *in* EUROPE *trading to* INDIA.

THE trade to the Eaft Indies was long carried on by the Ifraelites through the Red Sea and the Streights of Babelmandel, not only to the coafts of Africa on the weft; but alfo to thofe of Arabia, Perfia, and India on the Eaft; who reaped a prodigious profit thereby. King David was the firft who begun it; for having conquered the kingdom of Edom, and reduced it to be a province of his empire, he thereby became mafter of two feaport towns on the Red Sea, Elath, and Eziongeber, which then belonged to that kingdom; and feeing the advantage that might be made of thefe two places, he wifely took the benefit of it, and there begun this traffic. After David, Solomon carried on the fame commerce to Ophir, and had from thence, in one voyage, four hundred and fifty talents of gold. But the ufe of the compafs being

then

then unknown, the way of navigation was in thofe times only by coafting, whereby a voyage was frequently of three years, which now may be finifhed almoft in three months. However, this trade fo far fucceeded, and grew to fo high a pitch under Solomon, that thereby he drew to thefe two ports, and from thence to Jerufalem, all the trade of Africa, Arabia, Perfia, and India, which was the chief fountain of thofe immenfe riches he acquired, and whereby he exceeded all the kings of the earth in his time, as much as by his wifdom: but at length, the whole of this trade was engroffed by the Tyrians; who managing it from the fame port, made it by the way of Rhinocorura, a feaport, lying between the confines of Egypt and Paleftine; fo that it centered all at Tyre; from whence all the weftern parts of the world were furnifhed with the wares of India, Africa, Perfia, and Arabia, which thus, by the way of the Red Sea, the Tyrians traded to; who hereby exceedingly enriched themfelves during the Perfian empire, under the favor and protection of whofe kings they had the full poffeffion of this trade. But when the Ptolemies prevailed in Egypt, they, by building Bernice, Myos-Hermos, and other places on the Egyptian or weftern fea, and by fending forth fleets from thence to all thofe countries to which the Tyrians traded, foon drew all this trade into that kingdom, and there fixed the chief mart of it at Alexandria, which was thereby made the greateft mart in all the world; where it continued for a great many years after; all the marine traffic which the weftern parts of the world had with Perfia, India, Arabia, and to the eaftern coaft of Africa, being wholly carried on through the Red Sea, and the mouth of the Nile, until a way was found, about 280 years fince, of

failing

failing to thofe parts by the way of the Cape of Good Hope : after which the Portuguefe managed this trade; but now it is in a manner wholly got into the hands of the Englifh, French and Dutch.

THE ENGLISH EAST INDIA COMPANY. The united company of merchants of England trading to the Eaft-Indies, is the moft confiderable and florifhing company of trade in Great-Britain, and perhaps in Europe, for riches, power, and extenfive privileges ; as appears by the many fhips of burthen which they conftantly employ; the very advantageous fettlements they have abroad; their large ftorehoufes and fales of goods and merchandizes at home; and the particular laws and ftatutes made in their favor.

THIS company was originally formed in the laft years of queen Elizabeth, who granted letters patent to the London merchants, that entered into an affociation for carrying on this trade ; and the charter which fhe granted them in 1599, has ferved as a model for all thofe the company has obtained from her royal fucceffors.

THE Portuguefe and Dutch were in poffeffion of feveral large territories along the coafts of India, before this time ; as alfo in feveral other parts of Afia, proper for the profecution of this trade. The former, indeed, had no company, which is ftill the cafe : but the latter had formed feveral companies fo early as the year 1596, which were afterwards incorporated together.

THE firft fleet the Englifh fent to the Eaft-Indies confifted of four fhips, which fet fail in 1600, with Mr. John Mildenhal, who was employed as an agent to procure a trade, and carried a letter from queen Elizabeth to the Great Mogul, in behalf of her fubjects : which fhips returned fo richly laden, that in a few years near twenty others were fent there by the company.

AFTER the death of queen Elizabeth, king James the Firſt confirmed and augmented, by a new charter, all the privileges that had been granted the company in the preceding reign: and, to ſhew how much he had at heart this eſtabliſhment, he ſent ambaſſadors in 1608 and 1615 to the Mogul, the emperor of Japan, the king of Perſia, and ſeveral other eaſtern princes, to conclude, in his name and that of the company, different treaties of commerce, of which ſome are ſtill ſubſiſting.

It is well known how many privileges the king of Perſia granted the Engliſh company, for aſſiſting him in the expulſion of the Portugueſe from Ormus; who made uſe of that famous iſland, and its almoſt impregnable forts, as a citadel, to ſupport them in the uſurpation of the commerce of the Perſian Gulph, which they engroſſed for almoſt an age to themſelves.

The company's charter was renewed by king Charles the Second in 1662, whereby that monarch granted them abundance of privileges they had not before enjoyed; which charter is properly the baſis of the company, and was afterwards confirmed by king James the Second: however, there were charters of king Charles the Second, whereby the company were granted ſome new privileges.

The firſt was dated the 3d of April 1662, containing a confirmation of the former charters; or, it is rather a new one, which attributes to the company ſeveral rights it had not as yet enjoyed; and adds to, or ſets forth in a proper light, almoſt all thoſe granted to it by the charters of Elizabeth and James the Firſt, which will be more amply ſpoken of in the ſequel; becauſe it is properly the baſis of all the commerce of this company; and becauſe upon this charter are founded all the privileges

THE EAST-INDIES. 291

leges and policy of the company established in 1698.

THE second charter granted by Charles the Second, was dated the 27th of March 1669, whereby his Majesty made a cession to the company of the island of Bombay, with all its royalties, revenues, rents, castles, ships, fortifications, and enfranchisements: such as then belonged to him by the cession of his Portuguese Majesty, reserving only to himself the sovereignty, to be held in fee from the royal hospital of Greenwich, in the county of Kent; and for all duty, rent, or service, the sum of 10l. sterling in gold, payable yearly on the 30th of September, at the custom-house of London.

BY the third charter, of the 16th of December 1674, the king likewise made a cession to the company of the island of St. Helena, as belonging to him by right of conquest. This island, which afterwards served as a staple to the company's shipping, was discovered by the Portuguese in their first navigations to the East Indies by the Cape of Good Hope; but having abandoned it, the island was possessed by the Dutch; who quitted it in their turn to establish themselves at the Cape of Good Hope, and were succeeded by the English, who were expelled in 1672 by the Dutch company: but captain Monday, who commanded a British squadron, retook it the year following; and this was the right of conquest that Charles the Second made a cession of to the company by the charter of 1674. The fourth charter the company obtained from this monarch orders the erection of a court of judicature, composed of a civilian and two merchants, in all the factories and places possessed throughout the extent of its concession, to judge of all cases in seizures, and contestations, with regard to ships or goods going to the Indies, con-

U 2 trary

trary to the exclusive privilege granted by the letters-patent of 1662; as also to take cognizance of all causes regarding merchandise, marine, navigation, purchases, sales, exchange, insurance, letters of exchange, and other things; even of all crimes and misdemeanors committed at sea, or in the countries, states and territories belonging to the company; the whole, notwithstanding, pursuant to the usages and customs of merchants, and the laws of England.

These four charters were afterwards confirmed by James the Second, by a charter granted in the first year of his reign: but the charter of 1662 was the principal, and consisted of 28 articles, whereof the most material are as follow.

By the first his majesty erects the company into a corporation, or body politic, under the denomination of the governor and company of merchants trading to the East-Indies.

The third grants it a common seal to serve in all its expeditions; with a power of breaking and changing it at pleasure, and of making and engraving a new one.

The fourth establishes a governor, and 24 assistants, chose out of the proprietors, or stock-holders, of the company, to have the direction of affairs, and to give all necessary orders with regard to the freighting and sending away of ships, together with all particulars belonging to the commerce carried on throughout the extent of its concession.

The fifth, sixth, seventh, eighth, and ninth, nominate, for the first time, the governor and directors; and regulate for the future, the form to be observed in the election of the said governor and directors, and a deputy-governor, or sub-governor, to preside in the absence, or in case of the governor's death. They also ordain before
whom

THE EAST-INDIES. 293

whom the elected shall be obliged to make oath, and what this oath is to be; lastly, they fix the time that all these officers are to continue in their post; and when the general courts of the company are to be held.

THE tenth article fixes the extent of the concession, and allows all those that shall be of the company, their sons of one and twenty years of age, their apprentices, factors, and domestics, to trade and negotiate freely by sea in all the routes and passages already discovered, or that shall be so hereafter, in Asia, Africa, and America, beyond the Cape of Good Hope, as far as the streights of Magellan; and where any commerce can be exercised, so that it is before-hand concluded on by the company; and so that also the said commerce is not carried on in the places already possessed by the subjects of some other prince.

THE eleventh article empowers the company to enact all the laws and regulations it shall judge proper, to be observed by its factors, captains, masters of ships, and other officers in its service; to revoke them and make new ones; and, in case of contravention with regard to the said laws, to ordain for offenders such penalties, fines and punishments, as it shall judge to be just and reasonable, without being accountable to any one whatsoever, not even to his majesty's officers; provided that the said laws, and regulations, are not contrary to those in England.

BY the twelfth, his majesty wills, that for all the duties and customs, on goods coming from the East Indies in the company's ships, a whole year shall be allowed for their intire payment; that is, six months for the first moiety, and six months for the other, by giving notwithstanding a sufficient security; which shall hold good also for the

goods

goods exported from England for the East Indies, which goods shall pay no duty, if lost, before their arrival at the place of their destination; and, in case any duties are paid, a restitution shall be made, on the company making affidavit before the Lord High Treasurer of the kingdom, of the amount of the said loss; provided that if the goods imported be exported again in the space of 13 months, no duties shall be paid for such export, if it be done aboard British vessels.

THE thirteenth article allows the exportation of foreign specie out of the kingdom, to be employed in the commerce of the company; and even those of England coined in the Tower of London, provided that the total sum exceeds not 50,000 l. sterling in each year.

BY the fourteenth and fifteenth the company is allowed to have six large vessels, and six pinks, laden and equipped with all kinds of ammunition and provision, together with 500 good English sailors, to support its commerce throughout the whole extent of its concession; whereon his majesty cannot lay an imbargo upon any pretext whatsoever, unless he cannot absolutely do without the said vessels in some pressing and unforeseen want in time of war to augment his fleet.

THE sixteenth grants to the company an exclusive privilege of trade to the Indies, ordaining the seizure and confiscation of vessels and goods, which the other subjects of his Britannic majesty might send there; the imprisonment of the captains and masters of ships who brought them there; and lastly, a security of 1000 l. sterling of going no more within the limits of the company's concession, in contravention to this article.

THE nineteenth obliges the company to bring back into England at least as much gold and silver, as carried out every year; and assigns the
ports

THE EAST-INDIES. 295

ports of London, Dartmouth, and Plymouth, as the only places in the kingdom, from which it fhall be for the future allowed to export the fpecie it fhall have occafion for in its traffic, which fpecie of gold and filver fhall be entered in the faid ports, either going out or coming in; though without paying any duties.

By the twentieth, the cuftom-houfe officers are enjoined not to fuffer the entrance of any goods coming from the places within the extent of the company's conceffion, unlefs by a permit in writing.

THE twenty-firft fixes the fum in the capital ftock neceffary to have a vote in the meetings at 500 l. fterling, empowering notwithftanding thofe who fhall fubfcribe a lefs fum to join feverally together for the forming of one vote.

THE twenty-fourth article allows the company to fend fhips of war, and foldiers; to build caftles and forts in all the places of its conceffion; to make peace or war with all kinds of people that are not Chriftians; and to obtain fatisfaction by the force of arms from all thofe who prejudice them, or interrupt their commerce.

AND the twenty-fixth empowers it likewife to arreft and fecure all the fubjects of his Britannic majefty, who fhall trade in Indian or Englifh veffels, or who fhall dwell in any of the places of its conceffion, without a fpecial licence from the faid company.

AFTER the publication of this charter, the parliament feemed to diflike the exclufive privilege granted by the fixteenth article; which was no novelty, for it had been already agitated in the reign of James the Firft; but this prince, fearing to rifque his authority, chofe rather to repeal a like privilege, which he granted to the colonies of Virginia, than to uphold the royal prerogative.

U 4 THE

The shares, or subscriptions, of the company, were originally only of 50 l. sterling, but, the directors having a considerable dividend to make in 1676, it was agreed to join the profit to the original, instead of withdrawing it; whereby the shares were doubled, and became of 100 l. sterling. The first capital was only 369,891 l. 5 s. which, being thus doubled, amounted to 739,782 l. 10 s. to which, if 963,639 l. the profits of the company to the year 1685, be added, the whole stock will be 1,703,422 l.

The company, having sustained several losses by the Dutch and the subjects of the Great Mogul, began to be in a declining way at the Revolution; when the war with France put it into so desperate a condition, that appearing scarce possible to be supported, a new one was erected.

The rise of this new company was occasioned by the great case of the old company being taken into consideration by the parliament; which case had been depending several years; and because of its intricacy, had been first referred by the parliament to the king, and by him back to the parliament again, in the year 1698; when the old company offered to advance 700,000 l. at 4 per cent. for the service of the government, in case the trade to India might be settled on them exclusive of all others; and the parliament seemed inclined to embrace their proposal. But another number of merchants, of whom Mr. Shepherd was the chief, and who were supported by Mr. Montague, chancellor of the Exchequer, proposed to the house of commons to raise two millions at eight per cent. upon condition the trade to India might be settled on the subscribers exclusive of all others: they also proposed, that these subscribers should not be obliged to trade in a joint stock; but

but if any members of them fhould afterwards defire to be incorporated, a charter fhould be granted to them for that purpofe. The houfe judged this new overture not only to be more advantageous to the government, but alfo very likely to fettle this controverted trade on a better foundation than it was on before; a bill was, therefore, brought in for fettling the trade to the Eaft-Indies, according to thefe limitations, and fome further refolutions.

THE old Eaft-India company prefented a petition againft this bill; which, notwithftanding, was paffed in favor of the new company, who obtained a charter of incorporation, dated Sept. 5, 1698, by the name of " The general fociety intitled to the advantages given by an act of parliament, for advancing a fum not exceeding two millions for the fervice of the crown of England " Whereby the fum total of all the fubfcriptions was made the principal ftock of the corporation; and the new company was invefted with the fame privileges as were granted to the old company, by the charter of king Charles the Second. However, the old company was, by the act indulged with leave to trade to the Indies until Michaelmas, 1701.

THE fund of this new company became fo confiderable, and fubfcriptions were carried on with fuch facility, that, in lefs than two years, the company put to fea forty fhips equipped for its trade; which was double the number employed by the old company in the moft florifhing times of its commerce; and it fent annually a million fterling in fpecie to the Indies; whereas the old company had never fent above 500,000 l.

THE two companies fubfifted a few years in a feparate ftate; when, having a due regard to their common interefts, and for the prevention of feve-

ral

ral inconveniencies that might otherwife have happened, both to themfelves and the nation in general, they agreed upon feveral articles for the union of the faid companies.

ACCORDINGLY, in the year 1702, a new charter of union was granted the two companies by queen Anne, under the name of, " The united company of merchants trading to the Eaft-Indies," which was effentially the fame with thofe of king Charles, and king William; becaufe, by the union of the two companies, they have adopted all the regulations made for the government of the old company: fo that the united company fhould rather be deemed the old company continued, than a corporation erected upon a different eftablifhment. Which charter being fince expired, another charter, with new powers, was granted them in 1730; and, in the 17th year of king George the Second, was continued until the 25th of March, 1780; when, on three years notice, and repayment of the capital ftock borrowed by the government and the annuities, the company's right to the fole and exclufive trade to the Eaft-Indies is to ceafe and determine.

To the 2,000,000 l. advanced by the new company to William the Third, the united company, in the fixth year of queen Anne, lent the government 1,200,000 l. more; which made their whole loan amount to 3,200,000 l; being, what may properly be called, the capital ftock of the company: the firft loan of two millions was fecured by the government out of the duties upon falt; and the additional ftamp duties granted in the 9th and 10th years of William the Third, chargeable with the payment of 160,000 l. as an yearly fund for paying the intereft at 8 l. per cent. but, by the act of the 3d of George the Second, this annuity of
160,000 l.

160,000 l. was reduced to 128,000l. and tranſferred as a charge upon the aggregate fund; and in 1749, it was reduced to 3l. ½ per cent. until Chriſtmas 1757, and after that to 3l. per cent. But beſides this 3,200,000l. there is a million more due by the public to this company, being lent by them at 3l. per cent. in the ſaid 17th year of his late majeſty.

FOR the œconomy and policy of the united company, all perſons, without exception, are admitted members of it, natives and foreigners, men and women; with this circumſtance, that 500 l. in the ſtock of the company gives the owner a vote in the general courts, and 2000l. qualifies him to be choſen a director. The directors are 24 in number, including the chairman and deputy chairman, who may be re-elected for four years ſucceſſively. They have a ſalary of 150l. a year, and the chairman of 200l. The meetings, or courts of directors, are to be held at leaſt once a week; but are commonly oftener, being ſummoned as occaſions require.

OUT of the body of directors are choſen divers committees, who have the peculiar inſpection of certain branches of the company's buſineſs; as the committee of correſpondence, committee of buying, committee of treaſury, committee of warehouſes, committee of ſhipping, committee of accompts, committee of private trade, committee of houſe, and committee to prevent the growth of private trade.

THIS company is not only granted an excluſive privilege of trade to the Indies, and other extraordinary conceſſions from the government, by the charter; but there are alſo ſeveral acts of parliment made in its behalf, whereby all the Britiſh ſubjects are reſtrained from going to the Eaſt-Indies;

or

or from procuring, or acting under, any foreign commission, for failing to, or trading there; or from subscribing to, or promoting, any foreign company, for trading there, under severe penalties; though, upon the whole, this trade is monopolized by the company, and is generally esteemed highly injurious to the British navigation, as all monopolies are to that of every trading country. This is evident from the behavior of the parliament in the reign of Charles the Second, who, was more resolute, or more happy, than his grandfather; so that the question was debated in the court of common pleas, where it was decided in favor of the king.

I shall conclude my account of this company, with observing, that this, as well as every company which is designed for building forts and making settlements in foreign countries, should have been at first incorporated for ever; because it is not to be expected, that a corporation will be at any great expence in building forts or making settlements, when they are in danger of their corporation's being dissolved, before they can reap any benefit from the expence they have been at. This was foreseen by the administration at the end of queen Anne's reign; therefore they established the South-Sea company for ever, though they went a little too far in giving that company a perpetual exclusive privilege; for though this may be necessary at first, it ought never to be made perpetual. From an act made in the following session relating to the East-India company, it would seem, that there was then likewise a design to have established that company for ever; but how that design came to be laid aside does not appear; for had it been carried into execution, the French, in the last war, would not probably

bably have found it so easy to make themselves masters of Madrass: at least, if they had, the managers for the company would have been much more to blame.

CHAP. VII.

Of the other EUROPEAN *companies trading to the* EAST-INDIES. *The* DUTCH *East-India company. The* FRENCH *East-India company.* DANISH *East-India company.* OSTEND *East-India company. East-India company of* SWEDEN. EMBDEN *East-India, or* PRUSSIAN ASIATIC *company.*

REMARKS.

THE Portuguese first sailed round the Cape of Good Hope to the East-Indies, in the year 1498; and the first settlement they made on the continent of India was at Cochin, on the coast of Malabar, in the year 1502. The English and Dutch did not attempt to trade to India till about the year 1600, and then only to the islands at first; though it is true, several of their commanders had, before that time, been sent out upon discoveries, and sailed round the globe, through the streights of Magellan, particularly Sir Francis Drake in the year 1586, and Oliver Noort in 1598. Besides, in the year 1595, the province of Holland fitted out four ships for discovery, which sailed to Bantam, in the island of Java, and brought back with them such samples of the goods of the east, as induced the United Provinces to erect one general company for that trade, in the year 1594; but the Portuguese had, for 100 years, engrossed all the rich

rich trade of India to themselves, except that the Spaniards had a little interrupted their commerce, in the Moluccas and the Philippines, on their discovering a passage to the Indies through the South-Sea, in the year 1520; though, when the other European powers became sensible of the value and facility of this commerce, they soon began to participate the emoluments, by erecting the following companies.

The Dutch East-India company commenced in 1594, in the midst of those military confusions attendant on the revolt of the United Provinces from the allegiance of Spain. The Spaniards having shut up all their ports against these new republicans, whom they looked upon as rebels, and having even prohibited them all commerce to the East and West-Indies, of which they were then, in some sense, the masters; necessity inspired some Zealanders to go in quest of a new passage for China and the East-Indies by the N. E. and to coast, if possible, along Norway, Muscovy, and Tartary.

This enterprise was undertaken in 1594, 1595, and 1596, by fitting out ships three different times, but all without any success; the extreme colds of Nova Zembla, and the impenetrable ice of Weigats, having either destroyed the ships sent there, or discouraged the adventurers.

Whilst this passage was unsuccessfully attempting, a second company was formed at Amsterdam; which, under the direction of Cornelius Houteman, sent four ships, in 1595, by the usual way which the Portuguese went, with orders to conclude treaties with the Indians, for the trade of spice and other commodities; but more especially in the places where the Portuguese were not as yet established.

This small fleet returned, two years and four months after its departure, with little or no gain

in

THE EAST-INDIES. 303

in reality; but with good information, and large hopes.

The old company, and a new one juft eftablifh-ed at Amfterdam, being incorporated, they fitted out a fleet of eight veffels, which fet fail, under admiral James Vaneck, from the Texel in 1598; and another fleet of three fhips was fitted out, which weighed anchor the 4th of May 1599. Thefe were followed by feveral others; and fo many new companies were erected at Amfterdam, Rotterdam, and other places, that the States-General apprehended they muft prove detrimental to each other; which fear, juftified by fome fad confequences, caufed the directors of all the different companies to affemble: the refult of this meeting was the union of all, which was confirmed by the ftates the 20th of March 1602; whofe fuccefs was very great, both on account of the immenfe riches brought into the United Provinces, or the kingdoms and ftates which this company fubdued in fo many different countries of Afia.

The firft fund of this company confifted of 6,459,840 guilders, or 565,2361. fterling; of which Amfterdam advanced 3,674,915; Zealand 1,333,882; Delft 470,000; Rotterdam 177,400; Hoorn 266,868; and Enchuyfen 536,775: and the firft grant of the ftates was for 21 years, to commence from the date of the grant, which was the fame with that of the confirmation.

The company is governed by fixty-five directors, divided into thirteen different chambers. The chamber of Amfterdam has 18 directors, the chamber of Zealand 12, the chambers of Delft and Rotterdam 14: thofe of Enchuyfen and Hoorn 14; thofe of Haerlem, Leyden, Dort, Tergow, the provinces of Guelderland, Friefland, and Utrecht, each of them one director.

SEVEN-

SEVENTEEN directors were also chosen from among the sixty-five, for the common affairs of the chambers; eight out of the chamber of Amsterdam, four out of that of Zealand, two out of those of Delft and Rotterdam, and two out of those of Enchuyfen and Hoorn, the seventeenth being chosen alternatively out of Zealand, the Meuse, or North Holland; and it is this second direction that regulates the number, the fitting out, and the departure of ships.

THE company is privileged to contract alliances with the princes whose dominions are eastward of the Cape of Good Hope; to build fortresses there, and to establish governors, garrisons, and officers of justice and police: but the treaties are concluded in the name of the states; in whose name all officers, both military and civil take their oaths.

AT the expiration of each grant, the company is obliged to obtain a new one, which has happened four times since the first was granted; but the renewal of grants costs the company considerable sums of money.

BY the grant of 1698, which was also confirmed in 1717, all the subjects of the States-General are prohibited the sending of ships, and sailing throughout the whole extent of the company's concession, or carrying on a trade therein, either directly or indirectly; as also associating with strangers for this trade, or serving in their vessels.

NOTHING can be more wisely and prudently concerted, than the police and discipline, whereby every thing is regulated in this company, either for the election of the directors of the chambers, or for the fitting out, and returns of ships; the choice of the seventeen particular directors, the sale of merchandises, and the dividends of the profits; or, lastly, for the conduct of their sovereignties in the Indies.

THIS

THE EAST-INDIES.

This company has several large settlements, and many factories, for the support of their trade. They are in possession of the Cape of Good Hope, which serves them, as St. Helena does the English East-India company, for supplying their ships with water and other refreshments in their voyage. The island of Mauritius served them also for the same purpose. They have a factory at Mocha in Arabia, and two others at Gombroon and Ormus in Persia, as also one at Ispahan, the capital of that empire. They have likewise factories at Barak, Choule near Bombay, Rigapore Dunde, Baffaloco, or Baynenar, and Bodven, on the proper coast of India; at Cananore, Pamari, Crananera, Cochin, Porchatt, Carnapole, Quilon, and Tegapatan, on the coast of Malabar; at Negapatan, Porta Nova, Sadraffapatan, Cabelon, Pellicat, Catelore, Petipoly, Mafualapatan, and Bimlipatan, on the coast of Coromandel; at Balafore, and Pipley, farther up the coast towards Bengal; at Bafnagul, Malda, Huegley, and Dacca, in Bengal; and at Patna, up the Ganges.

They have also a settlement in the kingdom of Aracan: they trade along the coast up to Siam, where they have the city of Malacca; and from thence they trade up to China.

They engross the whole trade of the island of Ceylon; they have some trade in the islands of Sumatra and Borneo: but the whole trade of Java, and the Molucca islands, is in their possession; as is also some part of the trade of the Celebes and Banda islands; besides, they are the only persons who trade to Japan: so that no less than 40 factories, and 25 fortresses, are reckoned belonging to this company in the East-Indies; who employ, in this long and painful navigation, above 150 ships, from 30 to 60 guns, manned with 25,000 sailors,

sailors, comprehending officers, soldiers, and mariners; besides 12,000 troops of their own republic, to garrison the forts.

Though all these factories are very considerable, they are not to be compared with Batavia, the center of the company's commerce; and the Cape of Good Hope, the staple, or rather the place of refreshment, for all its shipping, either going or coming.

The Dutch East-India company carry out great quantities of specie, and of European goods, but chiefly of the latter, to India. From China, they bring home silks, both raw and wrought, China and Japan ware, tea, and arrack; from Bengal and Patna, silks, raw and wrought, diamonds, indico, and coris; from the other ports of India, silks, calicoes, muslins, and great variety of other manufactures of cotton and flax; also shell-lack, stick-lack, red-wood, salt-petre, dying stuffs, and many drugs; besides coffee, and some drugs, from Persia.

From the island of Japan they bring home all kinds of Japan work, and lacquered ware; as also gold-dust: from the Moluccas, they bring cloves: from the Banda islands, nutmegs and mace: from the Celebes, pepper and opium: from the Sunda islands, pepper, gold, coffee, and canes: and cinnamon from Ceylon.

These commodities being articles of luxury, and too great for the consumption of the parsimonious Dutch, they export them to all parts of the world where they have any commerce; particularly to France, Spain, Germany, Italy, Turky, Dantzic, Denmark, Sweden, and Russia.

French East India company. The proposals of this company in 40 articles, bearing date the 26th May 1664, were presented to the king at
Foun-

Fountainbleau, who confirmed them, by his letters patent, in form of an edict, and had them ratified in parliament the 1st of September following.

Their import, among other things, was, that the company should be formed of his majesty's subjects, even of the nobles, without any dread of derogating from their nobility.

That each share could not be less than a thousand livres, nor the augmentations under 500.

That strangers, of any prince or state whatsoever, might be incorporated with the company; and that those who should have in it 20,000 livres, should be reputed denizens, and in that respect should enjoy all the privileges of real subjects.

That a chamber of general direction should be established, composed of 21 directors; whereof 12 should be of the city of Paris, and 9 others of the provinces; and that the said chamber might establish particular ones, when and where it should judge proper.

That his majesty empowered the company to navigate solely, exclusive of his other subjects, in all the Indian seas, east and south, during the term of 30 years.

That it should have for ever the possession of the island of St. Laurence, or Madagascar, and of all the other lands, places and isles, it might conquer from the enemy, and the natives, to enjoy them in all property, seigneury, and justice, without reserving any thing therein, but sole fealty and liege-homage, with the duty, rent, or service, of a crown and scepter of gold, weighing 100 marks, upon each demise of a king: granting him also the power of nominating and establishing all officers, military and civil; though the company might have it in its power to nominate ambassadors in his majesty's name to the Indian kings and princes, and make treaties with them.

That the company might send the species of gold or silver it should have an occasion for in its commerce, notwithstanding the prohibitions enacted by the laws and ordonances of the kingdom; and this by a particular permission, and a writing granted in its favor.

That his majesty should advance, or defray out of his own revenues, the fifth part of the expence necessary for the three first equipments; for which he was not to be reimbursed till the expiration of the first ten years, and without interest; and in case it should be found, by a general accompt, that the company had sustained a loss in its capital, the loss should devolve upon the sum advanced by his majesty.

That the Indian merchandises consumed in France should pay but the half of the duties regulated by the tariffs; and that those designed for other countries, and the exempted provinces, either by sea or land, should pay no duties of importation or exportation; as also the timber, and other necessary articles for the building and fitting out of the company's ships.

Lastly, That his majesty should pay the company 50 livres per ton for the merchandise its ships should carry into the countries of its concession, and 75 livres for those brought back and discharged in the kingdom.

His majesty also granted the company a seal, having for legend, *Ludovici* XIV. *Franciæ et Navarræ Regis sigillum, Usum supremi consilii Galliæ Orientalis*; and for arms, an azure globe and flower-de-luce of gold, with this inscription, *Florebo quocumque ferar*; the supporters being two figures, one representing Peace, and the other Plenty.

The

THE EAST-INDIES. 309

The extraordinary funds eftablifhed, whereof the king advanced the greater part, and which amounted to no lefs than 7 or 8 millions of livres, though thefe were to have been 15: the departure of feveral fleets, either for the eftablifhment projected at Madagafcar, which was to be the company's chief ftaple, or for the eftablifhment of the factories it was defirous of having in the Indies; and laftly, the union and affiduity with which the French directors endeavored to uphold this enterprife, gave great ideas of this company, and vaft hopes of fuccefs.

But the ill choice of this firft ftaple in an unwholfome ifland, inhabited by cruel and unconquerable people, lefs rich, and lefs fruitful than it was believed to be upon exaggerated relations; the death of the moft able and experienced directors fent to the Indies, the divifion of others; a breach of faith in M. Caron, a Dutchman, inconfiderately fet over affairs in fo diftant a country; the wars of 1667 for the rights of the queen, and of 1672 againft Holland; the little fuccefs of the fquadron commanded by M. Defhays, whereof a part perifhed in 1672, at Trinquimale, in the ifland of Ceylon, where the faid Caron had unadvifedly engaged; and the other at the taking, defence, and furrender of St. Thomas, in 1673 and 1674, brought affairs into fuch a fituation, that what fubfifted afterwards of this company, or rather thofe formed out of its ruin, which the traders of St. Malo fupported with fome fuccefs to 1719, were no ways confiderable.

The company being thus incapacitated from fulfilling its engagements, and continuing its commerce, it was thought advifeable to give it a new form, whereby its credit, if poffible, might be reanimated: to fucceed wherein, a general affembly of the parties was held on the 29th of May 1684,

X 3 pur-

pursuant to a *lettre de cachet* of the 17th of April preceding.

This *lettre de cachet* ordained the election of a sufficient number of directors to fill the place of the deceased, or of those who could no longer acquit themselves of that function. It nominated commissioners, for the most part the same that had been nominated in 1675, to examine the company's books and accompts; signifying withal, that it was his majesty's intention a provision should be made of suitable gratifications for the directors, both of the general chamber of Paris, and the particular ones of the provinces.

The new directors being chosen pursuant to the *lettre de cachet*, the company's books were laid before the king's commissioners, and the director's gratifications being debated upon, were fixed at 3000 livres for each director of the general chamber of Paris, and 1000 livres for each director of the particular ones.

But this assembly, and the examination of the company's books, having served only to disclose its desperate condition, and the impossibility of subsisting without being reduced to another form, his majesty ordained, by an arret of his council of the 3d September of the same year, a speedy convocation of a new assembly; wherein, in presence of his commissioners, the books of the Indian factories, as also the clerks of the said factories newly arrived, should be heard and examined; and that out of the said books, and other memoirs, a new book of accompts of the quality and value of the company's effects should be made; which, when inspected into by his majesty, with the advice of his commissioners, he might be in a condition to resolve upon what was to be done.

In consequence of this assembly, it appeared, by the company's accompts, that its funds amounted

in

THE EAST-INDIES. 311

in all only to the fum of 3,353,966 livres, or about 136,255 l. fterling; and that only 80 actionifts had afforded their fourths over and above; whereupon the king iffued out a declaration, in the month of February 1685, whereby it was ordained,

1ft, THAT the edict of the month of September 1664, fhould be executed, purfuant to its form and tenor, for the benefit of the antient actionaries, who fhould have furnifhed their fourth over and above, as well for the fourth remaining of their actions, as for their new fund of the fourth over and above.

2d, THAT thofe who had not paid the faid fourth, fhould forfeit all the intereft they had therein.

3d, THAT the fum of 728,975 livres, to which the fupplement amounted, and unpaid by the actionifts, fhould be advanced by thofe nominated by his majefty, who were to take the place of thofe that had not fupplied the faid fourth, with the injunction of paying them a like fum of 728,975 livres for the fourth, to which all the actions had been reduced.

4th, THAT thofe who contributed new funds for this reimburfement, and for the continuation of the company's commerce, fhould be paid the intereft of their faid funds and reimburfements, upon the footing of payment ufed in maritime commerce, that is, upon the provifo of profits that might iffue from the faid commerce.

5th, THAT, to take care of the company, and its trade, 12 directors fhould be chofen from among the actionifts of the city of Paris, who fhould have at leaft furnifhed 30,000 livres of new funds.

6th, THAT, upon the deceafe of any of the faid directors, others fhould be nominated, by a plurality

rality of voices, as well from among the furviving directors, as from among the actionifts, who fhould have furnifhed at leaft 20,000 livres of actions.

7th, THAT the faid directors fhould have the fole management of the affairs, and commerce of the company; his majefty fuppreffing all the directors nominated in the general chamber of Paris, and in all the other chambers of the kingdom.

8th, THAT in cafe the company was willing to keep the ifland of Madagafcar, it fhould be held purfuant to the fealty, homage, and duties, owing to his majefty; or, on the contrary, fhould be acquitted and difcharged from the faid fealty.

BUT the company renounced its right to this ifland in 1686; when by an arret of council of the 4th January of the fame year, Madagafcar was united to the crown.

IT was upon this foundation that the company fubfifted, and was governed till 1719; at which time it was incorporated with the company of the weft, known afterwards by the name of the Indian company.

IN the month of April 1687, the number of directors was increafed to twenty; which new directors were to pay for their reception 40,000 livres, if they had already 20,000 livres of actions in the company, and 60,000 livres, if they had no actions therein.

BY this new form given to the company, its funds amounted to 2,100,000 livres, or about 104,000 l. fterling; whereof the directors advanced 1,200,000, being 60,000 livres each, and the actionifts about 900,000 livres.

IT feemed, that, under thefe new directors, the company became fomewhat vigorous; and, in effect, its commerce being profperous, two dividends
were

THE EAST-INDIES. 315

were made for its actionifts in 1687 and 1691, amounting together to 30 per cent.

AFTER 1691, its commerce was greatly interrupted by the war that followed the revolution in England, and that wherein France was engaged for the Spanifh fucceffion.

IMMEDIATELY after the peace of Ryfwick, the directors made more extraordinary efforts than ever before; but here may be properly dated the epocha of the company's fall, the war of 1700 having endangered it to fuch a degree, that when it was incorporated 19 years afterwards with the company of the weft, its debts, contracted both in the kingdom and in the Indies, amounted to upwards of ten millions of livres, or about 500,000l. fterling.

IT feems that, in 1701, the company having reprefented to the miniftry its unhappy fituation, obtained from his majefty a loan of 850,000 livres, provided that each of the directors would augment their fund to the amount of 40,000, and the actionifts to 50 per cent.

THE execution of thefe conditions caufed great troubles among the directors and actionifts; the former accepting them, and the latter refufing to execute them, notwithftanding two arrets of council, of the 21ft February, and 16th May 1702, that authorifed the refult of the general affembly held the 24th January of the fame year.

LASTLY, in 1704, all conteftations were terminated by an arret of council, of the 1ft of April; which, notwithftanding all other arrets fince that of the 16th of May 1702, ordained, that all the company's actionifts fhould be interefted in its commerce, both for the dividing of profits, and the fuftaining of loffes, each with regard to their fund, as well for the paft, as for the time to come.

THAT

That to be acquainted with the state of the company's affairs, the directors should immediately, and above all things, give in the accompts of their commercial transactions.

That, for the future, the actionists need not be engaged in any new loans, unless the deliberations were signed by three actionists from among the five that should be nominated by them for the examination of the said accompts; and in case of refusal, the parties should refer the matter to the Sieur Pontchartrain, according to whose report his majesty would proceed to a decision.

This stating of accompts reviving the directors and actionists contestations, and the company's affairs being daily upon the decline; two arrets were issued out, one of the 6th, and the other of the 12th of November 1708.

The first arret ordained, that within two months time, a general assembly of the company's directors and actionists should be held, in presence of the *prevot de merchands*, to expedite whatever was necessary for the upholding and augmenting of the commerce of the said company, that his majesty might be in a condition to know what regulations should be made.

The second ordained the execution of the former, and superseded all pursuits, compulsions, and executions, upon the company's effects, on account of its debts, and upon the persons and goods of the directors. Yet the creditors might indemnify themselves in the council, and might make therein whatever demand they should judge proper; with a prohibition of endeavoring to obtain justice by any other means, upon pain of nullity.

But things being not disposed as yet, to erect a new East India company in France, and the ministry willing that the French should continue their com-

commerce there with some reputation, the court allowed the company's directors to treat with the rich traders of St. Malo, and to give up to them their privilege upon certain conditions: in whose hands it was that the French trade began to reflourish in the Indies, till this company was incorporated with that of the west in 1719.

It should be observed, that, for a considerable time, the East India company was allowed to share its privilege with others, through the hopes that the profits accruing from its treaties might be a support to its commerce, or at least that it might have wherewithal to pay in France the interests of so many bills, and the credit of renewing them.

The first of these treaties was of the 4th January 1698, with the Sieur Jourdan, and his associates, for the Chinese trade; the second with the Sieur Crozat, and his company, in the month of December 1708, authorised by an arret of the 15th of the same month.

By this last treaty, the directors of the company allowed the Sieur Crozat to send to the Indies, in the company's name, two ships, upon proviso that the company should have 15 per cent. from the sale of the effects brought back by these ships, without any deduction: as also 2 per cent. accruing from the prizes the said ships might make beyond the line; with liberty for the said company to bring back in these two ships, freight free, to the amount of ten ton of Indian goods; the company reserving for itself the duty of tonnage, as well going as coming, granted by his majesty; that is, the duty of 50 livres per ton of the merchandises exported by these ships into the countries of its concession, and 75 livres per ton for those brought back to be unladen in the country; which his majesty acceded to by way of gratification for the company.

The conditions of the treaty with Jourdan were much the same with those of the Sieur Crozat.

PONICHERRY, which the French usually call Pontichery, or Pondicherry, is their chief Indian factory; the residence of the director-general of the company, and the center of their commerce: their other establishments being only factories, where few clerks are left, very often but one, except that of Surat, which is pretty considerable.

THE company secured Pondicherry in 1688, by a fort flanked with four towers; upon which was a battery of 24 pieces of cannon, with a good garrison.

THE Hollanders besieged it in 1693, and took it after a long siege: during which the Sieur Martin, director-general, who, two years before, was complimented with letters of nobility from the king, and who was afterwards of the order of St. Michael, signalized himself greatly, and obtained for himself and his garrison a very honorable capitulation, besides several advantageous articles for the company.

PONDICHERRY was four years after restored to the French by the treaty of Ryswick, and is, to this day, their chief establishment in the Indies: but the English, in the year 1748, under the conduct of admiral Boscawn, unsuccessfully attempted the reduction of it. The commodities imported to France by the French East India company, are the same as those imported into England by the English East India company.

DANISH EAST INDIA COMPANY. It is but of late that the Danes undertook long voyages, at least for the Indies; their flags making no appearance in the gulph of Bengal, and about the coasts of Pegu, till near the middle of the 17th century. Their chief factory is at Tranquebar, or Trincombar,

THE EAST-INDIES. 317

bar, where they fend two or three ſhips yearly, and where they have a conſiderable fortreſs; but they have lately extended their trade to China, and appointed Altena, near Hamburgh, for the port where the Eaſt India commodities are to be unloaded, and public ſales made of them.

OSTEND EAST INDIA COMPANY. As ſoon as the Spaniſh Netherlands were yielded to the emperor by the treaty of Raſtadt, the merchants of Oſtend, Antwerp, and ſome other towns of Flanders and Brabant, thought of reaping ſome advantage from the protection and power of their new maſter, for the eſtabliſhment of their commerce in the Eaſt Indies.

THEIR firſt ſetting out was without authority and letters-patent; yet with the hopes, at their return, of being made a regular company, like the Engliſh, Dutch, and French.

BUT the infant commerce of this company was immediately troubled by the Dutch; who, the 19th of December 1718, took, upon the coaſts of Africa, an Oſtend veſſel richly laden, though protected by a paſſport from the emperor.

TOWARDS the end of the year 1719, the emperor allowed the directors to receive ſubſcriptions, and began to encourage the ſubſcription of actioniſts : he alſo granted a deduction of 2¼ per cent. of all the duties accruing to him from the commodities imported by the company's ſhips, beſides ſeveral other privileges they were made to expect; and, about the ſame time, he demanded ſatisfaction from the States-General for the ſeizure of the Oſtend ſhip; but to no purpoſe, for the Dutch Eaſt India company ſeized another.

THE merchants of Oſtend, by commiſſion from the emperor, fitted out privateers to protect their commerce, took a Dutch ſhip, would not make
reſtitution,

restitution, and, in despight of the Hollanders menaces, fitted out for the East Indies in 1720 five ships richly laden, and in 1721 six more; three for China, one for Mocha, one for Surat and the coast of Malabar, and the sixth for Bengal; their principal station in the Indies being at Coblon, 56 miles N. of Pondicherry, on the coast of Coromandel.

The Dutch, on their side, to stop their progress, confiscated a ship fitted out for the East Indies by the traders of Bruges, notwithstanding the remonstrances of the imperial minister at the Hague.

The English pirates having taken, in the seas of Madagascar, an Ostend ship richly laden, and bound for Europe; this new loss seemed to discourage the Imperial company: but upon the safe arrival of four others, in 1722, it found itself in a condition, not only to repair its losses, but also to continue its commerce with more success and reputation.

At last his imperial majesty granted this company his letters-patent, in a most ample and authentic manner; the duration of its concession being 30 years, its limits the East and West Indies, with all the coasts of Africa, both beyond and on this side the Cape of Good Hope; as also all the ports, harbors, places, and rivers, where other nations had any freedom of trade.

The company's fund was fixed at six millions of guilders, or about 475,000 l. sterling, and at 6000 actions, of 1000 guilders each.

The news of these letters-patent made the English and Dutch unite to obtain their revocation; and the Dutch East India company presented two memorials on this head to the states; in the latter whereof, of the 9th August 1723, a liberty of disputing their rights by the force of arms was required.

quired. The Oftend company founded themfelves upon the natural liberty which all nations have of trading wherever it feems convenient, unlefs fome particular convention might deprive them of it; and the Dutch pretended that there was fuch a convention between them and thofe of Oftend, fpecified by the treaties of barrier, and that of Munfter.

THE courts of London and Paris, whofe fubjects had been allowed, by treaty, to import filks into Germany, and the emperor's hereditary dominions, backed the remonftrances of the republic; and France thought it neceffary to hinder her traders to intereft themfelves in this company; for which purpofe the French monarch iffued out a declaration, of the 16th Auguft 1723, among other things, impofing a penalty of 3000 livres, a confifcation of all funds and effects in the faid company, and three years banifhment in cafe of a fecond offence; which example was followed in Great Britain.

THE emperor, continuing his utmoft efforts to fupport the new company, entered into a treaty with Spain in 1725, whereby the Spanifh monarch engaged to allow greater advantages in trade to the imperialifts than to any other nation, particularly to the Oftend company. Whereupon the French infinuated, that there were ftill fome further fecret articles, much more prejudicial to the trade of Britain than thofe that appeared; which induced the Britifh miniftry to enter into an alliance with them, in oppofition to that of Vienna; whereby the contracting parties guarantied their refpective rights and privileges in relation to trade, which ftruck chiefly at the Oftend company; and the Dutch were afterwards induced to accede to this treaty, with a view to prevent the trade of this

company

company to the East Indies; while Great Britain commenced hostilities against Spain in the West Indies: so that the emperor being prevailed on by the Dutch, who acted as mediators, to consent that the charter should be suspended for seven years, preliminaries for a general peace were signed at Paris, in May 1727, between the allies of Vienna, and those of Hanover; since which time, the Ostend company has never been revived.

EAST INDIA COMPANY OF SWEDEN. In the year 1730, a Dutchman, named Van Asper, who had projected the same thing in Denmark, proposed the erecting of an East India company in Sweden; which being approved of, the king took upon himself to be its protector; and when the Dutch, who apprehended this would be as prejudicial as the Ostend company had been to their trade, complained of it, they were given to understand, that commerce was open to all nations, and that the Swedish kingdom had an equal right to it with others; since which time the Swedes have sent several ships to the Indies; and have been so successful in this trade, as to be under no necessity of purchasing the merchandise of India from their European neighbors, as they formerly did, unless it be the fine spices; which the Swedes, and all other nations, are obliged to purchase of the Dutch, who have robbed the rest of the world of them, and consequently set what prices they please upon those commodities.

EMBDEN EAST INDIA, or PRUSSIAN ASIATIC COMPANY. His Prussian majesty, sensible of the advantages resulting from a maritime interest, granted in 1751 a patent for 20 years, to Henry Thomas Stuart, and company, for establishing a Prussian Asiatic company at Embden, an imperial city, and port-town of Germany, in the circle of
                                                    Westphalia;

Westphalia; empowering it to send an indefinite number of ships annually to Canton in China; which grant was solemnly registered; and such effectual means were concerted for the prosecution of the design, that the adventurers were perfectly satisfied; for his majesty not only issued his letters patent for making the port of Embden a free port, but ordered memorials to be presented to the maritime powers, and such other princes whose subjects traded to the East-Indies, concerning the navigation of the ships belonging to the Embden company: upon which the States-General of the United Provinces declared, that his majesty's ships should have the same liberty as those of other nations, to trade to all the ports, except those which the Dutch East India company have the sole right of trading to: that they should be also at liberty even to put into those ports to refit, after bad weather, or to get provisions and water, in case they were in distress for them: but that, as the subjects of the Republic, employed in their India company, incur very severe penalties, by going into the service of any other power, they hoped his Prussian majesty would not permit such persons to sail in his ships to the East Indies, seeing, in such cases, the Dutch East India company could not avoid seizing them, and punishing them with the utmost rigor. The directors of this company resolved to send only two ships to China for the first year; and, upon the success of these, to regulate their future proceedings: accordingly one of their ships, called the king of Prussia, set sail from Embden on the 17th of February 1752; and as the other powers granted the same concessions with the Dutch, this company had more reason to expect a successful event than that of Ostend, which was circumvented by those very powers, who, in complaisance to his

Vol. I.   Y   Prussian

Prussian majesty, granted to the Embden company what the emperor could never obtain for the other.

REMARKS.

ONE of the reasons why the Dutch East India company flourishes, and is become more rich and powerful than all the others, is its being absolute, and invested with a kind of sovereignty and dominion, more especially over the many ports, provinces, and colonies, it possesses in those parts. For it appoints magistrates, admirals, generals, and governors; sends and receives embassies from kings and sovereign princes; makes peace and war at pleasure; and by its own authority administers justice to all; appoints tribunals to judge in their name, with plenary power and no appeal; punishes and remits offences; bestows rewards becoming the dignity of kings; settles colonies, builds fortifications, levies troops, maintains numerous armies and garrisons, fits out fleets, and coins money. And though there is acknowledged a dependance upon the States-General, it may be said they seldom exert their power; and while the republic preserves the right of sovereignty, it tacitly leaves the exercise and possession of it to the merchants of this company. These vast powers were, and are still, requisite to cherish and preserve this flourishing branch of trade: and the proprietors justly merited them; for by their own vigilance, care, and expence, they conquered, and preserve all the countries they possess in those parts of Asia; and their fortresses on the coast of Africa for the refreshment, refitting and protection of their ships.

THE power of the Dutch by sea and land is very great in the East Indies; where, by force, address, and alliances, they raised themselves, and still support a great superiority, in spite of the English,

English, Portuguese, and other Europeans, that have some trade there; but so inconsiderable, that, all together, is not equal to what the Hollanders singly enjoy, and who could give law to the very English in 1662, obliging them to a peace very advantageous to Holland, and their East India company in particular, after a bloody and expensive war that arose from jealousy and rivalship in commerce. Therefore it may be for the advantage of England, France, and even Portugal, to tolerate and encourage other companies, from reasons of state, and self-preservation, which put all princes and republics upon reducing the power of such as aspire after universal dominion, or have already acquired it; as the Assyrians, Chaldeans, Medes, Persians, Greeks, and Romans did, and against whom those nearest to danger usually form conspiracies, courting even distant alliances to ballance the great and ambitious power that threatens them; and to reduce it to an equality, or even lower, that all may live secure, and confined within their own limits. If the power of the Dutch, though great in Europe, does not put princes and states upon their guard, they must possess a kind of universal monarchy or dominion in the southern provinces, islands, and seas of Asia, from Arabia to Japan; subjecting, by all possible ways, many of the powers of Europe to their law, in every thing respecting that important branch of trade; a thing which, beside the dishonor of it, very much interferes with their interest. For, in those parts, Holland commands and directs every thing at pleasure, bringing sovereigns under subjection, conquering or reducing large and plentiful provinces, after it laid the foundation of its empire upon the spoils of Portugal, and enlarged it by prescribing narrow limits to the jurisdiction and commerce of the

English,

English, and disappointing or reducing that of the French and other Europeans. For this, and other reasons, good policy seems to suggest, that the English, French and Portuguese, interested and aggrieved, should unite, and not only tolerate, but encourage any proper new company, and receive it as an auxiliary and confederate power, to assist in humbling the pride of the Dutch, and weakening their universal dominion in the East Indies, that all may live independent, and not under a subjection that bears hard upon their honour and commerce.

The East Indies is a bottomless pit for bullion, which can never circulate back to Europe; and when bullion fails, that trade must cease. That this is the present situation of all the kingdoms of Europe, with respect to the trade which they carry on with the East Indies, is also asserted by the marquis Jerome Belloni, a celebrated merchant and banker at Rome; and this for no other reason, than that immense gulph of passive commerce, wherein they are involved by means of the commodities which the Europeans import from those parts. For, according to this author, not only the great quantities of jewels and manufactures, with the numberless liquors and spices, the greatest part whereof the luxury and pride of men have raised to high prices, render that trade so exorbitant, that the great advantage which the Europeans receive from America, and the great quantities of gold and silver, and other useful things, which are brought from thence, are not sufficient to compensate the loss sustained by that excessively expensive trade; but even the many commodities which come from the East Indies to Europe, and those inexpressibly vast sums of money, besides some few sorts of European commodities, which

are

are exhaufted by the importation of thofe Eaft Indian goods, give juft ground to make it a queftion, whether the money that is brought from America to Europe is more confiderable, than that which is exported from Europe to the Eaft Indies.

The baron de Montefquieu, in his " Spirit of Laws," fpeaking of the trade of Europe in general to the Eaft Indies, not only acknowledges this truth, but alfo gives reafons for it. " We at prefent, fays he, carry on the trade of the Indies merely by means of the filver we fend thither, which is exchanged for merchandifes brought to the weft. Every nation that ever traded to the Indies, has conftantly carried bullion, and brought merchandifes in return. It is nature itfelf that produces the effect. The Indians have their arts adapted to their manner of living. Our luxury cannot be theirs, nor their wants ours. Their climate hardly demands, or permits any thing which comes from ours. They go, in a great meafure, naked; fuch cloaths as they have, the country itfelf furnifhes; and their religion which is deeply rooted, gives them an averfion for thofe things that ferve for our nourifhment. Therefore they want nothing but our bullion, to ferve as the medium of value; and for which they give us in return merchandizes, with which the frugality of the people, and the nature of the country, furnifh them in great abundance."

CHAP.

CHAP. VIII.

Of ancient INDIA: *its inhabitants; their religion; government; and of the* BRACHMANS.

THE Greeks having heard that the southern Indians were black and swarthy, easily confounded them with the people of Ethiopia and of Colchis, and imagined that the first were a colony that had straggled from the east, as the Colchians were originally Ethiopian soldiers, whom Sesostris had left in that province to defend his conquests against the northern nations. Secondly, the Indies have ever been reckoned a country abounding in all sorts of riches; and we know that Colchis had its mines of gold, and that Ethiopia produced the same animals which are to be seen in the Indies. There needed no more than this conformity, to give occasion to authors little versed in geography, to confound together such remote countries as Colchis, Ethiopia, and the Indies.

WE have no real knowledge of the last, but of those provinces and cities through which the army of Alexander passed, and which Arrian has described with all possible exactness. The Hyphasis became the boundary of his conquests, on account of the opposition the Macedonians made to his farther progress. He only passed it, in order to erect those superb altars in imitation of the columns of Hercules. As we are indebted to the expedition of that hero, for what knowledge we have of this country, such as it then was, so we are entirely ignorant of all that existed beyond it to the Ganges. Arrian makes mention of two cities, Minnagora and Barygaxa, both which he celebrates

THE EAST-INDIES. 327

lebrates for their commerce. That vaft extent of country, now fo famous, which ftretches from the junction of all thofe rivers to the Indus, even to the bottom of the peninfula, was as little known to the ancients. They mention only the kingdoms of the Sabraques of the Sogdes, of Mufican, of the Preotes, of the Sabians, and that of Patala. Some of the inhabitants they called Indo-Scythians.

ALL that country had the name of India within the Ganges ; *India intra Gangem.* It contained one hundred and eighteen nations or provinces, in fome of which were three hundred cities, as in the kingdom of Porus; in others much fewer, and there were princes who reigned only over two. About forty rivers are faid to run through this country, moft of them navigable, and all of them throw themfelves into the Indus. After fwallowing up fo many others, we may form a judgment of its bignefs, by that of the Hydafpes, whofe channel is never lefs than twenty ftadia, or a great league. What then muft a river be, in which fo many others lofe themfelves ?

ALTHOUGH the Indians are defcended from Shem, whofe pofterity preferved the memory of the true God for a longer time than thofe of Ham and Japhet ; yet the darknefs which fpread itfelf over every human mind, effaced the idea which the Creator had imprinted there; and they transferred their homage to the fun, the moon, to trees, and other fenfible objects. The day-ftar had one of the moft magnificent temples that ever was built: the walls were of porphiry, covered within with plates of gold, on which were carved rays, that fhone diverging every way from whatever fide they were beheld. In the bottom of the temple was a figure of the fun, compofed of an infinite number of different forts of precious ftones, dif-

Y 4   pofed

posed in a very artificial manner ; and which one might have said came near the original ; if it was possible to imitate that wonder of nature. They paid their adoration to that star by dancing in a circle, in imitation of its course. This was the only idol which the Indians had among them, till being instructed by the Greeks in the worship of the heroes of fabulous antiquity, they consecrated an elephant, which they called Ajax, with two golden statues of Alexander, and two brazen ones representing Porus. However great the number of those princes of ancient India might be, no historian has given us a succession of them, and we know but a small part of their laws and customs. They were all obliged to make their appearance every day, in order to hear the complaints of their subjects, to judge of all differences arising among them, and to regulate the affairs of the state; and they were not permitted to rise from the audience, even to take refreshment, before every thing was ended. They could do nothing without the advice of their council: but when more important affairs, or what related to religion, were under agitation, they were to consult the Brachmans, that is the sages, who again consulted the Augurs. The fidelity which they observed in their negociations was inviolable; and to express the sacredness of them, they gave their heralds the sign of an anchor, the symbol of their firmness and constancy.

In the kingdom of Musican, near the delta of the river Indus, luxury and effeminacy were carried to as great a height, as ever they had been among the Persians in the dregs of the last ages of their empire. The king was continually surrounded by a train of women, whose manners, actions, songs and conversation, inspired nothing but the most shameful pleasures.

One

One muſt be at a loſs to underſtand, how, under princes ſo effeminate, ſo much order and diſcipline were neverthelefs preſerved in the ſtate, that they were admired on that account by the moſt civilized foreign nations. But it muſt be remembered, that luxury was not predominant in all the courts. A wife ſenate prefided over all the affairs of government: the numbers of it were choſen by the people: the king had only a voice in it; and, if that council was accuſed of error or injuſtice, the parties appealed to the people, who tried the cauſe afreſh, and amended the ſentence if neceſſary; in fine, the whole country was divided into ſeven claſſes, of which every one had its chiefs and ſuperintendants, who reſtrained particulars within the bounds of their duty. The firſt of theſe claſſes was, that of the Brachmans, or Sages; the ſecond of the huſbandmen; the third, of the ſhepherds; the fourth, contained the merchants and tradeſmen; the fifth, the ſoldiers; the ſixth, the ſuperintendants; and the ſeventh, the counſellors of the king and people.

THE prince was diſtinguiſhed above the Brachmans, by nothing but his ſceptre and the pomp of his purple. Their continual application in the ſearch of truth, the purity of their manners, the retirement and auſterity in which they lived, had acquired them all the honors and immunities which the prieſts enjoyed among the Egyptians, or the Magi among the Perfians. Theſe ſages were of two ſorts; the Brachmans properly ſo called, and the Germani or Samaneans: the firſt were of a particular family, and the laſt might be of any of the other orders.

THEY taught philoſophy, the immortality of the ſoul, the motions of the heavenly bodies, the conſtruction of the human body, and the ſecrets

of

of nature. They difcourfed of every thing relating to government, the laws, the authority of the prince, and the rights of the people; in a word, they gave rules for the conduct of manners, that they might learn to lead a hard and auftere life, which neither famine, folitude, the inclemency of the air, nor the rigor of the feafons, fhould difturb or incommode.

They were feen to pafs the greateft part of the night and day in prayer, in finging fongs and hymns in honor of the deity, and raifing their hands to heaven when they offered up their vows for the prince, the people, and the goods of the earth. During the reft of the day they kept themfelves retired in their cells, where they were employed in meditation on particular truths, in the ftudy of philofophy, and in making experiments ufeful to the public. If in that interval they happened to fpend too much time in converfation with their friends, they impofed on themfelves the penalty of keeping filence for feveral days. Fafting and mortification was another exercife to which they thought themfelves obliged.

A life thus entirely taken up in prayer and contemplation, attracted the confidence of the people.

The prince applied himfelf to them in difficult and extraordinary cafes, to learn from them in what manner he fhould give judgment. He went to the place of their abode; he eat with them herbs, fruits, and lentile; but nothing which had life; and the ftatelinefs of thofe philofophers was fuch, that they drew lots for their places, that they might not yield to him the pre-eminence. He thought himfelf too happy if they gave him a gracious reception. They fuffered him to ftay with them no longer than a day, and it was only during the night that they gave him audience.

THE

The laſt object of their philoſophy reſpected the regulation of manners. They began their ſtudies, as they ſaid, by the knowledge of themſelves, whether of the mind and diſpoſitions, or of the body: but as their whole conduct manifeſted an inexhauſtible fund of pride, their lights upon this point were turned into darkneſs. The reſult of their reflections upon themſelves was to be perſuaded, that out of their own ſect there was nothing but ignorance, effeminacy, and corruption; to believe that nothing was concealed from them, not even the thoughts and name of a ſtranger; to pretend to inſpiration from the deity and familiar converſation with him; to place themſelves above the reſt of mankind, and to look upon themſelves as gods.

That pretended ſtrength of mind to which philoſophy carried them, rendered life and death equally indifferent. They looked upon the good or evil, the pleaſure or pain which might happen to them, as dreams; ſince they paſſed ſo rapidly from one to the other. But they were aſhamed of thoſe diſtempers which brought a decay upon the body, and diſturbed the operations of the mind, regarding this life as the firſt moment of our conception, and death as the day of our real birth.

When they found themſelves attacked by a ſevere indiſpoſition, or worn out with old age, without heſitation, they put an end to their days by a voluntary death. They fitted up with their own hands the pile that was to ſerve them as an altar: they aſcended it decked with their richeſt ornaments; and after having ſung a few hymns, they lay down upon their faces, and ſuffered themſelves to be reduced to aſhes, without betraying the leaſt ſign of pain or ſenſibility. What a ſtrange philoſophy fophy was that, which led men to their own deftruction! " Equality, faid the Brachman Dindimus to Alexander the Great, places us all in independence; it banifhes from among us envy, jealoufy, ambition and hatred. We have no tribunals, becaufe we do nothing which deferves reprehenfion: and the juftice in which we live, has not yet given rife to the eftablifhment of the fevere laws by which vice is punifhed among the reft of mankind. We are even afraid that by introducing them, they fhould give birth to the thoughts of that evil which they prohibit. Our only law is, not to violate that of nature. Thus fhunning all manner of reproach, we are not under any neceffity to pardon others, in the hope we may be entitled to a mutual indulgence. Much lefs do we purchafe pardon or impunity by the force of money; fuch an act of grace granted through avarice, renders the judge more culpable than the criminal. Among us, idlenefs is feverely punifhed; we dread voluptuoufnefs as the fource of all frailty. We love labor; as it exercifes our bodies; and we deteft the man, who is a flave to his lufts. Our bufinefs has no other object but to procure us neceffaries: we abhor every other view, and we look upon it as the original of all evil. No land-mark or boundaries are to be feen in our fields for the diftinction of property: we are convinced that is an ufurpation contrary to nature; every one takes what he pleafes of the products of the earth. We fuffer the birds to fly unmolefted, the beafts to range the fields, and the fifh to fwim in the bofom of the waters. We poffefs all we can defire, becaufe we defire nothing beyond that which is neceffary. We dread nothing fo much as that infatiable defire to acquire property, which gives rife to a thoufand cravings in the heart of man, and make him poorer from

day

day to day, in proportion to the increafe of his riches. The fun warms us; the rain and dew cool us; the rivers quench our thirft; the herbs and roots nourifh us; the earth affords us a bed: anxious cares interrupt not our repofe; independence delivers us from fear, and all kinds of fubjection; and we look upon one another as brothers whom nature has rendered equal, and as the children of one fupreme God, our common Father, who ought to make us partakers of the fame inheritance. The heavens fupply us with our favorite fpectacle: we admire with joy their order, œconomy, regularity, and motions. We are tranfported when we behold the fun flying in its purple car, fpreading through every region his beaming rays of light, and returning every year to the place from whence he departed. From the heavens we pafs to the view of nature, whofe works appear to us equally beautiful, admirable and incomprehenfible. The finging of the birds, the fountains, a flower, the ftalk of an herb, ravifhes and afford an inexhauftible fund of reflection. Contented with the natural growth of our own country, we wander not elfewhere in fearch of the different rarities which an unknown fky and climate produce. Nothing affects us but that which is convenient for us. We defpife the flowers of eloquence, and condemn it as a pernicious art, only made ufe of to give falfhood the appearance of truth to fcreen villainy, accufe innocence, and fometimes juftify parricide. All our eloquence confifts in being fincere, and adhering ftrictly to truth."

THIS is an abridgment of their manners; and here follow the articles of their belief. The Brachmans held it as a maxim, " never to defile their facrifices with blood, by flaughtering innocent victims: they adorned not their temples with gold or filver, silver, or the splendor of precious stones. They thought it would be insulting the deity, should they attempt to give him that which he does not want; or to shew themselves as powerful as he, in ostentatiously displaying all the riches which he could have. God requires that we should honor him with a pure and not a bloody worship; and to be rendered propitious by the prayers and humiliations of men : he is that word itself by which he has created the visible world, by which he preserves, governs, and keeps it in being. He is a pure spirit, and consequently requires nothing but the offering of our good works, of our virtues and virtuous actions."

THIS country was liable to the same innundations with Egypt, and perhaps they were here more considerable. Whether from the snow of Paropamisa, Caucasus, mount Imaus, and the Emodes, or from the great quantity of rains that fell in the months of April, May, and June, it is certain, in that season the country was covered with water; and after they had gone off, it was difficult to distinguish the limits which divided the lands of each individual. To prevent disputes which might thence arise, there were men in all the districts, perfectly well acquainted with those matters, who marked over again those limits of the fields that had been effaced. As they preserve in Egypt a part of these waters in great lakes, to spread them afterwards over the land during those months in which there were no rains; it was the office of these inspectors to open these repositaries when necessary, and distribute the waters in sufficient quantity.

CHAP.

CHAP. IX.

Of the ancient revolutions in INDIA, *from the conquests of* BACCHUS *to those of* ALEXANDER *the* GREAT. *Of the settlement of the* MAHOMEDANS *in* India: *and of the* MOGUL *government. Of the climate of* India, *and its present inhabitants. With some remarks relative to trade.*

IT is certain, that the government of India was always monarchical; that the kings were more numerous there than in any nation of the world; and that some of them had acquired an empire over the rest. But we have no native writers of the country, who have given a succession of their ancient kings; so that it is not surprising it should be entirely unknown to us. Pliny, who had before him different relations, informs us, that the Indians reckoned one hundred and fifty three kings from the invasion of Bacchus to that of Alexander, which were two memorable æras. This number of sovereigns, however, become suspicious, by the exaggeration of the interval which it places between the two conquerors, in reckoning upwards of six thousand four hundred years; unless their years, at least in the primeval ages, were much shorter than ours, as they were among the ancient Egyptians.

FOR want of better lights, we must have recourse to some remarkable revolutions, which occasioned changes in the government of the western part of India. This country has always been the object of emulation to the heroes of Asia, Egypt, and Greece. Ancient tradition informs us, that Bacchus and Hercules carried their arms thither: but as there were several conquerors of that name, authors differ about those who penetrated first into the

the Indies; and after long difquifitions, they leave us in the utmoft uncertainties and difficulties upon that point. Yet it appears, that this Bacchus was the fon of Semele; though we can decide nothing about Hercules.

Although Arrian calls in queftion the expedition of Sefoftris into thefe remote provinces, it is fo formally attefted by others, that we cannot refufe affent to their teftimony. Indeed, it was attended with no confequence as to government, that prince not having rendered thofe nations tributary whom he had fubdued, but refting contented with having brought them under his power: nor did his fucceffors even attempt to preferve his conquefts. But the expedition of Darius the fon of Hyftafpes was attended with more real confequences. Confounded at his bad fuccefs in the defarts of Scythia, he turned his arms againft the Indians, whofe country he entered by furprife, reduced them to his obedience, and impofed a large tribute upon the inhabitants, whom he obliged to ferve as vaffals, and in that quality we find them in the mufters of the armies of Xerxes, Ochus, and Darius Codomannus, the laft of that monarchy.

It is probable the fon of Hyftafpes carried his conquefts no farther than the river Indus; but Alexander extended his to the Hyphafis, where his troops refufed to follow him any farther, and obliged him to return into Perfia.

The northern nations of India, although idolaters, were eafily induced to embrace Mahomedanifm, and are at this day the Affghams or Patans, who figure fo much in all the late revolutions of Delhi.

The armies which made the firft conquefts for the heads of the refpective dynafties, or for other incurfors, left behind them numbers of the Mahomedans,

THE EAST-INDIES. 337

homedans, who, feduced by a finer climate and a richer country, forgot their own.

THE Mahomedan princes of India naturally gave a preference to the fervice of their own religion; who, from whatever country they came, were of a more vigorous conftitution than the ftouteft of the fubjected nation; this preference has continually encouraged adventurers from Tartary, Perfia, and Arabia, to feek their fortunes under a government, from which they were fure of receiving greater encouragement than they could expect at home.

FROM thefe origins, time has formed in India a mighty nation of near ten millions of Mahomedans, whom Europeans call Moors: to them, under the authority of the Great Mogul, the greateft part of Indoftan is now fubject; but although the reigning nation, they are out-numbered by the Indians ten to one.

THIS inferiority of number has obliged the Mahomedans to leave, in all parts of Indoftan, many Indian princes in poffeffion of their refpective fovereignties, which they are permitted to govern without moleftation, on condition they pay the ftipulated tribute, and do not infringe any other of the articles of the treaties by which they or their anceftors have acknowledged the fovereignty of the Great Mogul. Thefe Indian princes are called Rajas, or kings; and more than one half of the empire is at this day fubject to thefe princes.

BESIDES the Indians, who refide in the territories of the Rajas, there are every where feen great numbers of them in thofe parts of the country, which are immediately fubject to the Great Mogul, without the interpofition of an Indian prince to govern them. They are the only cultivators of the land, and the only manufacturers of the im-

VOL. I. Z menfe

menfe quantities of linen which are made in the empire; infomuch, that at a diftance from the capital cities, the great trading towns, the encampments of armies, and the high roads, it is rare to fee in the villages or fields a Mahomedan employed in any thing excepting levying contributions, or acting in fome other refpect as an officer of the Great Mogul.

INTELLIGENT enquirers affert, that there are no written laws among the Indians; but that a few maxims, tranfmitted by tradition, fupply the place of fuch a code in the difcuffion of civil caufes; and that the ancient practice, corrected on particular occafions by the good fenfe of the judge, decides abfolutely in criminal ones. In all cafes derived from the relations of blood, the Indian is worthy to be trufted with the greateft confidence; but in cafes of property, in which this relation does not exift, as a cunning fubtil people, they are perpetually in difputes; and for the want of a written code, the juftice or injuftice of the decifion depends on the integrity or venality of the judge. Hence the parties prefer to fubmit their caufe to the decifion of arbitrators chofen by themfelves, rather than to that of the officers appointed by the government.

THE feudatory, by the acceptance of a certain title, and the penfion which accompanies it, acknowledges the great Mogul his heir. No man, from the vizier downwards, has any truft of importance repofed in him, but on thefe terms; and, on his deceafe, the whole of his property that can be found is feized for the ufe of the emperor, who gives back to the family what portion he pleafes.

IN thefe climates the name of fnow and froft is entirely unknown: the trees are never without leaves, and the fruit and bloffoms alternately fucceed

ceed each other: but here, as in other countries lying between the tropics, is a dry and wet feafon.

WITH the month of January returns the heat, which is cooled by breezes of the fea. The month of February is more hot, dry and unhealthful. In March the winds cool a little the fcorching heat of the fun. April is ftill hotter, and in the months of May and June is a fine feafon; but in which there blows a noxious land breeze, from feven in the morning till noon, as hot as the air of a furnace, which the ftrongeft conftitution has enough to do to bear, and Europeans can hardly at all. Some caufe themfelves to be fprinkled over from morning till night, to cool the fcorching heat. Here the nights are as unhealthful as the days. It is no uncommon thing to fee perfons rife paralytic, who had laid down in perfect health, in a place expofed to the evening damps. Such a feafon would deftroy the fruits of the earth, if amidft the heats of the month of June, the waters which rife in the mountains of Gad, did not gradually fwell. They are at their height in July, at which time the air becomes temperate.

THE autumn is the winter of Malabar, which is as moderate as our fpring. It rains, it is true, very much; but all is green after the fcorching heat of fummer is over. The trees bloffom in September, in which month and in October, is the firft gathering of fruit, when the air is both cool and perfumed, occafioned by the aromatic plants in bloffom, and commonly Europeans find this feafon the moft healthful. The fick, indeed, efpecially hypochondriacs, are principally moft affected in the months of November and December, when the cold and rains are at their height. In thefe months the Malabares, who go almoft naked, fhiver with cold, againft which they do not know how to fhelter themfelves, either by cloaths, or by burning wood, a very scarce commodity in this country, where they use little else, even in their kitchens, than dry cow dung. They are chilly in the same degree of heat, in which no Europeans can hardly bear to be covered.

The soil is fertile almost throughout, occasioned by the overflowing of the rivers, as Egypt is by that of the Nile. When the heat is most intense the rivers swell, which is apparently occasioned by the melting of the snow in the mountains where they rise: for the warmest climates, as the isle of St. Thomas and upper Ethiopia, have Alps covered with snow and ice. Then the farmers open their sluices, and each turns his part of the river on his rice grounds. If the rivers fail, the country is all a barren wilderness, and the natives die, by thousands, of famine. This disaster is often occasioned by the animosities among themselves, which hinder them from keeping their sluices in repair.

Here the air is very suffocating, and iron rusts ten times more than in Europe. The sun gives a stronger light at noon than the eyes can bear; even the stars shine brighter, and Venus has a very sensible shadow. The twilight is very short, and day and night appear almost at the same time. Before rain and fog there is commonly heard a hollow but very strong noise proceeding from the sea. There are often seen fiery meteors, resembling comets, but much lower in the air, through which they traverse very swiftly. The winds are so strong as to throw down houses and pluck up trees by the roots; and should any of these hurricanes overtake a man in the fields, he must lay himself along upon the ground.

The natural color of the inhabitants is black: but the Bramins, and generally the Morattoes, are yellowish, little differing from a tawnish Portuguese.

The

The chief plant in Malabar is rice, by which alone almost the bulk of the people are maintained; it serves for bread even to the rich, as corn does not come to perfection. Their agriculture almost solely consists in the culture of rice, which is reckoned an honorable occupation, and such as follow it have precedence of mechanics. It is sown in the month of June, in a soil that is a mere puddle, occasioned by the overflowing of the rivers on their grounds. When it is a hand high they take it up, and replant it in just such another soil. Their harvest is gathered in the beginning of winter. Their plough is a very simple machine, and a branchy bough serves for a harrow. When the rice is dry, it is boiled in water or milk, which they eat heartily. They use another method, by distilling it and extracting an aqua vitæ, which administers to the debaucheries of Europeans: for the natives abhor excessive drinking, which must shorten life, by super-adding a new fire to that of the climate.

It is to be understood, that the English East India company have the sole monopoly of trading to the east of the Cape of Good Hope: but this is a very large and uncertain description of their bounds; for as the world is round, they might go to the east of the Cape of Good Hope if no land intervened, till they came unto it again; and at that rate, Chili, Peru, and other parts of America, would be within their monopoly. Therefore this must certainly be a vulgar error, and there must be other bounds prescribed by the charter; which probably does not extend to the Molucca islands, the spice islands, or the Philippines; for I do not find that, since the act of parliament, the company ever traded to any of those places; and yet the advantage would be very great.

We

We may therefore suppose, their monopoly does not extend to New Guiney, New Britain, the isle Sabada, and other islands which captain Dampier sailed round in one of the men of war, and on which he landed about the year 1700, and where he met with gold, nutmegs, and other valuable things. For the same reason one also might suppose, that Corea and Japan are not within the company's charter, because they never traded to either of them, since the act of parliament.

These various regions afford the richest commodities, gold, jewels, spices, pearls, and drugs, of the most valuable kind. The East India trade is of such consequence, that the highest regard should be paid to it: for if this trade was enlarged, it would encrease such a demand for woollen goods, iron ware, and every other branch of business in England, as would employ all the manufacturers, who are now starving, and thereby relieve the poor.

This might be demonstrated, by the many places that are not yet traded to by the English. The company trades in the Red Sea but to one port, that is, Moca; but the Abyssinian empire, or Ethiopia, which lies on the west side of that sea, is not attempted to be traded to, although it is inhabitated by christians, and abounding with gold, myrrh, sena, alloes, avit, and numbers of rich dying and medicinal drugs, with other commodities. They have no iron nor woollen goods, but what are carried to them over land from Egypt or Turkey, and are mostly manufactured by the French, or at Damascus.

The company doth not trade to Siam, a rich and great kingdom; nor to Pegu, a kingdom that produces rubies, gum-lac, gum-dragon, and all the materials of the fine Indian varnish:

the

the inhabitants are very induſtrious, and great trade might be made there. Tonquin is alſo a kingdom full of induſtrious people; and the kingdom of Cochin-China would give vent to a great number of commodities. The kingdom of Corea, and the empire of Japan, are included among the richeſt in the world; yet with theſe our Eaſt India company have no commerce; though thoſe countries abound in raw-ſilk, gold, ſilver, ſpice-goods, tea, porcelain, Japan, and other things fit for European markets. Thoſe many ſpice iſlands unpoſſeſſed by the Dutch, and ſome of the Philippines unſubjected by the Spaniards, are a glorious field of induſtry for the Engliſh; numbers of adventurers might make their fortunes by ſuch a trade; hundreds of ſhips be employed; and immenſe ſums brought home in gold, ſilver, and rich goods in payment for our manufactures.

IT is neceſſary for us to think of theſe things; for if we do not, other nations will!

END OF VOLUME THE FIRST.

www.ingramcontent.com/pod-product-compliance
Lightning Source LLC
Chambersburg PA
CBHW031421230426
43668CB00007B/389